coming of age in a **HARDSCRABBLE WORLD**

coming of age in a

HARDSCRABBLE
WORLD
a memoir anthology

edited by NANCY C. ATWOOD
and ROGER ATWOOD

The University of Georgia Press
athens

Credits for previous publications included in this work
appear on pages 315–17, which constitute an
extension of this copyright page.

© 2019 by the University of Georgia Press
Athens, Georgia 30602
www.ugapress.org
All rights reserved
Designed by Kaelin Chappell Broaddus
Set in 10.25/13.5 Miller Text by Kaelin Chappell Broaddus
Printed and bound by Sheridan Books, Inc.
The paper in this book meets the guidelines for
permanence and durability of the Committee on
Production Guidelines for Book Longevity of the
Council on Library Resources.

Most University of Georgia Press titles are
available from popular e-book vendors.

Printed in the United States of America
23 22 21 20 19 P 5 4 3 2 1

Library of Congress Cataloging-in-Publication Data

Names: Atwood, Nancy C., 1933– editor. | Atwood, Roger, editor.
Title: Coming of age in a hardscrabble world : a memoir anthology /
    edited by Nancy C. Atwood and Roger Atwood.
Description: Athens : The University of Georgia Press, 2019. |
    Includes bibliographical references and index.
Identifiers: LCCN 2018057734| ISBN 9780820356655 (hardcover. : alk. paper) |
    ISBN 9780820355320 (pbk. : alk. paper) | ISBN 9780820355337 (ebook)
Subjects: LCSH: Working class writings, American. | Working class—
    Literary collections. | American literature—20th century. |
    American literature—21st century.
Classification: LCC PS508.W73 C76 2019 | DDC 810.8/09220623—dc23
    LC record available at https://lccn.loc.gov/2018057734

contents

chapter nine CLASS CONSCIOUSNESS

acknowledgments

We thank Bethany Snead, our acquisitions editor at the University of Georgia Press, whose response to an initial email query in 2017 conveyed enthusiasm, so appreciated then and still appreciated now, as it has taken the form of solid, trustworthy support for the preparation of our book.

Nancy: I had been reading memoirs for years, when I first realized that the books I read for fun were also a valuable resource for serious readers and human-service professionals like me. I had just finished reading a memoir by Fred Allen, a favorite radio and TV comedian from my youth and was sitting in the great reading room of the Boston Public Library waiting for the delivery of a book I had requested. A teenage boy deposited the book on the table in front of me, and that reminded me of Allen. As a poor boy in Boston Allen had an after-school job finding books in the stacks and delivering them to patrons. I knew that because I read about it in his memoir. That was a curiously compelling moment for me: readers can find out about the lives of others by reading memoirs. Once I realized the obvious—that memoirs are a source of information about life—I began studying them in earnest and organizing what I found into articles that I wanted to share with other readers. Members of my family were willing to read drafts, and Gwendolyn, Christopher, and Claire Atwood were characteristically perceptive in their comments. My former employer, Smith College School for Social Work, published my first work based on memoirs, "Experiencing Inequality: Memoirs, Hardship, and Working-Class Roots," in the fall 2014 issue of its journal. Importantly, to my delight, my oldest son, Roger, a writer-journalist, agreed to become coeditor of the anthology that I was planning as an outgrowth of that article. Throughout the process of working with him I have deeply appreciated the insights, writing skills, and hard work he has brought to the project.

I have consulted with others to help to shape the memoirs into an anthology especially suitable for college and university students. Two are English professors. Julia Prewitt Brown at Boston University guided me on how to place the memoirs within the context of other coming-of-age literature and to appreciate redemption as a key concept in both literature and psychology. Josh Cohen at Massachusetts College of Art and Design recognized how ethnic and socioeconomic diversity among memoirists can be a helpful source of identification for college students who are learning how to write personal essays. Professor of psychology Ellen Winner at Boston College had a deep appreciation for the talent of the memoirists and for the resilience they needed to succeed. Writer and memoirist Judith Nies validated differences in social class as a neglected and needed focus in narrative nonfiction. Personal essayist and former English teacher Janet Banks suggested sensible improvements in how to organize and present our material. Ernest Gonzales, professor of social work at New York University, confirmed my hunch that social-work students could learn from our anthology and urged us to add provocative questions to stimulate discussion. Lynne Benson drew on her experience teaching at a community college and public university in Boston to inspire a new conceptualization of the term "social class," one that avoids labeling and dry abstraction. Brandeis University professor emerita Janet Zollinger Giele raised my feminist consciousness once again when she critiqued an early version of the book. I was blessed that Jill Ker Conway (1934–2018) encouraged the early development of our anthology. I wish she were alive to see how helpful her ideas were to understanding the value of our readings. The first person, besides myself and Roger, to read every single word of the memoir excerpts and comment on them in person was Henry Shull, a researcher at the Radcliffe-Harvard Schlesinger Library. He found the readings interesting and made thoughtful remarks about the effects of economic pressures on young people. I also welcomed a collective response to the memoirs from the members of my Unitarian Universalist (UU) church. The audience at First Church in Boston was attentive to my talk called "Memoir from A to Z" (A being Angelou and Z being Zinn). Being typical UU parishioners, they had many comments and questions. I knew from their response that the topic of memoir is a crowd-pleaser.

Roger: Nancy had been sharing her enthusiasm for memoirs with me for years before she decided to turn her passion into a book. I assisted her with the early edits, proposals, and lists of titles to include. But it was not until 2016 that I really understood the need for an anthology of memoirs by writers from working families and agreed to join Nancy in this project as coeditor. That was the year I taught a class in memoirs as an adjunct professor in the English department at the University of the District of Columbia, the public university of the city of Washington. Although we read mostly non-American writers in that class, I was struck by how my students, nearly all from working-class backgrounds and a few hoping to embark on writing careers, hungered to read true stories that mirrored their own upbringings and lives as young adults. When we read passages by Brent Staples (included in this anthology), for example, my students came alive with that same passion that I had seen over so many years in my mother, that realization that memoir, when done well, can be a uniquely honest and brave inquiry into human feeling and experience. I am grateful to UDC for hiring me and particularly professors Matt Petti, Wynn Yarbrough, and Alex Howe.

Like all independent writers, I rely on a network of friends, colleagues, and editors for feedback on ideas, intellectual companionship, and occasionally a sympathetic ear. My thanks to Fred Thys, Sam Fromartz, Sonya Hepinstall, Steve Rasin, Rupert Shortt, Jarrett Lobell, Erik Ching, Riordan Roett, Ramón Borges-Méndez, Vincent Garay, Martin Oliver, Robert Berry, and Alejandro Cedeño for their support during the years when I was working on this project. My husband, Werner Romero, as always, was there through it all with his good sense, great cooking, and endless patience. *Que estemos siempre juntos.*

Editing anthologies requires obtaining permission from publishers and literary agents to reprint copyrighted material. Anyone who has ever participated in that process knows that it is time consuming, probably expensive, and potentially frustrating. Given that likelihood, it is a real pleasure to single out for special thanks those who acted as counterforces to bureaucracy and smoothed our way. The memoir author Mary Childers straightened out a glitch in a publisher's communication system and later praised the structure of our book. The permissions manager at Grove Atlantic was flexible about how we excerpted material and discounted the fee on material from Tobias Wolff's *This Boy's Life*.

But above all, when it comes to permissions, David A. Berkowitz and his children deserve our deep gratitude. Larry and Rachel facilitated their father's bequest for the support of our project, and Larry has efficiently managed all financial aspects of the permission-getting process. This project might well have run aground without David's unstinting support, both moral and financial. It is to him that we dedicate this book.

introduction

Hardscrabble: *Adj.*: Requiring or characterized by hard work and struggle . . .
   Noun: Rough or barren terrain that is difficult to work or make productive . . .

                                              —*Oxford English Dictionary*

As children, the authors in this anthology grew up tough. Some were scrappy fighters and others quietly resilient. Their stories are about coping with whatever their poor and working-class environments threw their way. Paul Clemens was tackled by gangs in his Italian neighborhood of Detroit, but years later he found that he missed the adrenaline-pumping fun of those years. After the sudden death of her millworker father, Monica Wood drew from trauma the first stirrings of a writerly imagination, creating families in which both parents were alive in homes with "no missing pieces." Brent Staples left an abusive home in a declining factory town for a career in academia and journalism, only to be laid low emotionally by the murder of his brother in a drug dispute. This anthology chronicles how talented writers remember their early years and how they shaped those memories into creative nonfiction that appeals to readers of every social class, rich and poor alike. It is a book about enterprising young people who grapple with the seemingly impossible and sometimes succeed.

OVERVIEW OF THE READINGS

The stories in this anthology are drawn from book-length memoirs by thirty authors. In contrast to autobiographers, who cover the full span of their lives, memoirists focus on a theme or select a portion of their lives to explore in depth. The central theme of these memoirs is coming of age, usually defined as the period of growth and development from childhood to young adulthood. Coming of age can also be defined metaphorically as a maturing experience or major psychological breakthrough that can occur at any age. Memoirs are inherently episodic, because life itself is a series of scenes. Each of the thirty excerpts from memoirs in this anthology represents an episode, or a cluster of episodes, in the life of the author.

We have organized the readings into sections that encompass significant experiences in the lives of the writers-to-be as they grew from children to young adults. The stories depict family life and neighborhoods and how the youthful memoirists made friends and tried to deal with enemies. The authors recount experiences at school, in church, and in the workplace and tell us about falling in love and experimenting with sex. They describe how their early identities as writers, scholars, and social activists began to form. And when the dark shadow of abuse fell over the lives of some, they tell us how they attempted to cope with trauma.

Stories in these memoirs have multiple layers, with emotional complexity and ambiguity. Their narratives can be understood as straightforward storytelling and also as literature that resonates with psychological and cultural meaning. Like most passages in this book, the story by Rick Bragg combines drama, introspection, and social commentary. He writes of the "darkest and ugliest time" of his childhood in the Jim Crow South as a poor white boy with an alcoholic father. The inner layer of his narrative is about what actually happened. His liquor-crazed father terrorized his mother, his siblings, and him and abandoned the family. Black neighbors, finding them destitute, shared food with the family, transforming an account of a desperate situation into a parable of interracial magnanimity.

Bragg places these occurrences within the context of social change and suggests that the civil rights movement led white people to question attitudes entrenched since childhood yet altered them only partially. As a self-scrutinizing memoirist with a conscience, he is honest enough to admit to a possible residue of prejudice, despite his efforts to change. He writes as a mature man aware of how he used to think and act, confessing that for many years he and his brothers physically tormented their black neighbors. They stopped after receiving their neighbors' gift of food: "we didn't throw no more rocks."

That grammatical lapse is a deliberate throwback to Bragg's earlier, ignorant way of talking. Thus, these stories combine interpersonal, cultural, and sometimes linguistic elements into complex, nuanced narratives about another time and place as told by writers who have thought deeply about the past.[1]

MEMOIR AS CRAFT AND ART

The books excerpted in this anthology exemplify the craft and artistry of memoir. What are the components of memoir-writing at its best? We identify five basic elements.

Voice. The voice of the narrator is distinctive and belongs exclusively to him or her as "a writer and a human being," writes Mary Karr.[2] Vivian Gornick uses the word "persona" to designate the unique identity—the narrator's voice—that organizes the narrative.[3] For example, memoirist Luis Rodriguez writes in a distinctive voice. As a twelve-year-old he delivered newspapers: "I got good at it. It was the first important accomplishment I remember as a child. I couldn't exactly talk with any coherency, or do sports, or show any talent for anything. But, man, I could deliver newspapers!" That voice is an endearing combination of modesty and bravado. He presents himself as an underdog, one who is spirited and irreverent. That same persona appears later when he refuses to envision Jesus as a "stringy blond-haired, blue-eyed icon" but prefers to see him as Mexican Indian, down-to-earth, and oriented to action.

Dramatic tension. Memoir is a category of creative nonfiction, a genre of writing based on fact that uses fiction-writing methods to shape those facts into narratives.[4] The stories have (1) dramatic tension associated with problems or conflict; (2) character development; and (3) a narrative arc—a beginning, a middle, and an end—built around addressing problems and resolving them. The resolution may be an action or event, or it may be internal, such as a penetrating insight into a troublesome situation. The narrative arc, also known as plot, applies to episodes or stories within the memoir and to the text as a whole. Memoir writers are sometimes upfront about what they have done to "enliven the narrative," to use Mary Childers's phrase: "I merge a few events in time, leap and fill in gaps in memory about sequence and details, and reconstruct dialogue that I could not possibly remember verbatim."[5] Whatever narrative liberties she takes, good memoir is always based on the author's ownership of the meaning derived from remembered experience. The reader feels the authenticity of these stories because the authors extracted memories from a potent psychological core.

Kate Simon's story in this anthology is prototypical creative nonfiction. It has dramatic tension, character development, and a narrative arc. Tension comes from the threat that the entitled visiting cousin from Poland posed to the well-being of an immigrant family in the Bronx. Character development occurs as daughter Kate went from initial naiveté about Cousin Yankel to unmovable resistance to his predatory ways. The narrative begins with his seemingly benign arrival; the middle is the onset of sexual abuse itself and Kate's defense against it; and the end is Yankel's premature departure, under the threat of exposure, thereby seemingly restoring the home to its original status quo, at least in outward appearances. The author's remembered experience has become an unfolding and suspenseful narrative with psychological power.

Balance between scene and summary. Good memoirs strike a satisfying balance between scene and summary; that is, they both *show* what happened and *tell* us its context and meaning. In *scene*, experience is presented through a verbal transcription of events as they unfold. Scene typically uses physical description, often detailed, to give verisimilitude. The surest sign of scene is dialogue, especially the verbatim quotation of characters.[6] The scene element is intended to give the reader an "I was there" feeling. In contrast, *summary* involves the retrospective summation of the author's experience.

E. Lynn Harris, like other memoirists in this anthology, skillfully combines scene and summary, titrating appropriate amounts of each in telling his story. An example is how he depicts his first day at IBM, where this twenty-one-year-old black man with an Afro went to work following his graduation from college. He describes the clothes he wore as he entered the office of his manager, also African American: "I wore a modest Sears & Roebuck gray pin-striped suit that had a certain shine to it, with a pink shirt and a brown and blue clip-on tie." He explains that he did not know how to tie a regular tie. Observing the new hire's clothes, the manager gave Harris an advance on his first month's salary and told him to go to Brooks Brothers to see a particular salesman: "Tell him I sent you, and don't leave until you've spent every penny." The final piece of dialogue and Harris's concluding summary complete the narrative's arc. His manager gave him another piece of advice: "'Lynn, when you leave Brooks Brothers, burn that suit,' he said, and smiled." Dialogue like this has the ring of truth, even though it is repeating a conversation that occurred decades before. It resonates as something that a person would be likely to remember. The summary of the story adds meaning: "On my first day at IBM, I had my first dress-for-success lesson. The first of many lessons I would learn." The summary puts the encounter into context, helps to illuminate the narrator's character, and propels the story along, preparing readers for what follows.

Double vision. Memoirists have double vision. They have a "being in it" voice and a "looking back" voice.[7] Their first vision is of the past, seen through the eyes of their younger self. The second vision is a reinterpretation of the past, based on the insights of the older, presumably wiser person they have become.[8]

For example, the Catholic girl who worshipped a martyred saint became the grown-up memoirist Sandra Scofield who uses a feminist framework to question her earlier piety. She writes of how as a twelve-year-old she adored Maria Goretti, an eleven-year-old Italian who died defending her virginity rather than submit to rape by a boy from a nearby farm. Young Sandra chose the canonized Maria as her confirmation namesake, admiring her for welcoming martyrdom and for praying for the repentance of her brutal attacker. The mature author has a different view, having herself been raped, and she reinterprets the Catholic version of Maria Goretti's death—that she intentionally died to preserve her purity—as church-serving hagiography. The real reason for that myth, Scofield reinterprets, was that females traditionally had few legitimate pathways to recognition from society, and martyrdom was the only respectable alternative available to them. The church's canonization rescued Maria not from death but from anonymity.

Moral justification. A memoir, like an autobiography, is a moral enterprise, in the sense that it is an explanation and justification for how one has led one's life. Readers will judge the writer not just aesthetically, but also for "the content of his character," to use the phrase of Martin Luther King Jr., in accordance with the cultural ideals and standards of the time.

Diane Bjorklund views autobiographical writing through a sociological lens and sees such writing as a presentation of the self to the public, and therefore subject to the writer's understanding of what the public expects and how the public makes judgments.[9] This is not to say that a good memoirist panders to perceptions or misperceptions of what the public wants. Rather, a skillful memoirist is aware of public conceptions of morality and ethical behavior and takes them into account in constructing a narrative. Such an awareness is compatible with an author's honesty, because candor and self-scrutiny are ethical norms in our culture. A memoirist might well describe an experience of which he or she is ashamed, but that narrative will transmute the shameful experience into a revelation of heightened understanding and possibly redemption.[10] At other times, a story of goodness is just that, an uncomplicated evocation of admirable or altruistic behavior in the past. Such narratives are not bragging; rather, they are an ethical accounting for the events described in the storytelling.

The narrative "voice" of memoirist Joe Queenan tends toward the sardonic, even flippant, but an underlying decency shines through when he recounts a summer of serving as a fellow altar boy with Jackie, his neighbor, at a nearby Catholic school. To get there the two boys walked a mile by themselves across empty fields and through a truck pass with no sidewalks. Queenan wonders why Jackie took the assignment: "Unlike me [he] had no clerical aspirations" and was "not a cerebral sort," but "somehow I managed to talk him into getting up every morning for three months straight an hour before sunrise." For his willingness to do this, young Joe appreciated Jackie as "sturdy and reliable." And in turn, we infer that Jackie saw Joe as a trustworthy friend that a ten-year-old boy would like to have.

In summary, a good memoir weaves together a distinct narrative voice, dramatic tension, scene and summary, the double vision of being in it and looking back, and a moral justification for how the author has led his or her life.

COMING OF AGE AND
INDIVIDUAL DEVELOPMENT

The literary concept of coming of age and the psychological concept of identity formation overlap. These readings exemplify both, yet coming of age in particular has a long pedigree in fiction. In German literature, coming of age is the theme of *bildungsroman* ("novel of education"), of which Goethe's *Wilhelm Meister's Apprenticeship* (1795) was the prototype. Coming-of-age stories focus on the personal development of a single individual, usually in youth. In English literature, Charles Dickens's novel *David Copperfield* (1850) is perhaps the best-known example of the form. Young David engages vigorously with his environment, confronts multiple obstacles and achieves success, becoming an established author and ultimately a happy husband. Like the memoirs excerpted in this anthology, his coming of age represents the book's narrative arc. From the perspective of psychology, he masters several developmental tasks, including finding an occupational identity and forming lasting relationships of trust and intimacy.[11]

The readings in this anthology follow a sequence consistent with milestones associated with healthy psychological development.[12] Each reading carries its own, unique interpretation on the coming-of-age theme, yet the progress toward maturity the readings describe falls into three basic categories: psychological, cognitive, and moral. Narratives from Brent Staples, Vivian Gornick, and Mary Childers illustrate those three distinct but overlapping developmental processes.

For African American Brent Staples, the psychological turning point in his pathway from boy to man was the night of his sixteenth birthday. His intoxicated father harassed him for not doing a household chore fast enough, struck him for talking back, and then punched him so hard that Brent lost consciousness. After that, Brent resolved to part company with his family: "Physically I remained with them, but mentally I was gone." He arranged to be out of the house "at every possible minute." As he describes in his memoir, after the events described in the passage in this book, being "mentally gone" meant staying out of trouble and drawing on the resources of Chester, Pennsylvania, the shipbuilding city where he lived. Through this branching out from home, Staples gained an unconventional education that ultimately led him to university and a successful career as a writer.

For Vivian Gornick, the break with girlhood was mainly cognitive. At City College in New York she discovered herself to be an intellectual surrounded by other intellectuals and began a permanent commitment to the life of the mind. This revelation proved so exciting that she felt overcome, paradoxically, by a physical sensation: "I discovered that people were transformed by ideas, and that intellectual conversation was immensely erotic."

Several memoirists reflect on their ethical lapses, but Mary Childers's remorse about participating in urban vandalism has a special resonance that suggests a moral coming of age. She was part of a posse of wild teenage girls who barged into a Chinese laundry and ripped shirts off the shelves and dragged them across the floor, screaming slurs in imitation Chinese. When she faced what she had involved herself in, she found an excuse to break away from the gang. Later, she fantasized about returning to the store to help the owner clean up, turning the ringleader in to the police, and spending more time with girls at school in the honors classes. Internal change is central to coming of age. She realized, "I am capable of reckless, random insolence" and was serious about stopping that behavior. She kept her vow.

IDENTITY FORMATION AND UPWARD SOCIAL MOBILITY

At a basic economic level the memoirists and their families were have-nots. The parents had low-paying jobs and no financial assets. Almost every story refers to or implies economic insecurity or to problems directly related to not having enough money. What the

memoirists did about that reality represents a merger of two concepts, one psychological and the other sociological. The concepts are
identity construction and upward social mobility, although the writers do not use these abstract terms.

Identity construction in this context means the memoirists' process of exploring who they are, what they value, and the direction
they will choose to follow in the rest of their lives. Upward social
mobility is movement from a lower social class to a higher social
class; for the memoirists, mobility is potential movement as adolescents or young adults out of poverty or the working class to middle-
or even upper-class status.

As readers considering these concepts and how the stories illustrate them, we need to remind ourselves that what we read in the
memoirs is the author's personal construction of past experience. It
is not observable reality but rather what the author wants us to understand about his or her identity formation and aspirations. The
author is constructing an identity through words and illustrating
upward mobility with narrative. This is a highly selective process of
determining what to record, emphasize, and elaborate. The author
starts with memories, but putting them all altogether into a pub-
lishable narrative involves deciding what is important, morally res-
onant, and interesting to the public. This is not to say that what we
read is untrue; rather, that the author makes selections that convey
the essence of the experience and its authenticity.

Identity formation and upward social mobility are often closely
linked, as two readings in particular demonstrate. Daisy Hernández was "determined not to become a teenage mother" because she
knew that the consequence would be "no high school graduation," a
notorious barrier to economic advancement. Her immediate objec-
tive, as spelled out in her memoir, was to get herself birth control;
her longer-term goal was to become a college student with a four-
year scholarship and thereby pave her way into the middle class. As
an "overachiever from a working-class home," as she describes herself, she accomplished both.

Rosemary L. Bray used her early years at Yale to contemplate
what she wanted to do with her life, sampling an array of academic
and extracurricular programs to find what especially suited her. Her
quest and its uncertainties point up the role of cultural context in

identity formation. Although writing was what she loved, she worried that majoring in English would deflect her from a more serious career, like law, that would pay back some of the huge investment she and her working-class family had made to get her into Yale and help her stay there. Other African American students were influenced, she writes, by an attitude of "grim professionalism" that led them to pursue lucrative careers in traditional fields. Rosemary resisted that animus, chose English as a major, and expanded her skills by becoming the photographer for a campus-based repertory theater company.

Despite their ambitions, a powerful preoccupation other than career choice influenced Bray and Hernández in those years, and that preoccupation was love. For Hernández love meant experiencing and acknowledging her bisexuality,[13] and for Bray it was establishing a committed relationship with a fellow student, an African American male. According to developmental theory, the tasks of late adolescence and young adulthood are two-fold: to establish a vocation or occupation that one cares about (or the potential for one) and to form an intimate relationship with another person.[14] These young women accomplished both.

Developing competence is crucial to identity formation.[15] Thirteen-year-old Esmeralda Santiago, newly arrived in the U.S. mainland, was determined to become an eighth grader in an American school, having completed seventh grade in Puerto Rico. That was her desired identity, whereas the school administrator pigeonholed her as a non-English speaking Puerto Rican who must repeat seventh grade. To escape that categorization, young Esmeralda gave herself a crash course in English vocabulary, spending hours in the library and borrowing as many illustrated children's books as she could to learn the names of familiar objects. "I figured that if American children learned English through books, so could I, even if I started later." She studied diligently and learned enough English to change her identity to the more advanced student she wanted to be. In the same vein, Oscar Hijuelos, in his memoir after the passage in this book, describes mastering the guitar as a teenager and gaining the confidence to perform in public. As a mature writer, his best-selling novel about a group of Cuban musicians drew on knowledge of popular music that its author had gained as a teenager.

Sixteen-year-old Russell Baker had a secret desire to become a writer. When he received an A-Plus on an English paper, his mother told him that she had always known he had a talent for words. After receiving that grade, he gained enough confidence in himself to believe that he could become a writer. His mother, widowed as a young woman and ambitious for her son to succeed, told him that he is now ready to "make something of himself." Thus, academic achievement helps to form identity and raises expectations for upward mobility.

For various reasons, especially lack of education beyond high school (and sometimes not even that), parents of the memoirists struggled financially. Employment was often sporadic. Immigrant parents might find work, but it was typically manual labor or for low pay in factories. If the family broke up because of divorce, death, or paternal desertion, the mother was left without a dependable wage and had to work long hours outside the home. Parents who drank alcoholically or had chronic diseases were unable to function as breadwinners. Large families meant not enough space and too many mouths to feed. Those are the facts.

Still, the memoirs about these families are not downbeat or morose. Rather, they are lively and interesting, as though the memoirists are looking back on their youth in a spirit of triumphant relief that they figured out how to survive and even to flourish. And flourish they did. Not only did all thirty authors write well-reviewed memoirs—several of them best sellers—but they also have had successful careers in journalism, academia, novel and short-story writing, essay and other nonfiction writing, poetry, social activism, and ministry. Their career biographies at the end of this book attest to their professional accomplishments.

THE MEMOIRS IN CULTURAL CONTEXT

The readings focus on individuals, but the writer's larger world is always implicit in the stories. Autobiographical writing, including memoir, is "culture speaking through the self."[16] Cultural forces influence whose voices become prominent and the scope and content of what they say. Historian and memoirist Jill Ker Conway identifies three such forces.[17]

Feminism. The women memoirists are not the "romantic hero-ines" of an earlier era who chronicle their pursuit of marital secu-rity.[18] Rather, in this anthology the narratives of heterosexual re-lationships are mainly cautionary tales about abuse, such as Mary Childers's account of marauding teenage males and Kim Barnes's story about the pathological possessiveness of her boyfriend. Rose-mary Bray describes an ultimately satisfying heterosexual pairing, but her account is filled with ambivalence. What is notable is not that the relationship was established but that it took Bray so long to recognize its potential for long-term commitment. She was skep-tical about the future, in keeping with her feminist belief that mar-riage was a suspect institution.

Postmodernism. Conway characterizes postmodern memoir as abandoning earlier cultural assumptions about the normative po-sition of power in American culture.[19] Instead of portraying famous individuals with mainstream backgrounds and characteristics, post-modern memoirs favor narratives based on ethnic subcultures, vic-timization, or deviance. Over a third of the readings in this anthol-ogy are written by people from historically powerless minorities: African Americans, Hispanics, and Asians. Several readings fit into Conway's category of "grim tales."[20] Many of the memoirs focus on issues of identity and coping with trauma. Some are by individuals who were abused, like Michael Keith, whose father's neglect bor-dered on the criminal, or Tobias Wolff, whose stepfather's bullying was sadistic. Pete Hamill and Michelle Tea acknowledge deviance—their own—in the form of alcohol abuse ("I got drunk," says Tea, "that was always fun").

Authors in this anthology who intentionally expose the darker sides of their pasts often want their work to serve a societal purpose. "Nobody was dealing with white working-class and poor people," states Michael Patrick MacDonald.[21] So he dug deep into the life of South Boston as he had experienced it in the 1970s and 1980s, not only for himself but for all those "back in Southie" as "a conduit for a story that needed to be told." Richard Hoffman acknowledges the "fear and shame" that derive from trauma but asserts that his story is "not about me. It's about what I'm able to see because of what I've been through."[22]

American ideology of self-made success. "Individualistic fulfillment," to use Conway's phrase,[23] is an American ideal. Benjamin Franklin wrote the prototypical autobiography of the talented self-made man who triumphs in life by taking initiative and energetically pursuing multiple interests. Stories of pulling oneself up by the bootstraps became an American literary tradition, typified by the Gilded Age novels of Horatio Alger.[24] They depict poverty as a bleak but noble experience that confers "character" and teaches such values as resilience, thrift, and honesty to the narrator as he struggles up the socioeconomic ladder. Stories in this anthology both follow and transcend that tradition. The authors are aware that they are fleeing poverty through their own efforts, yet several refer obliquely to the corroding effects of poverty on the psyche. They have no illusions about poverty, and most view their escape from the deprivation of their birth families with an ambivalence and introspection that are quite alien to the Horatio Alger tradition. Rather than disdaining those who remain in poverty for their supposed indolence, many authors have empathy for those less competent, ambitious, and lucky than they.

Yet these writers often show a sense of hard-won satisfaction in living more comfortable and worldly lives. Richard Rodriguez recounts how he and his three adult siblings, the children of Mexican immigrants, received the rewards that came from their drive for success. At their family Christmas gathering, the dinner conversation was about European travel, and the gift-giving was lavish. The family has assimilated into the middle class, yet the scene remains laced with ambiguity as seen in Rodriguez's reference to "useless and slightly ludicrous gifts." Other writers turn the kind of grit and persistence traditionally associated with upward mobility to their fight against injustice, such as Maya Angelou in her struggle to gain work as a streetcar conductor in segregated San Francisco.[25]

The memoirists' sense of responsibility extended to the wider society, including the labor unions that Bich Minh Nguyen, Monica Wood, Roxanne Dunbar-Ortiz, and Howard Zinn supported. Nor did the youthful memoirists isolate themselves. Their receptivity to help from others ensured that they would have collaborators along their pathways to success. African American bell hooks gratefully received solace from an older white church member and from a Catholic priest, and Esmeralda Santiago formed lasting relationships with the faculty at her school for the arts.

CLASS CONSCIOUSNESS

Although not all the memoirs excerpted in this book are principally about social class (some focus on race or gender, or other concerns altogether), all these writers hold a mirror to American society's treatment of working-class children and teenagers. Sometimes that mirror reveals decency and compassion; other times, cruelty and humiliation. Yet all these memoirists, with the possible exceptions of Zinn and Dunbar-Ortiz, show a basic faith in the ability of liberal democracy to address the societal problems that they experienced. They believe in the fundamental role of the institutions of democracy to act as correctives to the abuses of capitalism as it is lived in the United States. They are advocates for social justice and critics of institutional abuse. For most, their solution to the financial insecurity they grew up with was individualistic and based on accepting personal responsibility. They were exemplars of an upward mobility that germinated in the capitalistic culture that surrounded them. Fortunately, they had the aptitudes and characterological strengths to succeed within that system and to overcome impediments inherent in capitalism.[26]

Howard Zinn was well aware of the downside of capitalism and took to heart that people like his hard-working father, no matter how much they tried, were poor and always would be. Zinn himself as a teenager and young man held manual and semiskilled jobs for many years and lived in several "cramped and unpleasant places." He was offended that large parts of the population experienced lifetimes of unemployment and bad employment, even in the richest country in the world. To him, it was a lie of smug politicians that "if you were poor it was because you hadn't worked hard enough." Acutely conscious of economic injustice, he never stopped being class-conscious, even after becoming a college professor with an income adequate to support his family.

Daisy Hernández, born more than fifty years after Zinn, would agree with him that hard work alone is no guarantee of financial security, but she would also cite progress toward equality in the past several decades. Social changes have led to new opportunities for minority groups like hers. The civil rights, feminist, and LGBT movements "have opened the door to higher education, better laws, and supportive communities," she writes, for what would be "otherwise marginalized people" like herself.

Although American society has become more inclusive in some ways, the class divide remains and, by some measures, has widened. No matter what our rhetoric of equality and opportunity asserts, vast disparities exist between haves and have-nots. Memoirists recount coming into personal contact with those disparities as they are propelled into social and occupational contact with the affluent. While he was working at IBM, E. Lynn Harris was invited by a colleague to a dinner party at an Upper East Side apartment that looked as chic as pages from a glossy design magazine. He "secretly envied and despised" his fellow guests for their "seemingly perfect lives." They understood how to dress well and manage money, whereas he came from an Arkansas family that rarely had money to manage. Harris's experience suggests that consciousness of the reality of class can be more acute among those who, like him, have crossed class lines.

The authors in this book offer us their lives as examples of what it is like to grow up unprotected by privilege. They were fortified by their resourcefulness in finding opportunity in every environment, no matter how hardscrabble or inhospitable. There are many reasons to appreciate and respect the writers featured in this anthology, but surely among them is what they have in common: working-class roots and the talent to share their past in ways that broaden understanding and imagination for us all.

NOTES

1. Jennifer Jensen Wallach finds "a high degree of anxiety about what it meant to be a white southerner" among the three white memoirists whose work she analyzes in her literary/historical study, *Closer to the Truth Than Any Fact: Memoir, Memory, and Jim Crow* (Athens: University of Georgia Press, 2008), 101.

2. Mary Karr, *The Art of Memoir* (New York: Harper, 2015), xiii.

3. Vivian Gornick, *The Situation and the Story: The Art of Personal Narrative* (New York: Farrar, Straus and Giroux, 2001), 23.

4. Sue Hertz, *Write Choices: Elements of Nonfiction Storytelling* (Los

Angeles: Sage, CQ Press, 2016); Lee Gutkind, *You Can't Make This Stuff Up: The Complete Guide to Writing Creative Nonfiction—from Memoir to Literary Journalism and Everything in Between* (Boston: Da Capo Press, 2012).

5. Mary Childers, *Welfare Brat: A Memoir* (New York: Bloomsbury, 2005), 263.

6. G. Thomas Couser, *Memoir: An Introduction* (Oxford: Oxford University Press, 2012), 68–69.

7. Karr, *The Art of Memoir*, 182.

8. Sven Birkerts, *The Art of Time in Memoir: Then, Again* (Saint Paul, Minn.: Graywolf Press, 2008)

9. Erving Goffman, *The Presentation of Self in Everyday Life* (Garden City, New York: Doubleday, 1959). Diane Bjorklund, *Interpreting the Self: Two Hundred Years of American Autobiography* (Chicago: The University of Chicago Press, 1998), 42.

10. Dan P. McAdams, *The Redemptive Self: Stories Americans Live By* (Oxford: Oxford University Press, 2006).

11. Julia Prewitt Brown, in her *Reader's Guide to the Nineteenth-Century English Novel* (New York: Macmillan, 1985), 106, notes that *David Copperfield* was Freud's favorite novel.

12. Laura E. Berk, *Exploring Lifespan Development*, 2nd ed. (Boston: Allyn & Bacon, 2010); Erik H. Erikson, *Identity and the Life Cycle* (W. W. Norton, 1980), 51–107; Howard Gardner, *Developmental Psychology: An Introduction* (Boston: Little Brown, 1982).

13. As noted, Daisy Hernández identifies as bisexual; Michelle Tea and E. Lynn Harris identify themselves as lesbian and gay in their memoirs excerpted in this anthology; and Richard Rodriguez publicly came out as gay following the publication of his memoir.

14. Freud famously summarized what a "normal person should be able to do well" with the words, "Lieben und arbeiten [to love and to work]." (Erikson, *Identity and the Life Cycle*), 102.

15. Robert W. White, *The Enterprise of Living: Growth and Organization in Personality* (New York: Holt, Rinehart and Winston, 1972)

16. Bjorklund, *Interpreting the Self*, 158.

17. Jill Ker Conway, *When Memory Speaks: Reflections on Autobiography* (New York: Alfred Knopf, 1998).

18. Conway, *When Memory Speaks*, 40.

19. Conway, *When Memory Speaks*, 151–52.

20. Conway, *When Memory Speaks*, 151.

21. Melanie Brooks, *Writing Hard Stories: Celebrated Memoirists Who Shaped Art from Trauma* (Boston: Beacon Press, 2017), 36.

22. Brooks, *Writing Hard Stories*, 79.

23. Conway, *When Memory Speaks*, 23.

24. Carol Nackenoff, *The Fictional Republic: Horatio Alger and American Political Discourse* (New York: Oxford University Press, 1994).

25. Paul Tough associates "grit" with success in his research-based study, *How Children Succeed: Grit, Curiosity, and the Hidden Power of Character* (Boston: Houghton Mifflin Harcourt, 2013).

26. For most of the memoirists there is evidence of a youthful "giftedness" that led educational systems to single them out for special rewards and opportunities. Most received consistently high grades, and several were admitted to a class, program, or school for gifted, talented, and/or fast learners. For characteristics of gifted children, see Ellen Winner, *Gifted Children: Myths and Realities* (New York: Basic Books, 1996).

chapter one
FAMILIES

Paul Clemens

b. 1973

From *Made in Detroit: A South of 8 Mile Memoir*

(2005)

> Paul Clemens grew up in an Italian section of Detroit.
> The city became predominantly black during the decade
> of his birth. Race, cars, and family attachment are
> themes that emerge from his memories of early child-
> hood.

The t-shirt and magazine collections had begun in our first Detroit
bungalow, near the intersection of 6 Mile Road and Gratiot Avenue.
It was the sort of house you saw all of upon entering: look around
for a second or two as you stood in the doorway, politely nodding,
and you'd taken the entire place in, the whole scope of its seven
hundred square feet. Straight ahead was the kitchen. Up and to the
right was the bathroom. On either side of the bathroom, at opposite
ends of a five-step hallway, were the front and back bedrooms. And
that—"We told you it was small," my mother would say, smiling—
was about it. Not much to remark on, really, or compliment, unless
you cared to take as your conversation piece the white aluminum
siding that covered the home's exterior.

A half-mile to our north was Assumption Grotto, the neighborhood Catholic church, where my father had gone for his first few
years of grade school and where I would attend kindergarten; a
mile to our south were City Airport, Mt. Olivet Cemetery, and De
La Salle Collegiate, the storied Christian Brothers high school that
was attended, in the early 1960s, by my father and my Uncle Tony
and which, during the Depression, had denied Coleman Young ad-

mission because of his race. "A Brother in the order asked if I was Hawaiian," Young once said, recalling his admissions interview of decades before. Detroit's first black mayor was light-skinned with freckles, and the product of a Catholic grade school. "I told him, 'No, Brother, I'm Colored.' He tore up the application form right in front of my nose." According to my father, Coleman Young may have been better off. The Christian Brothers, in his affectionate reading, were a bunch of heartless Irish bastards given to dispensing discipline in unorthodox ways, like pushing students down stairwells or having them hold heavy textbooks at arm's length for hours, until the limb became leaden and the spirit was crushed.

I was born a few miles from this bungalow, on the fourth floor of St. John's Hospital, on 7 Mile, in the late winter of 1973. There was an ice storm that March, just after St Patrick's Day, and so my father drove my mother and me the three miles home from the hospital over slick, dangerous roads. Because he is of that variety of man who believes that we were put on this earth, above all else, to do things *right*, my father no doubt performed this function as responsibly, as meticulously, as he has performed every other function required of him in the thirty-plus years of fatherhood that have followed. Each March my mother tells the story of my difficult birth, and how, after enduring thirty-two hours of labor, an emergency C-section, and six days of uncomfortable bed rest, she had to suffer through a knuckle-whitening ride back into the inner city in a '65 Chevy Carryall truck, a baby boy resting on her sore belly. "They used to just hand the baby to you," my mother said recently. "No car seat. Driving home in an ice storm with no car seat." My mother was born Margaret Mary Saulino, and over the years I've often asked her, when there's been special pleading to be done, to pray on my behalf, believing no God worth His salt can deny a sincere request made by a girl so named.

The garage behind our house was two-car, accessible from the alley, and home to my father's 1970 Plymouth Barracuda. I would watch him work on it from a high padded stool—he had to lift me onto it—and once his work was completed he would pay me a nickel to hop down, grab a push broom, and sweep the metal shavings out into the alley. Because he often failed to wear safety goggles when grinding, he occasionally had to visit an ophthalmologist at 8 Mile and Gratiot and have the shavings ground out of his eye.

My father worked a good many late hours and frequently on Saturdays—the words "time and a half" had a magical ring out of my mother's mouth—and he returned home in the evening in any of a dozen of his plaid work shirts, his hands stained with oil, his body, which I would bury my head in while hugging him, smelling of hot metal, mineral spirits, and a masculine, earned sort of sweat. The place where my father worked was always referred to by my parents as "the shop." Some men, I understood, worked at "the office," or "the station house." My father worked at the shop. "How was it at the shop today?" my mother would ask when he got home, and I could tell by looking at him how it was: it was tiring.

Until a few weeks after my birth, my mother was working as a secretary at the Uniroyal Tire plant on Jefferson Avenue. Next to the factory was the Belle Isle Bridge (the MacArthur Bridge, officially, though no one called it that), its lovely half-mile span connecting the wooded island in the middle of the Detroit River exclusively to the American mainland. My father had worked at Belle Isle over summers in the early sixties, selling cans of pop and sweeping sidewalks with my Uncle Tony, who had introduced him to my mother, helping to keep clean what the French settlers had originally called Hog Island. Across from the factory, and altogether less picturesque than the bridge—though perhaps more prophetic of the city's future—was one of Detroit's first methadone clinics. After I was born my mother tried to go back to work but cried all day from separation anxiety, and my father told her to quit: they'd make ends meet on one paycheck.

My mother, too, knew how tiring my father's workday was, especially as he was now the sole source of income, and so always had dinner ready for him, along with some strategy or other to downplay the day's bad news. These always failed, for my father possessed what Hemingway would say every writer needed: a built-in, shockproof shit detector. My father could detect sugarcoating a mile off and had an absolute, raging impatience for having the silver lining pointed out when it was the goddamn cloud that concerned him.

The summer I was three and a half I walked off with a friend while my mother was on the telephone. When she hung up we were gone, and though frantic she was unable to search for us: my sister, a year old at the time, was sound asleep in her crib. My mother called the neighbors and then my father at work, who sped home, only to pull up at the same time I did, in the back of a Detroit Police cruiser. The cops had seen my friend Danny and me several blocks over, and, as I'd been taught to do, I gave the police my name, address, and telephone number. Danny didn't even know his last name. He and his older brother lived a few blocks over with their unmarried mother, a woman whose kids ate the wrappers to candy bars and never had clean clothes, children who always stayed for dinner and seemed to be under no instruction to come home when the streetlights came on, as the rest of us were. They were kids, as my mother said, you felt bad for.

Holding my baby sister, Beth, in her arms, she began to cry when the cops opened the back door of the squad car. My father gave me a hug, gave my mother a look, and went back to work. He wouldn't speak to her for days.

Life, I learned, hangs by the slenderest of threads: this was the lesson of my growing up. Chaos is out there, and only the constant application of common sense—a misnomer, I was to learn: not many had it—could keep disorder at bay. "*Think!*" my father would say, tapping the side of my head, when my actions made it clear to him that I'd needed to and hadn't. Fighting tears and swallowing hard, I'd tell him the next time I would, whereupon his tone would soften and I'd receive a hug. The value of a life accrues slowly, or so said the example he set, not through backslapping and bluster but by the daily meeting of one's responsibilities, however dull they may be. This seriousness, born of worry, was the result of his being the son of a similar father, someone whose childhood in a Catholic orphanage had been harsh and who, as a result, had come to see the two—reality, harshness—as synonymous. [. . .]

Across the street lived the Shannons, an old couple whose five children were grown and whose favorite pastime was to make the trip down to Eastern Market each weekend, where Mr. Shannon would buy more produce than he and his wife could possibly eat, most of it from old Italian men who, if asked the price of any item, would point a short, chubby finger and say, "F'you?" Most of this produce was then given away to the neighborhood kids, with a coerciveness we knew well from our own mothers. "If you don't eat it," they'd say, the force of ancestral famine and coffin ships behind them, "we'll just have to throw it away."

The Shannons had a double-wide yard, so their next-door neighbors, a family of rednecks, were actually two lots down. There weren't many such people on the east side of Detroit—people who for all the world appeared to hail from the north of Kentucky—but there were many of them on our street, and they all lived next door to the Shannons, where they hung out of windows, huddled around stalled cars, and slammed doors all the hours there are. I lost my first street fight at the age of five to one of their fat daughters, a girl twice my age and triple my weight. She sat on me, and that was that.

On the patch of grass between the Shannons and the rednecks, the boys of the neighborhood, myself included, played our simple, violent games, the fun of which was not to be matched for the rest of our days. The best game, in which the guy with the football runs for his life until he is gang-tackled by seventeen of his friends, went by several names—Smear the Queer, Kill the Man with the Ball—but we'd condensed it to Kill the Man.

My father was not bothered that I came home dirty and bleeding after such outings—this would help make a man of me—but he did not like a bit what I learned to yell when we jumped onto the guy we'd just gang-tackled. "Nigger pile!" we'd all holler, loud enough for the whole block to hear. The night my father finally caught wind of what was being said he came out of the house and motioned from the front porch for me to come home for a minute. "What did I hear you yelling out there?" he asked when I came in, grass stains on the knees of my pants. I knew I'd done something wrong from his tone. "Nigger pile," I said, my head lowered. "Do you know what that word means?" My father couldn't bring himself to repeat it, so it was simply "that word." I shook my head. "Well, it's a not-very-nice word for a black person," he said. But even the black kids say it, I said. "I don't care what they say," my father said sharply. "You're my son, and you won't say it. Do you understand me?" He took my chin between his index finger and thumb and forced me to look him in the eye. I said that I did and tried to remember that when I went back outside, where everyone was still yelling it while piling onto the guy on the ground, who invariably had the wind knocked out of him.

Ninety-five percent of this story can be chalked up to my father's inherent goodness; there was simply very little malice in the man. His temper was tremendous, but it was mostly directed at inanimate objects—cars that didn't run, faucets that dripped, drainpipes that wouldn't drain—and those members of his immediate family, himself included, whose behavior had been less than bright. "Not very bright, was it?"—this was my father's worst put-down, his five-word rhetorical condemnation for leaving a screen door open or a bicycle unlocked. But malice for people against whom he had no specific grievance was more or less unknown to him.

Richard Hoffman

b. 1949

From *Half the House: A Memoir*
(2005)

Siblings are important in memories of family life.
Recalling his early years, Richard Hoffman evokes the
closeness of his bond with his younger brother Bob. But
the traumas of disability and ultimately death suffuse
his account of childhood in Allentown, Pennsylvania.

For many years my mother's hair was lacquered blacker than it was
when she was young. Once she was embarrassed when I came home
from college a couple of days early and she hadn't gotten to the sa-
lon and her roots were showing. Shame, that goes to the roots: my
mother bore two congenitally ill, doomed sons. For her, muscular
dystrophy was a mythic curse: only males are afflicted by it, and only
females carry it. A genetic defect. I can imagine my mother washing
her face in the morning, looking at herself in the mirror, protecting
herself, vigilant against the gray or silk-white roots that prove the
past, that say that time is once, once, once. For so many years she
knew her sons would die before her that she had to deny time every day to be there for them, to feed them, wash them, bring them
books, papers and pencils, change the channel, bring the pisspot.
Michael screamed in the night most every night for five or six years,
waking everyone. She slept in a chair downstairs so she could wake
him faster from his nightmares. How could she possibly believe one
lifetime is all there is? She went to the cemetery, often. She had kept
them alive inside her once before. "We'll be together again someday,"

she would insist, holding up her index finger. "Nobody can say it's not true." [...]

In the morning, Bob and I would wake in our bed and laugh and fight. If he woke before me, he would nudge me, poke me, kick me, and if all else failed, open my eyelids with his fingers, asking, "Dick, are you awake yet?"

I remember hanging my foot out from the covers on a morning when I could see my breath, pinching my nose shut to keep from laughing, seeing how long I could stand it, letting my foot get colder and colder, intent on how he would shriek when I placed it on his sleeping back, anticipating his counterattack and readying my pillow for a shield. Mom would be in to wake us any minute, and when I heard her on the stairs I did it, right up under the back of his pajama top.

"Hey! Quit it! Quit it! Mom!"

"Let's go, you two monkeys. Time to get up!"

Sometimes she sang reveille:

> *"You gotta get up*
> *You gotta get up*
> *You gotta get up*
> *In the morning!*
>
> *You gotta get up*
> *You gotta get up*
> *You gotta get*
> *Out a' bed!"*

She stood in the doorway, already dressed for the day, in a shapeless pink homemade dress, with a Chesterfield in the same hand as her coffee cup and an ashtray in the other.

Dad was usually gone to the brewery by the time we came downstairs in the morning. All day he loaded tall brown bottles into wooden crates on a conveyor belt, or loaded passing cardboard cartons with cans. Some days he loaded the delivery trucks, a job he liked better because he could be outside.

"It's good for your muscles," he'd say. "Here. Feel that." And Bob and I would marvel at his big, hard biceps.

"Watch me make a muscle!" one of us would say, and both of us would flex our arms. Dad would pinch my biceps between his thumb and first knuckle and say, "You're getting strong!" and squeeze it till my knees buckled and I fell on the floor laughing, hurting, and rubbing my arm. And then he'd do the same to Bob.

He told us stories of bottles of beer that had come down the line with things inside: a rag, a cigar butt, a dead mouse. When either of us fetched him a beer, we were allowed the first swig, but we always held the bottle to the light first.

Our house was a narrow brick row house painted with a thick cream enamel, and we had the last slate sidewalk on the block. The slate was broken and heaved up by the roots of a huge tree that shaded the front of the house. Dad called it "that god-damned hemlock," because the roots were cracking the walls of the storm sewer in front of our house and threatening the foundation. He'd already had to call a plumber to pump water out of the cellar.

Bob and I knew right where the crack was because the concrete bunker underneath the sidewalk was what we called "our secret hiding place." The crack was just below the corrugated metal drainpipe, an echoing darkness wide enough for skinny kids to crawl in and to back out. It led from the vault to wherever we decided on a given day: the sea, the center of the earth, China.

We took turns crawling into the pipe: I remember reaching ahead with my hands, feeling my way as far in front of me as possible, worried that the horizontal pipe might suddenly turn vertical and I'd find myself falling, plummeting toward the answer to our arguments.

"I think I heard the ocean!" I'd say to Bob as I backed out of the pipe. Or I'd tell him I saw a pair of glowing eyes in there. I was just as afraid whether I was in the cramped dark tube or waiting in the vault. A year older than Bob, I felt responsible for him. And of course each of us, once out of view, tried to scare the other by keeping silent.

We're going on a trip: Mom, Dad, baby Joey, Mammy Etta [maternal grandmother], Bob, and me. We're in a big, round, shiny black '50 Pontiac, my dad's first car. Joey's on Mom's lap; Bob, me, and Mammy are in the back. Bob and I want to sit next to each other, so *we* can fight, Mammy says. She lets us. Lancaster is two hours from Allentown, four hours to look at things and places out the window! We look and fight till Dad says, "Etta, what the hell is going on back there?" We stop for gas; get back in the car with Mammy between us.

Bob cried all the way home, a bandage wrapped around his right leg, Mammy Etta's arms around him. I looked out the window, trying to get excited about the hills, the farms, the cows, the other cars, the billboards. Except for Bob, I don't remember anyone, all the way home, making a sound.

They'd done a biopsy, slit the back of Bob's right calf and snipped a bit of muscle from it. Minor surgery: to a child there's nothing more terrifying—the needle itself is terror, then a stranger, a grown-up, cuts you! My father decided to remove the sutures himself, a week or so later. Mom and I held Bob on the bed; Dad, with his tweezers, kept saying, "Keep still, damn it," while Bob screamed and cried. It must have been too early for the stitches to come out, because he bled; he had a tender, raised scar on his leg after that.

It always took a while to quiet down at bedtime, and my parents were always shushing us and telling us not to wake our baby brother, Joey, who slept in the crib in my parents' bedroom. Sometimes we stayed up playing chestnut football. On the embossed linoleum floor, a purple and pink floral design, patterned after an Oriental carpet, horse chestnuts were arranged in rows. The object of the game was to roll your running back, your roundest chestnut, down a cardboard ramp, and through eleven squat defenders, flat-sided chestnuts that had to be at least four fingers apart, without touching any of them. The further object of the game was to stay up as late as possible having fun, but without making enough noise to anger Dad and bring him upstairs.

In autumn we collected the chestnuts from around the neighborhood, prying them from their spiky cases and polishing them on our sweaters. Dad, inventor of chestnut football, told us they were called horse chestnuts because, like "horse corn," they were fit only for horses to eat, while another kind of chestnut, the kind that Nat King Cole sang about at Christmas, was delicious roasted. Horse chestnuts, Dad told us, were poison. Bob and I, daring each other, ate a little piece of one, and although it tasted awful, like a bad pistachio, and dried out your mouth like a crab apple, neither of us got sick from it.

Other times we knelt together at the floor register, a grate that allowed heat to rise from downstairs, and listened to the television and to our parents talking. Sometimes they argued, often about money.

"All I know's my mother raised the five of us on *half* of what you spend," Dad said. "I'm bustin' my ass, pulling double shifts, and, what the hell, look at this god-damn TV set. The picture tube's going; then what? I got a piece of linoleum plugging the hole in my shoe. We're eating Spam, for Christ's sake."

"You said you liked Spam."

"When I was in the Army, I said. I liked it when I was in the Army. Jesus, Dolly, we ain't got a pot to piss in!"

"So let me go to work! I could help with lunch at the high school. My mom said she'd watch the kids."

"No, god damn it, I said no. Wait. What's that? Is that those sneaky kids again?"

We dove back into bed and lay there, trying not to make a sound. After a while, we looked at each other, pulled imaginary zippers across our mouths, and crept back to the grate.

My mother stayed home; my father went out. It seems incredible to me, the energy he had. At times he worked two jobs. One he still remembers with pride was laying track for a diesel roundhouse at Bethlehem Steel. For a time he worked in a brewery and then unloaded sacks of spices at a warehouse in the evenings. When he wasn't working in the evenings he was always doing something— coaching baseball in summer, refereeing basketball in winter—I went along, a batboy in summer, and in winter a lonely spectator at basketball games between teams I didn't know. He knew, the former promising lefthanded pitcher from the Boys' Club, that Bob's illness was called Duchenne's muscular dystrophy, and that it was progressive and lethal. He ran up and down the court, blowing his whistle, pointing his finger, shouting. "Foul on number nineteen. Hacking. On the arm. Two shots." Sometimes people booed, and I sat behind the scorer flushed with anger and embarrassment.

My mother stayed home. And wanted a girl this time, a Catherine Marie; carrying Michael Steven, who never learned to walk. [...]

The nuns at school were sure Russia was the enemy. Russians hated Jesus, and they loved to torture people to test their faith. They would try to make us deny Jesus, like St. Peter. If we were caught alone, they would try to make us lead them to our families so they could kill them too.

Otto Schlemcher was my idea of a Russian. He was big—an eighth-grader—who bullied Bob and me almost daily. Dark and ugly, he walked with a sort of lurch and he mumbled; it was hard to make out what he said. We knew that the other eighth-graders laughed at him. Bob and I feared and hated him; we thought his name was as weird and ugly as he was.

It was that spring of 1957 that Bob began to weaken. Stairs gave him trouble. One day he fell on the way home from school. I was giving him a hand getting up, when Otto was suddenly there. He pushed me, and Bob went down again. "Leave us alone, you Commie," I said.

"What you call me?"

"You're a Commie Russian," Bob said. He'd gotten himself on all fours, and Otto grabbed him by the hair. "Take that back," he said and pulled.

Bob started crying. "I take it back, okay, I take it back."

Otto let go.

"Leave him alone," I said.

"What it to you, punk-face?" He came after me and got me in a headlock and rapped my head with his knuckles until I cried. When he let me go, I swung at him and hit him as high as I could reach, on the shoulder. "You can't even talk right," I yelled at him and ran across the street. Bob tried to run. Otto caught him and knocked him down, hard on a low picket fence that bordered someone's front yard. He shouted something across the street at me and lurched away.

Bob's shirt was torn and his back and ribs were scraped and bleeding. Dad called the Schlemchers while Mom painted Bob's ribs with Mercurochrome. He must have got Otto's father on the phone. He started yelling. "Don't give me that crap. That's no excuse. Next time I'll call the cops. Oh, yeah? You better hope I don't come over there, that's all I have to say." My mother called the school.

The next day Bob was absent from school, but Otto and I had to go to the principal's office and apologize to each other. There were four nuns in the room, looking sternly at us and slowly shaking their heads. After Sister Elizabeth Mary told Otto he could leave, they all sat down and explained to me that I should never make fun of Otto again, because he couldn't help the way he walked and slurred his words. He had a terrible disease called palsy.

The year I turned nine, Bob was fitted with brown leather braces to wear at night. Dad always laced them too tightly, and Bob would cry out that they pinched him. "They won't work, damn it, if they're not on tight!" Dad would scold him. There was going to be a cure, a rescue, if we could only hang on. But if Bob allowed the tendons in his calves to tighten up, the cure, when it came, would be too late. So Dad tied the rawhide laces tight and Bob did his best not to complain. We lay in our bed in the dark.

"The left one hurts."

"Go to sleep."

"It's killing me. It's pinching. Can you fix it?"

"It has to be on tight or it won't work."

"Just pull it away from the skin where it pinches."

I could just get my index finger under the leather collar that choked Bob's calf; by working it around, I could free the skin that had been caught. Often the collar was too tight to get my finger under it.

"Fix it!"

"I can't. Shut up and go to sleep."

"I can't."

"Well, just shut up till Dad gets back."

This was the routine: after half an hour Dad would climb the stairs to feel Bob's toes. If they were cold, he turned on the light to look at them; if they were blue, he loosened the laces.

Not long after that, Bob slammed my shin with one of the heavy braces and I knocked him out of bed. Mom and Dad came running. Dad straddled me on the bed and grabbed me by the front of my pajamas. "Selfish," he called me. A smack in the face. And "lucky."

Smack. I was a "bully." He was going to teach me. Smack. My mother stopped him. Bob was crying on the floor. Dad picked him up and put him back in the bed, where I lay with my face turned to the wall.

Another night or two and Bob was sleeping on a cot in the middle room downstairs. Soon our toys and games were divided between what was now my room and a tall metal wardrobe next to the cot downstairs. I was alone. I kept the crystal radio that Dad had helped us assemble from a kit when we had the chicken pox. I kept the Swiss Army knife we used to saw flashlight batteries in half. The reason they didn't work, Dad said, was they were out of juice. Whenever a battery didn't work, we cut it open. Dad was right. No juice in it. We never cut open a battery that still worked; that would have been stupid. Besides, if we cut one open that still had juice in it, we were sure Dad wouldn't buy another one. We believed he knew how long a battery should last, how much juice it had, and how long it took to dry up. "Batteries don't grow on trees," he said.

I don't think I knew then, at least not in a way I understood, how much I missed Bob, especially at bedtime. After all, he was still around, still there to fight with at the breakfast table, still there to play Parcheesi on the floor, still my brother. [. . .]

At St. Francis we learned about the souls in purgatory and that we could help them get to heaven by suffering and offering it up for them. They in turn would remember us when they ascended to heaven and would intercede for us. [. . .] I took to folding my legs back under me in a painful way, and I tried to withstand the pain a little longer each night, counting how many decades of the rosary I recited before I had to give up and unbend my legs. Gradually I became less afraid. The rosary's incantatory power brought a kind of peace to me; after a while the cyclical sounds were released from their meanings, and I was released from my yearning—for my brother and for things to return to normal—and I slept.

In a comic book I read about telepathy, and I showed it to Bob. I don't remember if it was my idea or his, but we tried it for a while, long enough to arrive at some rules. The trouble was that we fought all the time, because we each believed that if the other would only quit *sending* so much and spend more time trying to *receive*, it would work. I remember one time when I convinced myself that he had agreed to give me his Warren Spahn and Eddie Matthews base-ball cards. He denied it. I took the cards, but my mother made me give them back. We decided to start out more simply. We each kept a tablet and pencil next to our beds to write down what we wanted to send as well as anything we thought we had received. In the morning we would compare our pages. We never matched, so we decided to try to send single words. As we tired of the whole thing, we each began to write long lists of all the words that occurred to us once we were in our separate beds. Every morning we would find that some of our words matched, just enough of them for us to believe, with each other's help, that we were getting somewhere. After a while we gave up.

I believed that Bob was the problem, though I knew it wasn't his fault. Maybe it was part of his illness, like falling down all the time.

So I lay in bed and tried to contact aliens: Martians or Venusians. This was similar to praying, except that, while I took it for granted that God heard me, I wasn't sure if any aliens were listening, or if I had telepathic powers strong enough to reach them. There was no formula that I knew of for communicating with aliens, no Hail Mary's or Glory Be's. This hit-or-miss dimension made it even more exciting. And then there was the element of listening; though God sometimes spoke to people, they were almost always grown-ups. In any case, I didn't expect a reply, from God. I would know, however, that the aliens had "heard" me only if they answered. I don't know what I expected, maybe something like, "Check. We read you, earth boy. We are standing by."

I remember that Bob was alarmed when I let on what I was up to. How would I know if they were friendly aliens? What if they sent me a whole brainful of scary thoughts? What if they tried to take over my mind?

What I thought but never told him—and this, I suspect, I got from a *Twilight Zone* episode on TV—was that the alien I was trying to contact was a superior intelligence, probably with a huge head like a light bulb, who would give me the cure for whatever had made him sick. I kept the tablet and pencil next to the bed. I imagined the cure would be too complicated for me to grasp, but that the alien would send me the message slowly so I could write it down and give it to scientists who would understand it. On the other hand, the cure might be something simple, something we were overlooking, and the alien would point it out, and I would tell my mother the next morning and everything would be okay.

I knew that Bob's sleeping downstairs was permanent, but it was the kind of knowledge I wouldn't, or couldn't, surrender to. With so much changing so fast, how could I believe anything was "for keeps," as we called it? There were braces, there were prayers, there was telepathy, and there was hope.

In a few more months the school year would be over. By the end of that summer, Bob was in a wheelchair. In September he was going to a different school. [. . .]

The growing distance between Bob and me was partly my need to believe that he could learn, if only he would try a little harder, how not to get hurt. I wanted him to practice with me. "Let's go outside and play paratrooper," I'd say, but he never felt like it. I knew he was sick, but I needed to hold him responsible for at least some part of it. If my brother's disease could slam him into the ground at any moment, bloodying his nose and blacking his eyes, there was no hope. If he were completely helpless, I would have to feel it: not only the sidewalk smashing him in the face, but also his outrage and humiliation, and, worst of all, my grief. No. Not my brother. He's too smart. He could get the hang of it if he would try. [. . .]

Several years ago, on a visit home, I sat in the kitchen looking through the shoe box with my mother. Most of the pictures were facedown, so looking through them was like turning over cards. I came to understand why my mother never used the album I'd bought her. To arrange the pictures chronologically, or any other way, would be a fiction. A memory is something that happens. To arrange memories in a particular order is to protect oneself, to substitute form for feeling. Better to reach in the box and pick a card at random. My mother's shoe box was an emblem of her courage.

I turned over a snapshot taken on my First Communion day. My head and shoulders almost fill the picture, but I'm out of focus. On the concrete walk, very small in the background, just below my right ear, Bob has fallen and is trying to get back on his feet. I remembered those times, how Bob spoke to himself, impatient but encouraging, "Come on now, *push.* Now keep your balance, *nnnh.* Good. There. Okay."

And I remembered other times, when I was responsible for bringing Bob home from school. I was in fourth grade, he in third. By then he walked on his toes; the tendons of his calves were tightening, pulling his heels off the ground. And I remember one day in particular: Bob is on the ground; I want to get home because I'm supposed to play football with Pete and his friends. They've never asked me to play with them before, and Bob is ruining everything. I grab him by the arm; he screams and won't let me pull him to his feet. I hit him. He cries. I try to pull him up and he screams again. I kick him. He lies there and cries among the horse-chestnut cases and yellow leaves stuck to the sidewalk on Ninth Street. A neighbor called my parents. My father said he'd "beat me within an inch of my life" if I ever laid a hand on Bob again.

I was holding the picture and shaking. I handed it to my mother. "Oh, who took this one? You're all blurry," she said. If she noticed the scene in the background, she didn't comment; she turned it face-down on the pile of those she'd already looked at. "Here's a good one of Bob," she said. He is sitting in his chair, a blank look on his face, at the end of the concrete walk, where we always wheeled him when he wanted to be outdoors.

Kate Simon

1912–1990

From *Bronx Primitive: Portraits in a Childhood*

(1982)

Kate Simon grew up in a crowded Bronx tenement with her Polish-born parents and an older brother. As a girl she was vulnerable to predation by an older relative. When he joined their household, would she continue to be exploited, or could she resist?

My father arranged passage for a nephew, the grown son of one of his numerous elder sisters. My mother wasn't especially eager to welcome him; when she had suggested that one of *her* unmarried sisters be brought from Warsaw, my father had said he was spending *his* money on *his* family, not hers. She went into one of her silent, glowering times. Cousin Yankel (addressed occasionally by my father, never my mother, as Yankele, the affectionate diminutive of his name) was nineteen or twenty, lanky and awkward, with a big Adam's apple that I liked to watch riding his throat. He had a long thin nose, cheeks scored with pits and pimples, and the shortest stubble of hair on his head when he arrived. A number of immigrants arrived with shaved heads, we were told, to get rid of head lice and the trouble they might cause if immigration officials found them. Other than his Adam's apple, I liked the fact that he was double-jointed, as he demonstrated in one light moment by pushing his thumb down to touch his forearm. We thought it might be a family trait, like curly hair, and when we couldn't do it, we felt disinherited. Yankel was bedded down on an old army cot my father found in a Third Avenue junk store and placed under the window in the dining-living room, an arrangement my mother didn't like because a country cousin, a young man, would probably not be careful of her china closet, her stone birds, her rose-covered tablecloth, the ugly sullen rubber plant she loved and wiped with castor oil to keep it shiningly healthy, and he might even in his carelessness kick the piano. Clearly, she had it in for him, and we might automatically have taken his side, shown him some favor, if he hadn't been so indifferent to us. He had other fish to fry. He immediately registered in a night-school English class and was gone after supper most evenings. The remaining evenings he spent with my father to make the rounds of acquaintances with marriageable daughters. Yankel expressed dissatisfaction with them all; a spoiled bastard who had been brought up in a crooning nest of women, as my father had been, he found none of the girls pretty enough for him or, judging from their houses and dress, rich enough. He wanted a good-looking girl with prosperous parents, as promised him by rich America. [. . .]

My mother's irritation with Yankel fed and battened on his inconsiderate habits: his dirty socks on the polished piano, his night-school books pressing the breath out of the embroidered roses on her tablecloth, his habit of carefully squeezing pimples before the bathroom mirror while my brother was twisting his legs trying to hold in his pee. He wouldn't eat lung or liver, and she couldn't tell him he had to, as she did us. He ate all the farmer cheese meant for morning breakfast during his night raids on the icebox. The *klops*, a huge hamburger stewed in onion, Polish style, disappeared in one sitting, leaving nothing for the next day's lunch sandwiches. And pausing between heaping spoonfuls of *kasha*, he described the delicious things his mother, a good mother and a wonderful cook, made for him. My mother listened sourly.

There were other night raids that my mother knew nothing about. Deep in the night, Yankel would appear in his underwear at our bedroom door. He stood looking at the bed and my sister's crib for a moment, like a careful Indian scout. He came in, gently nudged my sleeping brother to the far side of our bed, nearer the wall, and waited to make sure he was still asleep. One knee on the bed, he nudged me for space. When I clung to the edge of the bed to keep him out, he stretched one long leg, and then the other, across me and settled in the middle between my brother and myself. [. . .]

Fiercely whispering at me not to make any noise, he pulled off my underpants and got on top of me. He pushed his big thing, pulsating like a machine, as near as he could to my opening but never went in. Near, on top, to the side, he pressed and rose, pressed and rose, and then stayed while warm gluey stuff spilled down my thighs. He got up, said nothing, and tiptoed down the hall to his dining room cot. Once, when a noise came from the baby's crib, he ran on tiptoe to the bathroom to make it appear, I suppose, that he had just gotten up to pee.

After several nights of this—I can't remember how or if they were spaced—I decided that this was bad and dangerous. There were adult phrases around the street and on park benches about the girl who died because Fatty Arbuckle had torn her. I seemed also in danger of being torn. When my brother and sister were fast asleep, I took the extra blanket hanging over the end of the bed, wrapped myself in it, and sat down in the chair on which we had draped our clothing, determined to spend that night, and all others if necessary, sitting up. He came in, stared, groped in the bed, and turned to find me sitting. He began to plead with me to go back to bed. He wouldn't touch me, never again. What would my mother think if she found me that way? Please go back to bed. Please don't say anything. He could be arrested and sent back to Poland if I said anything. He'd give me a beautiful present, a gold ring, if I went back to bed. Please. Please. I stared at him and said nothing. He looked at me out of his pimpled face for a while—waiting for what?—and then tiptoed down the hall.

Since my mother didn't like him and my brother was totally indifferent to him, the fact that I stopped talking to him at all made no conspicuous change in our lives. Not too long after I felt it safe to sleep in my bed again he said he had found a man from his province with whom he was going to share a room as a boarder, nearer the factory. I knew he was lying but only stared at him insolently. [. . .]

The next day, when I came home from school, he was gone and my mother was practicing her mandolin in her dining room, with the red tablecloth roses fluffed, the birds pecking in their white stone bowl, the rubber plant gleaming with castor oil.

Bich Minh Nguyen

b. 1974

From *Stealing Buddha's Dinner: A Memoir*

(2007)

The mother of Bich Minh Nguyen was left behind when
Bich, her father, sister, grandmother, and uncles fled
Saigon in 1975 and settled in Grand Rapids, Michigan.
Her factory-worker father married Rosa, the daughter of Mexican migrant farmworkers. Rosa brought a
daughter of her own into the family and then gave birth
to a son, Bich's half-brother. The blended family was
interracial, intergenerational, and intercultural, but
media-driven consumerism had a special grip on this
Vietnamese girl hungry for Americanization.

Just as I was about to enter fifth grade, the public school teachers
went on strike. To show her support, Rosa refused to let any of us
kids go to school until the teachers had returned. I called my best
friend Holly, who confirmed that everyone had shown up on the
first day except for me.

"Who's going to teach them?" I asked Rosa.

"Scabs," she hissed.

I pictured dry purplish scabs, like the ones that formed over my
skinned knees, pacing in front of a chalkboard.

Anh and Crissy [the writer's sister and stepsister] were thrilled
about missing school, and Vinh [brother] seemed glad enough to
stay at home with his Transformers and *He-Man* reruns, but I felt
uneasy: the first days were foundational; friendships for the whole
year could be cemented. I told Rosa that I needed to get back to

school, but she said no way, José. "No one in our house is going to cross the picket lines."

Rosa loved a good strike. Her great hero was César Chávez, whom I learned about when she announced that we were all boycotting lettuce, grapes, and everything made by Campbell's. She wore buttons on her blazers: "Lettuce Stick Together" and "Down with Grapes." Campbell's and grapes: those were her enemies, and for a long time not a single grape appeared in our household, unless smuggled in by our uncles and grandmother. Rosa spoke of the fruit—picked in California by underpaid and exploited migrants—with such resentment that for years, even after the migrants had won a bit of victory and Rosa stopped boycotting, I still looked at grapes with apprehension. César Chávez had organized the migrant workers in California, a move that must have taken Rosa straight back to her own childhood, when her parents' wages depended on the seasons and the sums doled out by farms and orchards up and down the coast of Lake Michigan. Rosa explained how the workers had no say and no power, and that only unions ensured that they would be paid fairly.

César Chávez appealed to my sense of justice, stirred from reading *The Grapes of Wrath*. It was one of my favorite books for its descriptions of dust, greasy food, and soulful characters. The biscuits were "high" and "bulbous"; Ma Joad "[lifted] . . . curling slices of pork from the frying pan." I found myself charmed by Tom Joad, a good man in spite of the years he'd done in prison. I felt his hunger when he came back from a day of picking peaches and shouted, "Leave me at her," while reaching for his dinner plate. The way he wolfed down his three hamburger patties and white bread with drippings drizzled on top. "Got any more?" he asked Ma. She kept the whole family going, but she didn't have any more food for Tom that night, not when wages were so little and store prices so high. They had seen families making their way eastward, back out of California, to go home to die in the dust they had tried to escape.

So my heart beat a little faster when Rosa decided to take Vinh and me to the picket line in front of Fountain Street Elementary School in downtown Grand Rapids. Against the backdrop of the old brick school and a sky-blue day, a small group of women clustered about the sidewalk, holding up signs. "Who are they?" I asked Rosa.

"Who do you think they are? The picketers, of course."

They carried plain signs—"FAIR WAGES! SUPPORT YOUR TEACHERS!"—as they walked back and forth, looking nothing like Tom Joad or Casey or Ma or Rosasharn. Things only got exciting when parents drove by, at which point the teachers started jumping and waving their signs. If they saw a scab they screamed, "Scab!" No one paid them any attention. No paid-off cops came to arrest them.

Vinh and I marched alongside Rosa and the other women for a while. It was early September and hot out, and we soon lamented not having any candy to keep us going. Other teachers showed up with thermoses of coffee, talking in serious tones about the lack of response from the superintendent. They looked indignant, and I rallied myself to feel the outrage I had felt when cops tried to arrest Tom's friend for "agitating," and when Casey got hit with the pick handle. I thought about how big corporations kept lowering wages, knowing that there were people waiting, and hungry enough, to take any worker's place. I tried to imagine Ma Joad among these teachers, walking heavily in her faded calico print dress.

The teachers ended the strike two weeks later with only some of their demands met. I started school mostly worried that my class-mates were already sailing far ahead of me. Cliques might have been formed, desks decorated and arranged. I would be the odd one out, the one anxious to find a seat in the cafeteria, the one having to court all over again the blue-eyed girls who held the keys to popularity.

As it happened, Holly said the scabs had been like substitute teachers. They'd spent the days reading and drawing and going over last year's easy math. I hadn't missed much at all. At recess on my first day back I felt so comfortable that I bragged that I had joined the picket line, until Jamie Taylor, who always dressed up as a prin-cess for Halloween and whose mother had once sent her to school with a platter of homemade rosette cookies dusted with powdered sugar, called me a Communist. When I denied it she shrugged and said, "Your *mom's* a Communist."

"She is not," I said, thinking of how Rosa spoke of Communists with foreboding in her voice, and how she warned me that if they "took over" we would have no more liberties.

Jamie Taylor pointed out, "You're the only one whose mom didn't let her come to school during the strike."

Her words reinforced the shame I already felt: I did not have a mother who stayed home to clean the bathrooms and bake angel food cakes. Rosa worked downtown, near the "bad" part of the city, directing GED and ESL classes at the Hispanic Institute. She liked to bring us kids there on weekends and after school, to help run the mimeograph machine and tidy up the classrooms. The building had been an elementary school in the sixties and now it seemed to soak up dust on every surface. Grime coated the windows and gritted the vinyl floors. Inside the main hall, someone had painted a fantastic mural in the style of Diego Rivera. A bald eagle and a brown-faced man faced each other, and around them groups of American Indians, African-Americans, and Latino-Americans looked on, wearing proud, impassioned expressions. Above them a banner unscrolled the words "We the People of America" and *"Viva la raza"* The vending machines stood near the mural, so I spent a lot of time staring at it. I felt the bold eyes watching me; the colors—all browns and russets streaked with red—followed me down the hall as I wandered in and out of classrooms, looking for something to read, teaching myself the Spanish words for the months and days. I scanned bilingual education phrase books. We had some at home, including one devoted to explanations of American idioms like "go jump in a lake" or "get out of town." My father always got these wrong. When he didn't know the answer to something he'd shrug and say, "Beat me."

The previous year Rosa had enrolled me in an evening cake-decorating class. While she caught up on paperwork in her office, I and a half dozen middle-aged Mexican-American women learned how to mix buttercream frosting and use silver nozzles fastened onto pastry bags to create stars, letters, and flowers. For my final project I decorated a cake with a pink unicorn prancing in a field of violets. I enjoyed the class—the murmur of the ladies fretting over their scalloped borders, the swirl of dye into frosting, the effort involved in each sugar rose. But it frustrated me that I could never frost a cake in even waves the way the women on commercials and in the Sunday coupons did. Their round two-layer confections, lavishly coated in Betty Crocker whipped frostings, never sloped or showed crumbs. I became convinced that such talents lay only in the hands of white mothers in aprons. To me, life lived in commercials *was* real life. Commercials were instructions; they were news. They showed me what perfection could be: in the right woman's hands, the layers of a cake would always be exactly the same size. In the right woman's kitchen, a cartoon rabbit would visit the children and show them how to slurp down a tall glass of Nestlé Quik with a straw. A shaken cruet would spill a stream of Good Seasons over hills of lettuce leaves. Commercials had a firm definition of motherhood, which almost all of my friends' mothers had no trouble fulfilling. They swept floors and scrubbed bathtubs. They cooked casseroles and washed dishes. They had smooth, sensible pageboy hairstyles and serene smiles. They set the dinner tables every night and sang Cinderella songs and taught their children where to sit.

My siblings and I were always plaguing Rosa to buy things we saw on TV. Instead of the generic raisin bran and Toasty-O's, which came in big bags that were slung onto the bottom shelf of the cereal aisle, we campaigned for Trix, Cookie Crisp, Franken Berry, and Count Chocula. We begged for any kind that came with buried trinkets—stickers, spokes, tattoo stamps. We created our own ads for orange juice, reenacted the commercials for Life cereal (Vinh always played Mikey), and sang the Carnation Instant Breakfast song: "You're gonna love it in an instant!"

On rare weekends, Rosa or Crissy made pancakes or French toast with blueberries we had picked and frozen the previous summer. That's when the trusty bottle of Mrs. Butterworth's syrup came out. I loved that her body was the bottle, which seemed both perverse and alluring. In the commercial, when kids talked to her she came to life, her arms gesturing regally as she spoke. I waited for her to speak to me, too, staring at the placid face to will her to life. Sometimes, too, I shouted "Hey, Kool-Aid!" but the giant pitcher of Mr. Kool-Aid never did come crashing through a wall of our house.

Most of all, I would have given so much to have the Pillsbury Doughboy appear in our kitchen. He would bounce across the counter like a living marshmallow and wave his wee rolling pin at me. His puffy white chef's hat would almost fall off and he would spread his arms to welcome me to his world. Then, at last, I would reach out and poke his belly with the tip of my finger, making him coo and giggle, his round eyes scrunching up with laughter.

Tobias Wolff
b. 1945

From *This Boy's Life: A Memoir*
(1989)

Tobias Wolff and his divorced mother lived with two women friends in Seattle. Smart and precocious, he was nicknamed Jack, after the writer Jack London. His mother received no financial support from Tobias's erratic father and worried about her son's potential for delinquency. When Tobias was about eleven, his mother's friend Marian told her that he needed a father and encouraged her to consider remarriage. His mother followed Marian's advice, involving herself and her son in a relationship that ended in divorce.

A few months after we moved into the house Marian got engaged to her marine boyfriend. Then Kathy got engaged to a man in her office. Marian thought my mother should get engaged too, and tried to fix her up. She set in motion a brief parade of suitors. One by one they came up the walk, stared at the broken steps, went around to the back; then, entering the kitchen, braced themselves and put on joviality like a party hat. Even I could see the hopelessness in their imitation of gaiety though not its source in their belief, already sufficiently formed to make itself come true, that this woman too would find them unacceptable.

There was a marine who did tricks for me with lengths of string tied to his fingers, and seemed unwilling to leave the house with my mother. There was a man who arrived drunk and had to be sent away in a cab. There was an old man who, my mother told me later, tried to borrow money from her. And then came Dwight.

Dwight was a short man with curly brown hair and sad, restless brown eyes. He smelled of gasoline. His legs were small for his thick-chested body, but what they lacked in length they made up for in spring; he had an abrupt, surprising way of springing to his feet. He dressed like no one I'd ever met before—two-tone shoes, hand-painted tie, monogrammed blazer with a monogrammed handkerchief in the breast pocket. Dwight kept coming back, which made him chief among the suitors. My mother said he was a good dancer—he could really make those shoes of his get up and go. Also he was very nice, very considerate.

I didn't worry about him. He was too short. He was a mechanic. His clothes were wrong. I didn't know why they were wrong, but they were. We hadn't come all the way out here to end up with him. He didn't even live in Seattle; he lived in a place called Chinook, a tiny village three hours north of Seattle, up in the Cascade Mountains. Besides, he'd already been married. He had three kids of his own living with him, all teenagers. I knew my mother would never let herself get tangled up in a mess like that.

And even though Dwight kept driving down from the mountains to see my mother, every other weekend at first, then every weekend, he seemed to sense the futility of his case. His attentions to my mother were puppyish, fawning, as if he knew that the odds of getting his hands on her were pathetically slim and that even being in her presence was a piece of luck that depended on his displaying at every moment deference, bounce, optimism, and all manner of good cheer.

He tried too hard. No eye is quicker to detect that kind of effort than the eye of a competitor who also happens to be a child. I seized on and stored away every nuance of Dwight's abjection, his habit of licking his lips, the way his eyes darted from face to face to search out warning signs of disagreement or boredom, his uncertain smile, the phony timbre of his laughter at jokes he didn't really get. Nobody could just go to the kitchen and make a drink, Dwight had to jump up and do it himself. Nobody could open a door or put on a coat without his help. They couldn't even smoke their own cigarettes, they had to take one of Dwight's and submit to a prolonged drama of ignition: the unsheathing of his monogrammed Zippo from its velvet case; the snapping open of the top against his pant leg; the presentation of the tall flame with its crown of oily smoke— then the whole ritual in reverse.

I was a good mimic, or at least a cruel one, and Dwight was an easy target. I went to work as soon as he left the house. My mother and Kathy tried not to laugh but they did, and so did Marian, though she never really abandoned herself to it. "Dwight's not that bad," she would say to my mother, and my mother would nod. "He's very nice," Marian would add, and my mother would nod again and say, "Jack, that's enough."

We spent Thanksgiving in Chinook with Dwight and his kids. Snow had fallen a few nights earlier. It had melted in the valley but still covered the trees on the upper slopes, which were purple with shadow when we arrived. Though it was still late afternoon the sun had already set behind the mountains.

Dwight's kids came out to meet us when we drove up. The two oldest, a boy and a girl, waited at the bottom of the steps as a girl about my age ran up to my mother and threw her arms around her waist. I was completely disgusted. The girl was pinch-faced and scrawny, and on the back of her head she had a bald spot the size of a silver dollar. She made a kind of crooning noise as she clutched my mother, who, instead of pushing this person away, laughed and hugged her back.

"This is Pearl," Dwight said, and somehow freed my mother from her grasp. Pearl looked over at me. She did not smile, and neither did I.

We walked up to the house and met the other two. Both of them were taller than Dwight. Skipper had a wedge-shaped head, flat in the back and sharp in front, with close-set eyes and a long blade of a nose. He wore a crew cut. Skipper regarded me with polite lack of interest and turned his attention to my mother, greeting her with grave but perfect courtesy. Norma just said "Hi!" and ruffled my hair. I looked up at her, and until we left Chinook two days later I stopped looking at her only when I was asleep or when someone walked between us.

Norma was seventeen, ripe and lovely. Her lips were full and red, always a little swollen-looking as if she'd just woken up, and she moved sleepily too, languidly, stretching often. When she stretched, her blouse went taut and parted slightly between the buttons, showing milky slices of belly. She had the whitest skin. Thick red hair that she pushed sleepily back from her forehead. Green eyes flecked with brown. She used lavender water, and the faint sweetness of the smell got mixed up with the warmth she gave off. Sometimes, just fooling around, thinking nothing of it, she would put her arm around my shoulder and bump me with her hip, or pull me up against her.

If Norma noticed my unblinking stare she took it for granted. She never seemed surprised by it, or embarrassed. When our eyes met she smiled.

We brought our bags inside and took a tour of the house. It wasn't really a house, but half of a barracks where German prisoners of war had been quartered. After the war the barracks had been converted to a duplex. A family named Miller lived on one side, Dwight's family on the other, in three bedrooms that faced the kitchen, dining room, and living room across a narrow hallway. The rooms were small and dark. Her arms crossed over her chest, my mother peered into them and gushed falsely. Dwight sensed her reserve. He waved his hands around, declaring the plans he had for renovation. My mother couldn't help but offer a few suggestions of her own, which Dwight admired so much that he adopted them all, right then and there.

After dinner my mother went out with Dwight to meet some of his friends. I helped Norma and Pearl do the dishes, then Skipper took out the Monopoly board and we played a couple of games. Pearl won both of them because she cared so much. She watched us suspiciously and recited rules at us while she gloated over her rising pile of deeds and money. After she won she told the rest of us everything we'd done wrong.

My mother woke me when she came in. We were sharing the sofa bed in the living room, and she kept turning and plumping the pillow. She couldn't settle down. When I asked what was wrong she said, "Nothing. Go to sleep." Then she raised herself up on one elbow and whispered, "What do you think?"

"They're okay," I said. "Norma's nice."

"They're all nice," she said. She lay back again. Still whispering, she told me she liked them all, but felt a little hurried. She didn't want to hurry into anything.

That made sense, I said.

She said she was doing really well at work. She felt like she was finally starting to get somewhere. She didn't want to stop, not right now. Did I know what she meant?

I said I knew exactly what she meant.

Is that selfish? she asked. Marian thought she should get married. Marian thought I needed a father in the worst way. But she didn't *want* to get married, not really. Not now, anyway. Maybe later, when she felt ready, but not now.

That was fine with me, I said. Later would be fine.

The next day was Thanksgiving. After breakfast Dwight packed everyone into the car and drove us around Chinook. Chinook was a company village owned by Seattle City Light. A couple of hundred people lived there in neat rows of houses and converted barracks, all white with green trim. The lanes between the houses had been hedged with rhododendron, and Dwight said the flowers bloomed all summer long. The village had the gracious, well tended look of an old military camp, and that was what everyone called it—the camp. Most of the men worked at the powerhouse or at one of three dams along the Skagit. The river ran through the village, a deep, powerful river crowded on both sides by deep mountains. These mountains faced each other across a valley half a mile wide at the point where Chinook had been built. The slopes were heavily forested, the trees taking root even in granite outcroppings and gullies of scree. Mists hung in the treetops.

Dwight took his time showing us around. After we had seen the village, he drove us upstream along a narrow road dropping sheer to the river on one side and overhung by boulders on the other. As he drove he listed the advantages of life in Chinook. The air. The water. No crime, no juvenile delinquency. For scenery all you had to do was step out your front door, which you never had to lock. Hunting. Fishing. In fact the Skagit was one of the best trout streams in the world. Ted William—who, not many people realized, was a world-class angler as well as a baseball great, not to mention a war hero— had been fishing here for years.

Pearl sat up front between Dwight and my mother. She had her head on my mother's shoulder and was almost in her lap. I sat in the backseat between Skipper and Norma. They were quiet. At one point my mother turned and asked, "How about you guys? How do you like it here?"

They looked at each other. Skipper said, "Fine."

"Fine," Norma said. "It's just a little isolated, is all."

"Not that isolated," Dwight said.

"Well," Norma said, "maybe not *that* isolated. Pretty isolated, though."

"There's plenty to do here if you kids would just take a little initiative," Dwight said "When I was growing up we didn't have all the things you kids have, we didn't have record players, we didn't have TVs, all of that, but we were never bored. We were never bored. We used our imaginations. We read the classics. We played musical instruments. There is absolutely no excuse for a kid to be bored, not in my book there isn't. You show me a bored kid and I'll show you a lazy kid."

My mother glanced at Dwight, then turned back to Norma and Skipper. "You'll be graduating this year, right?" she said to Skipper.

He nodded.

"And you have another year," she said to Norma. "One more year," Norma said. "One more year and watch my dust."

"How's the school here?"

"They don't have one. Just a grade school. We go to Concrete."

"Concrete?"

"Concrete High," Norma said.

"That's the name of a *town?*"

"We passed it on the way up," Dwight said. "Concrete."

"Concrete," my mother repeated.

"It's a few miles downriver," Dwight said.

"Forty miles," Norma said.

"Come off it," Dwight said. "It's not that far."

"Thirty-nine miles," Skipper said. "Exactly. I measured it on the odometer."

"What's the difference!" Dwight said. "You'd bellyache just as much if the goddamned school was next door. If all you can do is complain, I would thank you to just stow it. Just kindly stow it." Dwight kept looking back as he talked. His lower lip was curled out, and his bottom teeth showed. The car wandered the road.

"I'm in fifth grade," Pearl said.

Nobody answered her.

We drove on for a while. Then my mother asked Dwight to pull over. She wanted to take some pictures. She had Dwight and Norma and Skipper and Pearl stand together on the side of the road with snowy peaks sticking up behind them. Then Norma grabbed the camera and started ordering everyone around. The last picture she took was of me and Pearl. "Closer!" she yelled. "Come on! Okay, now hold hands! Hold hands! You know, *hands?* Like on the end of your arms?" She ran up to us, took Pearl's left hand, put it in my right hand, wrapped my fingers around it, then ran back to her vantage point and aimed the camera at us.

Pearl let her hand go dead limp. So did I. We both stared at Norma. "Jeez," she said. "Dead on arrival."

On the way back to Chinook my mother said, "Dwight, I didn't know you played an instrument. What do you play?"

Dwight was chewing on an unlit cigar. He took it out of his mouth. "A little piano," he said. "Mainly sax. Alto sax."

Skipper and Norma looked quickly at each other, then looked away again, out the windows.

When Dwight first invited us to Chinook he'd won me over by mentioning that the rifle club was going to hold a turkey shoot. If I wanted to, he said, I could bring my Winchester along and enter the contest. I hadn't fired or even held my rifle since we left Salt Lake. Every couple of weeks or so I tore the house apart looking for it, but my mother had it hidden somewhere else, probably in her office downtown.

I thought of the trip to Chinook as a reunion with my rifle. During art period I made drawings of it and showed them to Taylor and Silver [friends from Seattle], who affected disbelief in its existence. I also painted a picture that depicted me sighting down the barrel of my rifle at a big gobbler with rolling eyes and long red wattles.

The turkey shoot was at noon. Dwight and Pearl and my mother and I drove down to the firing range while Skipper went off to work on a car that he was customizing and Norma stayed home to cook. Not until we reached the range did Dwight get around to telling me that in fact there would be no turkey at this turkey shoot. The targets were paper—regulation match targets. They weren't even giving a turkey away; the prize was a smoked Virginia ham. *Turkey shoot* was just a figure of speech, Dwight said. He thought everybody knew that.

He also let drop, casually, as if the information were of no consequence, that I would not be allowed to shoot after all. It was for grown-ups, not kids. That was all they needed, a bunch of kids running around with guns.

"But you said I could."

Dwight was assembling my Winchester, which he apparently meant to use himself. "They just told me a couple of days ago," he said.

I could tell he was lying—that he'd known all along. I couldn't do a thing but stand there and look at him. Pearl, smiling a little, watched me.

"Dwight," my mother said, "you did tell him."

He said, "I don't make the rules, Rosemary."

I started to argue, but my mother gave my shoulder a hard squeeze. When I glanced up to her she shook her head.

Dwight couldn't figure out how the rifle fit together, so I did it for him while he looked on. "That," he said, "is the most stupidly constructed firearm I have ever seen, bar none."

A man with a clipboard came up to us. He was collecting entry fees. After Dwight paid him he started to move off, but my mother stopped him and held out some money. He looked at it, then down at his clipboard.

"Wolff," she said. "Rosemary Wolff."

Still studying his clipboard, he asked if she wanted to shoot.

She said she did.

He looked over at Dwight, who busied himself with the rifle. Then he dropped his eyes again and mumbled something about the rules.

"This is an NRA club, isn't it?" my mother asked.

He nodded.

"Well, I am a dues-paying member of the NRA, and that gives me the right to participate in the activities of other chapters when I'm away from my own." She said all of this very pleasantly.

Finally he took the money. "You'll be the only woman shooting," he said.

She smiled.

He wrote her name down. "Why not?" he said suddenly, uncertainly. "Why the heck not." He gave her a number and wandered off to another group of shooters. Dwight's number was called early. He fired his ten rounds in rapid succession, hardly pausing for breath, and got a rotten score. A couple of his shots hadn't even hit the paper. When his score was announced he handed my mother the rifle. "Where'd you get this blunderbuss, anyway?" he asked me.

My mother answered. "A friend of mine gave it to him."

"Some friend," he said. "That thing is a menace. You ought to get rid of it. It shoots wild." He added, "The bore is probably rusted out."

"The bore is perfect," I said.

My mother's number should have been called after Dwight's, but it wasn't. One man after another went up to the line while she stood there watching. I got antsy and cold. After a long wait I walked over to the river and tried to skip rocks. A mist drifted over the water. My fingers grew numb but I kept at it until the sound of rifle fire stopped, leaving a silence in which I felt too much alone. When I came back my mother had finished her turn. She was standing around with some of the men. Others were putting their rifles in their cars, passing bottles back and forth, calling to each other as they drove away into the dusk.

"You missed me!" she said when I came up.

I asked her how she had done.

"Dwight brought in a ringer," one of the men said.

"Did you win?"

She nodded.

"You won? No kidding?"

She struck a pose with the rifle.

I waited while my mother joked around with the men, laughing, trading mild insults, flushed with cold and the pleasure of being admired. Then she said good-bye and we walked toward the car. I said, "I didn't know you were a member of the NRA."

"I'm a little behind in my dues," she said.

Dwight and Pearl were sitting in the front seat with the ham between them. Neither of them spoke when we got in. Dwight pulled away fast and drove straight back to the house, where he clomped down the hall to his room and closed the door behind him.

We joined Norma and Skipper in the kitchen. Norma had taken the turkey out of the oven, and the house was rich with its smell.

When she found out that my mother had won, she said, "Oh boy, now we're really in for it. He thinks he's some kind of big hunter."

"He killed a deer once," Pearl said.

"That was with the car," Norma said.

Skipper got up and went down the hall to Dwight's room. A few minutes later they both came back, Dwight stiff and awkward. Skipper teased him in a shy, affectionate way, and Dwight took it well, and my mother acted as if nothing had happened. Then Dwight perked up and made drinks for the two of them and pretty soon we were having a good time. We sat down at the beautiful table Norma had laid for us, and we ate turkey and dressing and candied yams and giblet gravy and cranberry sauce. After we ate, we sang. We sang "Harvest Moon," "Side by Side," "Moonlight Bay," "Birmingham Jail," and "High above Cayuga's Waters." I got compliments for knowing all the words. We toasted Norma for cooking the turkey, and my mother for winning the turkey shoot. [. . .]

Dwight drove us down to Seattle early the next morning. He stopped on the bridge leading out of camp so we could see the salmon in the water below. He pointed them out to us, dark shapes among the rocks. They had come all the way from the ocean to spawn here, Dwight said, and then they would die. They were already dying. The change from salt to fresh water had turned their flesh rotten. Long strips of it hung off their bodies, waving in the current. [. . .]

Dwight drove down that weekend. They spent a lot of time together, and finally my mother told me that Dwight was urging a proposal which she felt bound to consider. He proposed that after Christmas I move up to Chinook and live with him and go to school there. If things worked out, if I made a real effort and got along with him and his kids, she would quit her job and accept his offer of marriage.

She did not try to make any of this sound like great news. Instead she spoke as if she saw in this plan a duty which she would be selfish not to acknowledge. But first she wanted my approval. I thought I had no choice, so I gave it. [. . .]

I had agreed to move to Chinook partly because I thought I had no choice. But there was more to it than that. Unlike my mother, I was fiercely conventional. I was tempted by the idea of belonging to a conventional family, and living in a house, and having a big brother and a couple of sisters—especially if one of those sisters was Norma. And in my heart I despised the life I led in Seattle. I was sick of it and had no idea how to change it. I thought that in Chinook, away from Taylor and Silver, away from Marian, away from people who had already made up their minds about me, I could be different. I could introduce myself as a scholar-athlete, a boy of dignity and consequence, and without any reason to doubt me people would believe I was that boy, and thus allow me to be that boy. I recognized no obstacle to miraculous change but the incredulity of others. This was an idea that died hard, if it ever really died at all. [. . .]

Dwight made a study of me. He thought about me during the day while he grunted over the engines of trucks and generators, and in the evening while he watched me eat and late at night while he sat heavy-lidded at the kitchen table with a pint of Old Crow and a package of Camels to support him in his deliberations. He shared his findings as they came to him. The trouble with me was, I thought I was going to get through life without doing any work. The trouble with me was, I thought I was smarter than everyone else. The trouble with me was, I thought other people couldn't tell what I was thinking. The trouble with me was, I didn't think.

Another trouble with me was that I had too much free time. Dwight fixed that. He arranged for me to take over the local paper route. He had me join the Boy Scouts. He gave me a heavy load of chores, and encouraged Pearl to watch me and let him know if I was laggard or sloppy. Some of the chores were reasonable, some unreasonable, some bizarre as the meanest whims of a gnome setting tasks to a treasure seeker. [. . .]

After school I delivered newspapers. Dwight had bought the route for almost nothing from a boy who was sick of it and couldn't find any other takers. I delivered the Seattle *Times* and the *Post-Intelligencer* to most of the houses in Chinook and to the barracks where the single men lived. The route paid between fifty and sixty dollars a month, money that Dwight took from me as soon as I collected it. He said that I would thank him someday, when I really needed the money.

I dawdled along the route, seizing any chance to delay going home. I sat in the bachelors' quarters and read their magazines (GENT GOES UNDERCOVER AT VASSAR! MY TEN YEARS AS A SEX-SLAVE OF THE AMAZONS OF THE WHITE NILE!). I fooled around with kids from school, played with dogs, read both papers front to back. Sometimes I just sat on a railing somewhere and looked up at the mountains. They were always in shadow. The sun didn't make it up over the peaks before classes started in the morning, and it was gone behind the western rim by the time school let out. I lived in perpetual dusk.

The absence of light became oppressive to me. It took on the weight of other absences I could not admit to or even define but still felt sharply, on my own in this new place. My father and my brother. Friends. Most of all my mother, whose arrival seemed to grow more and more distant rather than closer. In the weeks since Christmas she had delayed giving Dwight a definite answer. She wanted to be sure, she told me. Marrying Dwight meant quitting her job, giving up her house, really burning her bridges. She couldn't rush into this one.

I understood, but understanding did not make me miss her less. She made the world seem friendly. And somehow, with her, it was. She would talk to anyone, anywhere, in grocery stores or ticket lines or restaurants, drawing them out and listening to their stories with intense concentration and partisan outbursts of sympathy. My mother did not expect to find people dull or mean; she assumed they would be likeable and interesting, and they felt this assurance, and mostly lived up to it. On the bus ride from Salt Lake to Portland she had everybody talking and laughing until it seemed like some kind of party. [...]

My mother finally gave Dwight a date in March. Once he knew she was coming he began to talk about his plans for renovating the house, but he drank at night and didn't get anything done. A couple of weeks before she quit her job he brought home a trunkful of paint in five-gallon cans. All of it was white. Dwight spread out his tarps and for several nights running we stayed up late painting the ceilings and walls. When we had finished those, Dwight looked around, saw that it was good, and kept going. He painted the coffee table white. He painted all the beds white, and the chests of drawers, and the dining-room table. He called it "blond" when he put it on the furniture, but it wasn't blond or even off-white; it was stark, industrial strength, eye-frying white. The house reeked of oil.

My mother called a few days before Dwight was supposed to drive down and pick her up. She talked to him for a while, then asked to speak to me. She wanted to know how I was.

Okay, I told her.

She said she had been feeling kind of low and just wanted to check with me, make sure I felt good about everything. It was such a big step. Were Dwight and I getting along all right?

I said we were. He was in the living room with me, painting some chairs, but I probably would have given the same answer if I'd been alone.

My mother told me she could still change her mind. She could keep her job and find another place to live. I understood, didn't I, that it wasn't too late?

I said I did, but I didn't. I had come to feel that all of this was fated, that I was bound to accept as my home a place I did not feel at home in, and to take as my father a man who was offended by my existence and would never stop questioning my right to it. I did not believe my mother when she told me it wasn't too late. I knew she meant what she said, but it seemed to me that she was deceiving herself. Things had gone too far. And somehow it was her telling me it wasn't too late that made me believe, past all doubt, that it was. Those words still sound to me less like a hope than an epitaph, the last lie we tell before hurling ourselves over the brink.

After my mother hung up, Dwight and I finished painting the dining-room chairs. Then he lit a cigarette and looked around, his brush still in his hands. He gazed pensively at the piano. He said, "Sort of stands out, doesn't it?"

I looked at it with him. It was an old Baldwin upright, cased in black walnut, that he had bought for twenty dollars from a family on the move who'd grown tired of hauling it around. Dwight did a victory dance after bringing it home. He said the stupid cornpones had no idea what it was worth, that it was worth twice that much. Dwight sat down at it one night with the idea of demonstrating his virtuosity, but after making a few sour chords he slammed it shut and pronounced it out of tune. He never went near it again. Sometimes Pearl banged out "Chopsticks" but otherwise it got no play at all. It was just a piece of furniture, so dark in all this whiteness that it seemed to be pulsing. You really couldn't look anywhere else.

I agreed that it stood out.

We went to work on it. Using fine bristles so our brush strokes wouldn't show, we painted the bench, the pedestal, the fluted columns that rose from the pedestal to the keyboard. We painted the carved scrollwork. We painted the elaborate inlaid picture above the keyboard, a picture of a girl with braided yellow hair leaning out of her gabled window to listen to a redbird on a branch. We painted the lustrous cabinet. We even painted the foot pedals. Finally, because the antique yellow of the ivory looked wrong to Dwight against the new white, we very carefully painted the keys, all except the black ones, of course. [...]

Mother and Dwight weren't getting along. They hadn't gotten along since the night they returned from their honeymoon in Vancouver, two days early, silent and grim, not even looking at each other as they carried the suitcases into the house and down the hall to Dwight's room. That night Dwight sat up drinking and went to sleep on the sofa. He did this often, sometimes three or four nights in a row, weekends especially. I was always the first one up on Saturday and Sunday because the papers came in early on those days, and when I got up I usually found Dwight asleep on the sofa, a test pattern hissing on the TV.

For the first few weeks my mother was utterly cast down. She slept late, something she had never done before, and when I came home for lunch I sometimes found her still in her bathrobe, sitting at the kitchen table and staring dazedly down the bright white tunnel of the house. I had never seen my mother give up. I hadn't even known the possibility existed, but now I knew, and it gave me pause. It made me feel for a little while the truth that everything good in my life could be lost, that it was all drawn day by day from someone else's store of hope and will. But my mother got better, and I found other things to think about.

She did not give up. Instead, she chose to believe that she could still make a life in Chinook. She joined the PTA and persuaded the head of the rifle club to admit her as a member. She took a part-time job waitressing in the bachelors' mess hall. She filled the house with plants, mothered Pearl, and insisted that all of us spend time together like a real family.

And so we did. But our failure was ordained, because the real family we set out to imitate does not exist in nature; a real family as troubled as ours would never dream of spending time together.

Richard Rodriguez

b. 1944

From *Hunger of Memory:*
The Education of Richard Rodriguez,
an Autobiography
(1982)

Richard Rodriguez reflects on how the publication of
his autobiographical writing has affected his parents,
Mexican immigrants who value family privacy above
all. At Christmastime, he gathers for dinner and a gift
exchange with his parents and adult siblings who now
have children of their own. There's a glow from the family's togetherness, the professional and material success
of his siblings, and the satisfaction he draws from being
a successful writer and raconteur. But the holiday cheer
is tempered by his awareness of the unbridgeable gulf
that still separates him from his parents.

It is to those whom my mother refers to as the *gringos* that I write.
The *gringos*. The expression reminds me that she and my father
have not followed their children all the way down the path to full
Americanization. They were changed—became more easy in public, less withdrawn and uncertain—by the public success of children.
But something remained unchanged in their lives. With excessive
care they continue today to note the difference between private and
public life. And their private society remains only their family. No
matter how friendly they are in public, no matter how firm their
smiles, my parents never forget when they are in public. My mother
must use a high-pitched tone of voice when she addresses people

who are not relatives. It is a tone of voice I have all my life heard her use away from the house. Coming home from grammar school with new friends, I would hear it, its reminder: My new intimates were strangers to her. Like my sisters and brother, over the years, I've grown used to hearing that voice. Expected to hear it. Though I suspect that voice has played deep in my soul, sounding a lyre, to recall my "betrayal," my movement away from our family's intimate past. It is the voice I hear even now when my mother addresses her son- or daughter-in-law. (They remain public people to her.) She speaks to them, sounding the way she does when talking over the fence to a neighbor.

It was, in fact, the lady next door to my parents—a librarian— who first mentioned seeing my essay seven years ago. My mother was embarrassed because she hadn't any idea what the lady was talking about. But she had heard enough to go to a library with my father to find the article. They read what I wrote. And then she wrote her letter.

It is addressed to me in Spanish, but the body of the letter is in English. Almost mechanically she speaks of her pride at the start. ("Your dad and I are very proud of the brilliant manner you have to express yourself.") Then the matter of most concern comes to the fore. "Your dad and I have only one objection to what you write. You say too much about the family ... Why do you have to do that? ... Why do you need to tell the *gringos*? Why do you think we're so separated as a family? Do you really think this, Richard?"

A new paragraph changes the tone. Soft, maternal. Worried for me she adds, "Do not punish yourself for having to give up our culture in order to 'make it' as you say. Think of all the wonderful achievements you have obtained. You should be proud. Learn Spanish better. Practice it with your dad and me. Don't worry so much. Don't get the idea that I am mad at you either.

"Just keep one thing in mind. Writing is one thing, the family is another. I don't want *tus hermanos* hurt by your writings. And what do you think the cousins will say when they read where you talk about how the aunts were maids? Especially I don't want the *gringos* knowing about our private affairs. Why should they? Please give this some thought. Please write about something else in the future. Do me this favor."

Please.

To the adult I am today, my mother needs to say what she would never have needed to say to her child: the boy who faithfully kept family secrets. When my fourth-grade teacher made our class write a paper about a typical evening at home, it never occurred to me actually to do so. "Describe what you do with your family," she told us. And automatically I produced a fictionalized account. I wrote that I had six brothers and sisters; I described watching my mother get dressed up in a red-sequined dress before she went with my father to a party; I even related how the imaginary baby sitter ("a high school student") taught my brother and sisters and me to make popcorn and how, later, I fell asleep before my parents returned. The nun who read what I wrote would have known that what I had written was completely imagined. But she never said anything about my contrivance. And I never expected her to either. I never thought she *really* wanted me to write about my family life. In any case, I would have been unable to do so.

I was very much the son of parents who regarded the most innocuous piece of information about the family to be secret. Although I had, by that time, grown easy in public, I felt that my family life was strictly private, not to be revealed to unfamiliar ears or eyes. Around the age of ten, I was held by surprise listening to my best friend tell me one day that he "hated" his father. In a furious whisper he said that when he attempted to kiss his father before going to bed, his father had laughed: "Don't you think you're getting too old for that sort of thing, son?" I was intrigued not so much by the incident as by the fact that the boy would relate it to *me*.

In those years I was exposed to the sliding-glass-door informality of middle-class California family life. Ringing the doorbell of a friend's house, I would hear someone inside yell out, "Come on in, Richie; door's not locked." And in I would go to discover my friend's family undisturbed by my presence. The father was in the kitchen in his underwear. The mother was in her bathrobe. Voices gathered in familiarity. A parent scolded a child in front of me; voices quarreled, then laughed; the mother told me something about her son after he had stepped out of the room and she was sure he couldn't overhear; the father would speak to his children and to me in the same tone of voice. I was one of the family, the parents of several good friends would assure me. (Richie.)

My mother sometimes invited my grammar school friends to stay for dinner or even to stay overnight. But my parents never treated such visitors as part of the family, never told them they were. When a school friend ate at our table, my father spoke less than usual. (Stray, distant words.) My mother was careful to use her "visitor's voice." Sometimes, listening to her, I would feel annoyed because she wouldn't be more herself. Sometimes I'd feel embarrassed that I couldn't give to a friend at my house what I freely accepted at his.

I remained, nevertheless, my parents' child. At school, in sixth grade, my teacher suggested that I start keeping a diary. ("You should write down your personal experiences and reflections.") But I shied away from the idea. It was the one suggestion that the scholarship boy couldn't follow. I would not have wanted to write about the minor daily events of my life; I would never have been able to write about what most deeply, daily, concerned me during those years: I was growing away from my parents. Even if I could have been certain that no one would find my diary, even if I could have destroyed each page after I had written it, I would have felt uncomfortable writing about my home life. There seemed to me something intrinsically public about written words. [. . .]

I continue thinking about what she has asked me—and what she cannot comprehend. My parents seem to me possessed of great dignity. An aristocratic reserve. Like the very rich who live behind tall walls, my mother and father are always mindful of the line separating public from private life. Watching a celebrity talk show on television, they listen for several minutes as a movie star with bright teeth recounts details of his recent divorce. And I see my parents grow impatient. Finally, my mother gets up from her chair. Changing the channel, she says with simple disdain, "Cheap people."

My mother and my father are not cheap people. They never are tempted to believe that public life can also be intimate. They remain aloof from the modern temptation that captivates many in America's middle class: the temptation to relieve the anonymity of public life by trying to make it intimate. They do not understand, consequently, what so pleases the television audience listening to a movie star discuss his divorce with bogus private language. My father opens a newspaper to find an article by a politician's wife in which she reveals (actually, renders merely as gossip) intimate details of her marriage. And he looks up from the article to ask me, "Why does she do this?"

I find his question embarrassing. Although I know that he does not intend to embarrass me, I am forced to think about this book I have been writing. And I realize that my parents will be as puzzled by my act of self-revelation as they are by the movie star's revelations on the talk show. They never will call me cheap for publishing an autobiography. But I can well imagine their faces tightened by incomprehension as they read my words.

(Why does he do this?)

Many mornings at my desk I have been paralyzed by the thought of their faces, their eyes. I imagine their eyes moving slowly across these pages. That image has weakened my resolve. Finally, however, it has not stopped me. Despite the fact that my parents remain even now in my mind a critical, silent chorus, standing together, I continue to write. I do not make my parents' sharp distinction between public and private life. With my mother and father I scorn those who attempt to create an experience of intimacy in public. But unlike my parents, I have come to think that there is a place for the deeply personal in public life. This is what I have learned by trying to write this book: There are things so deeply personal that they can be revealed only to strangers. I believe this. I continue to write.

"What is psychiatry?" my mother asks. And I wish I could tell her. (I wish she could imagine it.) "There are things that are so personal that they can only be said to someone who is not close. Someone you don't know. A person who is not an intimate friend or a relation. There are things too personal to be shared with intimates."

She stands at the ironing board, her tone easy because she is speaking to me. (I am her son.) For my mother that which is personal can only be said to a relative—her only intimates. She makes the single exception of confessing her sins to a Catholic priest. Otherwise, she speaks of her personal life only at home. The same is true of my father—though he is silent even with family members. Of those matters too jaggedly personal to reveal to intimates, my parents will never speak. And that seems to me an extraordinary oppression. The unspoken may well up within my mother and cause her to sigh. But beyond that sigh nothing is heard. There is no one she can address. Words never form. Silence remains to repress them. She remains quiet. My father in his chair remains quiet. [. . .]

My brother and sisters recognize a different person, not the Richard Rodriguez in this book. I hope, when they read this, they will continue to trust the person they have known me to be. But I hope too that, like our mother, they will understand why it is that the voice I sound here I have never sounded to them. All those faraway childhood mornings in Sacramento, walking together to school, we talked but never mentioned a thing about what concerned us so much: the great event of our schooling, the change it forced on our lives. Years passed. Silence grew thicker, less penetrable. We grew older without ever speaking to each other about any of it. Intimacy grooved our voices in familiar notes; familiarity defined the limits of what could be said. Until we became adults. And now we see each other most years at noisy family gatherings where there is no place to stop the conversation, no right moment to turn the heads of listeners, no way to essay this, my voice.

I see them now, my brother and sisters, two or three times every year. We do not live so very far from one another. But as an entire family, we only manage to gather for dinner on Easter. And Mother's Day. Christmas. It is usually at our parents' house that these dinners are held. Our mother invariably organizes things. Well before anyone else has the chance to make other arrangements, her voice will sound on the phone to remind us of an upcoming gathering.

Lately, I have begun to wonder how the family will gather even three times a year when she is not there with her phone to unite us. For the time being, however, she presides at the table. She—not my father, who sits opposite her—says the Grace before Meals. She busies herself throughout the meal. "Sit down now," somebody tells her. But she moves back and forth from the dining room table to the kitchen. Someone needs more food. (What's missing?) Something always is missing from the table. When she is seated, she listens to the conversation. But she seems lonely. (Does she think things would have been different if one of her children had brought home someone who could speak Spanish?) She does not know how or where to join in when her children are talking about Woody Allen movies or real estate tax laws or somebody's yoga class. (Does she remember how we vied with each other to sit beside her in a movie theatre?) Someone remembers at some point to include her in the conversation. Someone asks how many pounds the turkey was this year. She responds in her visitor's voice. And soon the voices ride away. She is left with the silence.

Sitting beside me, as usual, is my younger sister. We gossip. She tells me about her trip last week to Milan; we laugh; we talk about clothes, mutual friends in New York.

Other voices intrude: I hear the voices of my brother and sister and the people who have married into our family. I am the loudest talker. I am the one doing most of the talking. I talk, having learned from hundreds of cocktail parties and dinner parties how to talk with great animation about nothing especially. I sound happy. I talk to everyone about something. And I become shy only when my older sister wonders what I am doing these days. Working in Los Angeles? Or writing again? When will she be able to see something I've published?

I try to change the subject.

"Are you writing a book?"

I notice, out of the corner of my eye, that my mother is nervously piling dishes and then getting up to take them out to the kitchen.

I say yes.

"Well, well, well. Let's see it. Is it going to be a love story? A romance? What's it about?"

She glances down at her thirteen-year-old son, her oldest. "Tommy reads and reads, just like you used to."

I look over at him and ask him what sort of books he likes best.

"Everything!" his mother answers with pride.

He smiles. I wonder: Am I watching myself in this boy? In this face where I can scarcely trace a family resemblance? Have I foreseen his past? He lives in a world of Little League and Pop Warner. He has spoken English all his life. His father is of German descent, a fourth-generation American. And he does not go to a Catholic school, but to a public school named after a dead politician. Still, he is someone who reads. . . .

"He and I read all the same books," my sister informs me. And with that remark, my nephew's life slips out of my grasp to imagine.

Dinner progresses. There is dessert. Four cakes. Coffee. The conversation advances with remarkable ease. Talk is cheerful, the way talk is among people who rarely see one another and then are surprised that they have so much to say. Sometimes voices converge from various points around the table. Sometimes voices retreat to separate topics, two or three conversations.

My mother interrupts. She speaks and gets everyone's attention. Some cousin of ours is getting married next month. (Already.) And some other relative is now the mother of a nine-pound baby boy. (Already?) And some relative's son is graduating from college this year. (We haven't seen him since he was five.) And somebody else, an aunt, is retiring from her job in that candy store. And a friend of my mother's from Sacramento—Do we remember her after all these years?—died of cancer just last week. (Already!)

My father remains a witness to the evening. It is difficult to tell what he hears (his hearing is bad) or cannot understand (his English is bad). His face stays impassive, unless he is directly addressed. In which case he smiles and nods, too eagerly, too quickly, at what has been said. (Has he really heard?) When he has finished eating, I notice, he sits back in his chair. And his eyes move from face to face. Sometimes I feel that he is looking at me. I look over to see him, and his eyes dart away the second after I glance.

When Christmas dinner is finished, there are gifts to exchange in the front room. Tradition demands that my brother, the oldest, play master of ceremonies, "Santa's helper," handing out presents with a cigar in his hand. It is the chore he has come to assume, making us laugh with his hammy asides. "This is for Richard," he says, rattling a box next to his ear, rolling his eyes. "And this one is for Mama Rodriguez." (There is the bright snap of a camera.)

Nowadays there is money enough for buying useless and slightly ludicrous gifts for my mother and father. (They will receive an expensive backgammon set. And airplane tickets to places they haven't the energy or the desire to visit. And they will be given a huge silver urn—"for chilling champagne.")

My mother is not surprised that her children are well-off. Her two daughters are business executives. Her oldest son is a lawyer. She predicted it all long ago. "Someday," she used to say, when we were young, "you will all grow up and all be very rich. You'll have lots of money to buy me presents. But I'll be a little old lady. I won't have any teeth or hair. So you'll have to buy me soft food and put a blue wig on my head. And you'll buy me a big fur coat. But you'll only be able to see my eyes."

Every Christmas now the floor around her is carpeted with red and green wrapping paper. And her feet are wreathed with gifts.

By the time the last gift is unwrapped, everyone seems very tired. The room has become uncomfortably warm. The talk grows listless. ("Does anyone want coffee or more cake?" Somebody groans.) Children are falling asleep. Someone gets up to leave, prompting others to leave. ("We have to get up early tomorrow.")

"Another Christmas," my mother says. She says that same thing every year, so we all smile to hear it again.

Children are bundled up for the fast walk to the car. My mother stands by the door calling good-bye. She stands with a coat over her shoulders, looking into the dark where expensive foreign cars idle sharply. She seems, all of a sudden, very small. She looks worried.

"Don't come out, it's too cold," somebody shouts at her or at my father, who steps out onto the porch. I watch my younger sister in a shiny mink jacket bend slightly to kiss my mother before she rushes down the front steps. My mother stands waving toward no one in particular. She seems sad to me. How sad? Why? (Sad that we all are going home? Sad that it was not quite, can never be, the Christmas one remembers having had once?) I am tempted to ask her quietly if there is anything wrong. (But these are questions of paradise, Mama.)

My brother drives away.

"Daddy shouldn't be outside," my mother says. "Here, take this jacket out to him."

She steps into the warm of the entrance hall and hands me the coat she has been wearing over her shoulders.

I take it to my father and place it on him. In that instant I feel the thinness of his arms. He turns. He asks if I am going home now too. It is, I realize, the only thing he has said to me all evening.

commentary for chapter one: FAMILIES

In this section memoirists use a "being in it" voice—the voice that describes the past as if it were the present, with dialogue and an eye for telling details, although clearly based on memory—to evoke family relationships that are charged with both intimacy and alienation, security and anxiety. Paul Clemens remembers an affectionate relationship with his father, burying his head in his father's body when he came home from work and smelling "hot metal, mineral spirits, and a masculine, earned sort of sweat." As an adolescent, Tobias Wolff sensed that his mother's impending marriage to her suitor Dwight was doomed to fail, but Tobias felt such emotional distance from her that he could not bring himself to warn her against it. These accounts point to how conflict ridden, even poisonous, our relationships can be with birth families, even when there is an underlying dynamic of love. They show working-class families coping with economic adversity, the challenges of child raising and, for immigrant families, the pressures and promises of assimilation into American society.

Some of these stories show parents trying to give their children a moral compass. When Bich Minh Nguyen wanted to go to her fifth-grade class instead of missing school because of a teachers' strike, her stepmother Rosa insisted she stay home out of solidarity with the strikers. "No one in our house is going to cross the picket line," Rosa said. Clemens's father chastises his son for using a vile racist epithet with other kids during a tackle game in his neighborhood. Richard Hoffman's father demands Richard treat his handicapped brother with respect and decency, at a time when their family is grappling with severe economic hardship. Low wages or unemployment can strain families to the breaking point, and as these stories suggest, setting ethical standards can be one of the few areas where working parents can give lasting guidance and exhibit authority to their children, even if opinions vary about proper ethical norms outside the home.

In half the families in this section, the children or parents are immigrants. Integration into American society brings its own pressures, both financial and cultural. Kate Simon's narrative hints at the economic stringencies of emigrating from Eastern Europe in the 1920s; their apartment building was overcrowded and the furniture bought at a junk store. Nguyen recounts her fascination with figures in TV commercials, which she saw as faithful, if sometimes comical, representations of life in their adopted country. Richard Rodriguez's Mexican-born parents were mystified at the way American celebrities and politicians would reveal secrets of their marriages and family lives publicly. The writer Rodriguez finds a balance between these competing values—a Mexican attention to discretion, the American penchant for self-revelation—by concluding with a touch of irony that "there are things so deeply personal that they can be revealed only to strangers."

Families vary in their capacity to function in a manner that nurtures the development of children. Five of the six families depicted here could be seen as basically functional. In those families, the members feel a sense of responsibility toward one another that sustains family cohesion and helps them meet challenges. Although Hoffman's mother knew that Richard's younger brother was showing symptoms of terminal disease, she kept up family morale, awakening her sons with a spirited reveille: "You gotta get up in the morning!" Rosa, head of the household in Nguyen's family, was an overextended working mother but the atmosphere at home supported congenial relationships among step-siblings and half-siblings. Simon's family had its share of dysfunction but its members colluded in sustaining the family by conforming to its patriarchal structure. By the time Kate's older cousin starts forcing himself on her sexually, her mother has already soured on Yankel's selfish ways and wants him to leave. But knowing of her father's affection for his nephew, Kate instead silently shames Yankel into leaving. Thus she keeps peace in the family. Just as her mother restored physical order to the household after Yankel left, Kate maintained interpersonal order by getting rid of her cousin completely on her own.

The one family that, as described by the writer, would be considered dysfunctional by almost any standard was that of Wolff. He looks back on the family formed by the marriage of his mother and the hostile, emotionally stunted Dwight and sees divorce as inevitable: "a real family as troubled as ours would never dream of spending time together." Rooted in the zeitgeist of the 1950s, the marriage was a loving but misguided effort by his mother to provide a "normal," two-parent family. The Women's Liberation movement would later give women more confidence to raise children on their own. If Tobias had been born ten years later, perhaps his mother would have made a different decision.

QUESTIONS FOR DISCUSSION

1. The authors of these stories remember their parents or stepparents as important in many ways: for example, as nurturers, as disciplinarians, or as role models. Regarding any particular episode that you select, what role did the parents play? How was the child affected?

2. Children over time come to learn that their own family is different from other families. What did the authors of these stories learn about differences between themselves and other families with which they had contact?

3. In what ways did adverse economic circumstances affect the lives of these families?

4. In all of these stories the authors describe how their parents acted toward them when they were children. Some also reflect on how their parents act toward them in the present. What do you note especially about the change in perspective?

5. Children are not just acted upon; they themselves influence relationships with parents and stepparents. Can you find examples of how these authors as children affected relationships with, or between, their parents?

chapter two
NEIGHBORHOODS

Oscar Hijuelos

1951–2013

From *Thoughts without Cigarettes: A Memoir*

(2011)

In the 1940s Oscar Hijuelos's parents emigrated from Cuba to New York City, where Oscar was born. His father worked as a cook at the Biltmore Hotel. During a family visit to Cuba, four-year-old Oscar contracted a severe kidney infection, leading to a year's hospitalization in Connecticut and prolonged semiconfinement to his apartment under his mother's care. Finally, at age twelve, Oscar escaped from all the "shouting and arguments" between his parents and discovered what his Upper West Side neighborhood, near the campus of Columbia University, had to offer.

Once I hit the streets with the other kids, I doubt that my mother was happy about that transition. It just happened: My afternoons were soon spent prowling about up and down the block, climbing railings, hiding in basements, and learning how to play basic games like handball against the wall. Eventually, I joined in rougher activities, like a game called Cow in the Meadow, the source of whose pastoral name I haven't the faintest idea of, which involved a simple-enough premise. The "cow" (someone) stood out in the street (the "meadow") and his task involved approaching the sidewalk on either side to pull a kid off the curb, into the meadow, which sounds easy enough except for the fact that once the cow left his meadow and ventured onto the sidewalk, the kids could beat the living hell out of him. What victories, of a Pyrrhic nature, one managed left arms and legs covered with bruises and cuts, and occa-sionally, as well, someone who didn't like you or thought that you were lame or just had it in for you would go after you for real, and in such instances, the ferocity escalated and what had begun with a good-natured beating intended to strengthen one's character (if there was any motivation at all) turned into an out-and-out fight between the cow and his assailant, though at a certain point, time might be called and the two would be pulled apart until tempers cooled, and the more earnestly intended beatings could begin again.

As distasteful as it might sound, that game, for all its potential for inflicting pain and damage—bruised limbs, cut lips, and boxed ears—always seemed fun: I particularly took to it, what with hav-ing so much pent-up *something* inside of me. I'm proud to say that I never went home crying afterward, even felt good that such a for-merly sick wimp could hold his own, though I would get beaten with a belt by my mother if I came back with a broken pair of eyeglasses or a tornup and/or bloodied shirt.

Mainly, I will say this about my block: A lot of tough working-class kids lived on it, and while there were a few serious delinquents among them who spent time away in juvenile facilities for burglary, and in one instance, for dropping a tile off a tenement rooftop on a passerby, blinding him, the majority were merely mischievous, though a few were simply mean. I almost had my eyes put out by this older fellow named Michael Guiling, the kind of teenager ca-pable of fastening what were called cherry bombs, a high explosive, to pigeons. (I know, it's hard to imagine the process, let alone the outcome, but I once saw him tying one of those bombs to a pigeon and lighting the fuse; he let that bird go, and, flying away, it blew up in midair.) He had a thing for fireworks and, for the hell of it, a happy smile on his face, once flung a cherry bomb at my face; if I hadn't stepped aside, who knows what would have happened. (He was just one of those cruel lost souls—years later, sometime in the early 1970s, he'd die of a heroin overdose in the men's room of a bar on 110th Street, most popular with Columbia University students, a dive called the Gold Rail.) Down the street, toward the drive, lived a giant fellow—six feet five and probably weighing three hundred pounds, his nickname, naturally was "Tiny"—who had some vague aspirations of becoming a football player. It was he who grabbed me by the back of the neck one lovely spring morning and, holding me there, dropped a dime onto the sidewalk, ordering me to pick it up. When I did, he stomped on my hand, crushing two of my fingers, the nail on one of them to this day oddly distended toward the right. (Despite hating his guts for that, fifteen or so years later, I would be saddened to hear that Tiny, while having had some success with a second-tier football team in Pennsylvania, died prematurely in his thirties of cancer.)

The Irish were everywhere in the neighborhood in those days (at least down to 108th Street, below which the streets became more Puerto Rican), but so were Hispanics and what census polls would now call "Other." Unlike some neighborhoods, like around the West Sixties, where different ethnic groups were at one another's throats, waging block-to-block turf wars of the sort commemorated in B movies, the older kids around there seemed to get along. In earlier times, in fact the late 1950s, when I, still camped at home, could have hardly been aware of such things, there had been periods in which gangs like the Sinners and the Assassins occasionally ventured south from their uptown Harlem neighborhoods—north of City College—to stage "rumbles" against the local "whiteys." These were fights born of grudges that began at high school dances with some insult, or a face-off between two tough guys getting out of hand, or because someone was banging someone else's girl, or quite simply out of pure poverty-driven anger and, as well, at a time when the word *spic* was in common usage in New York City, from the deep memory of old, bred-in-the-bone resentments. I'm not quite sure where the Latinos or, for that matter, the other ethnicities in my neighborhood placed their loyalties, but I'm fairly sure that in such instances they joined their white counterparts in these face-offs against that common enemy.

Over those years, blacks had also made incursions onto our block from the east, gangs of them climbing up the terraces of Morningside Park, intending to swarm over the neighborhood, though without much success. Down in the park on 118th, there was a "circle," a kind of stone embattlement that looked out over Harlem, and it is from there, I've been told, that the locals fended off such attacks by raining down bottles, rocks, and garbage cans on whoever tried to race up to the drive by a stone stairway or to climb those walls.

Nevertheless, though those days had passed, but not the prejudices, the possibility of such confrontations still hung in the air, and as a consequence, it was a common thing for the police to patrol Amsterdam Avenue regularly in their green and white squad cars, with an eye to breaking up any large groups gathered on a street corner, no matter what they were up to—usually just smoking cigarettes and bullshitting about girls. Still, the neighborhood definitely identified with that gang-era mythology. When a recording of the musical *West Side Story* first came out, my brother threw a party in our apartment for his friends, with my father, incidentally, stationed in the kitchen, allowing an endless supply of beer and other refreshments into the house, while in the living room, the lights turned low, couples danced to songs like "I Feel Pretty" and "Maria," the record playing over and over again, along with other music—of the Shirelles and the Drifters—but repeating so often that, looking back now, I am sure there was a pride about it, as if, in a neighborhood where mixed couples were already as common as interethnic fights, its songs amounted to a kind of personal anthem for a lot of the older kids. (And to think that the musical itself had been put together by a group of theatrically brilliant middle-class Jewish folks, who, in all likelihood, had viewed such a world from a safe distance!)

Now, the first party I ever attended, at Halloween, took place in the basement apartment of my father's pal Mr. Martinez, who lived up the street. His son, Danny, later a sergeant in the NYC police department, decorated the place with candlelit jack-o'-lanterns and tried to make their basement digs seem scarily festive, but what I mainly remember is that he provided a plain old American diversion, something I had only seen on TV, a bowl filled with apples for which one would bob, as well as a game of blindfolded pin-the-tail-on-the-donkey, which I had never played before. (Thank you, Danny.) One of their upstairs neighbors was a Mexican woman, Mrs. Flores, who seemed terrified of allowing her little boy, dressed always so nicely and wearing white patent leather shoes, to mix with the other kids. (In his daintiness he seemed another version of my younger self, darker, but just as bewildered as I had once been.) There also happened to be another Latino kid from that block, a diabetic, who, sharing my name, was called Little Oscar. Having apparently narrowly escaped diabetes myself, it amazed me to watch him sitting on

his stoop as he, with resignation, administered himself a shot of in-
sulin with a syringe. While it fascinated some of the kids, his condition did not bring out pity in them. Unfortunately, so frail and truly
weightless, he, just skin and bones, seemed an easy victim to the
bullies, and those kids, to my horror, were always picking on him—
and cruelly; on at least one occasion, as he stood with his hand tied
behind him to a signpost, they tried to force him to take a bite from
a dried piece of dog turd stuck on a twig. "Come on, leave the guy
alone," I remember saying, but they didn't relent. (Whatever happened to Little Oscar, for his parents, catching wind of such things,
soon got him the hell out of that neighborhood, I hope his future life
went well, though I will never know.)

Slowly, in the years after my illness, I had made my own friends
from around, among them Richard, the youngest smoker I would
ever know. I can recall seeing him, a few months after I had returned
from the hospital, standing outside my front window and showing
off the snappy cowboy outfit and medallion-rimmed black hat that
his father, often away, had just brought back from his travels. One
of the few kids around who'd take the trouble to come visit me in
the days when I couldn't really leave the apartment, he'd sometimes
climb the rickety back stairway to my window from the courtyard,
crawling inside to play and scrambling out when my mother heard
us from down the hall. The youngest of a large family, the Muller-
Thyms, who occupied two bustling first-floor apartments, one next
to the other, across the street, he had four brothers and five sisters
(though I knew hardly any of the older ones at all). As families went,
they were locally famous for both the brightness of the children and
the slight eccentricities of their genius father, Bernard, who had a
high sloping forehead and a vaguely Hubert Humphrey pinched-in
cast to his face, though with a Dutchman's side whiskers (the only
thing missing would have been a meerschaum pipe).

   Mr. Muller-Thym had first come to the neighborhood during
the Second World War, when he taught swimming to naval re-
cruits at the university. After the war, armed with a Ph.D. disserta-
tion in the mystical thinking of Meister Eckhart, he had drifted into
the business world and, with a brood of growing children, had decided to stay on that block, presumably to save the money he would
have spent in a better neighborhood. The aforementioned eccen-

tricities included his tendencies to occasionally parade in front of his windows, which were visible from the street, in nothing but a shirt, sometimes less—and though one would think that his physically candid persona would have scandalized the neighbors, even my mother, crying out *"Ay!"* at the sight of him, at worst found him more amusing than offensive. Publicly, he was civil, always well dressed, and if he stood out in any way from the working-class fathers on that street, it was for both his reclusiveness—I think my father, coming home from work, would say hello to him from time to time, but little more—and the lofty company he kept. (He was actually quite a nice man, always seemed interested in what I had to say, asking about me in a manner that neither of my parents did. "What do you want to do with yourself one day?" "I don't know." "Well, you should start thinking about it soon enough.") A former classmate of his from Saint Louis University, Marshall McLuhan, often frequented that apartment, well into the 1960s before the family moved away; and among the other figures who visited with Mr. Muller-Thym and sat for dinner at his table—doubtlessly on some of those evenings when my pop was sitting around with the likes of Martinez and Frankie the exterminator—happened to be Wernher von Braun, the rocket scientist then with the fledgling organization of NASA, with whom Mr. Muller-Thym had a professional relation as a consultant. (It cracks me up now to imagine this haughty rocket scientist, with his Nazi pedigree and physicist's brilliance, walking up my block to Richard's while screaming kids, cursing their hearts out and jumping onto cars to make a catch, played stickball on the street; why do I see the legendary Von Braun, shaking his head in bemusement over the apparent decline of civilization?)

Once I'd gotten my wings, I'd often go over there, usually in the afternoons, simply because I wanted to get out of the house. They lived humbly enough—there was nothing fancy about the trappings of their apartment—though what first caught my eye, always caught my eye, was the abundance of books in their home. Richard's older brother Tommy, an expansive sort with a bit of Brando about him and much street-inflected bonhomie for his fellow man, to say the least, had his own place with one of his other brothers, Johnny, next door, the floor beside his bed covered with dozens of novels, some of them science fiction but many I suppose, culled from American classics: Twain, Hemingway, Fitzgerald, and yes, Iceberg Slim are names I recall. Richard himself, the sharpest kid around, had at some ridiculously young age become consumed with history and ancient literature, no doubt because of his father's erudite influence. What can one say about a nicely featured kid, half-Italian and half-Dutch, who reads Gibbons and Thucydides, and the poetry of Catullus and Martial in the Loeb classical editions for his leisure? (At first in translation, and then later, once he had mastered them, in the original Greek and Latin.) His narrow room by the front door was always stacked with piles of such books, which sat atop his bunk bed and on his dresser, the floor, and anywhere else they might fit. He would get a kick out of reciting aloud some particularly grizzly account of a battle or, on the bawdier side, some risqué Roman couplets, a slight and naughty euphoria coming over his expression.

And while it might seem, given the calling I've unpredictably drifted toward, that this exposure to a household where books were so cherished and to a friend with such a voracious mind might have inspired in me some scholarly bent or an early love for reading, to the contrary, I regarded those books in the same manner I would while walking down Broadway with my father when we'd stop to quizzically peer into a bookstore window, never buying any, as if such volumes were intended only for others, like the college students through whose worlds we simply passed.

On that end, while I tended to dip into my school textbooks and always did well enough to pass from one grade to the next, I continued to read mostly comics, in which I would lose myself, and certainly nothing as complicated as the poems and narratives of the distant past, which, as far as I was concerned, may as well have been written on the planet Mars. In fact, that bookish world always seemed remote to me. During the few trips I'd made (with my mother) over to the 125th Street library, with its musty interior, I always found the sheer multitude of volumes intimidating and chose my books on the basis of whether they had ornate covers. (My mother, by the way, would wait in another aisle, perusing somewhat tentatively a few books that had caught her eye but never taking any out—I don't think she had a card—and if anything, she always left that place annoyed over the way the librarian, a heavyset black woman who, as I recall, always wore a large collared sweater and a strong of costume-jewelry pearls around her neck, sometimes watched her, probably, in my mother's view, with suspicion as if she "would take one without her knowing, *que carajo!*") For the record, one of the books I can recall borrowing—well, the only one I recall— happened to be an old edition of Peter Pan. I can remember feeling very impressed by the clustered, floridly set words on its opening pages, entangling to me like the vines of a briar patch—a purely visual impression—into which I thought I might delve; but I never made such headway; accustomed to the easy leisure of comics, I found Mr. Barrie's novel, however famous as a children's classic, too strictly word-bound to hold my attention long. (Or to put it differently, I was either too lazy or too distracted by my emotions to freely enter that world.)

Nevertheless, I liked the fact that my friend had so many books around, including an arcane collection of the writings of Aleister Crowley, in which his father was interested—all so incredibly for removed from my parents' beginnings. On some level, I suppose, I developed a kind of respect and admiration for the intelligence one needed for such things. But if I did so, it was from the distance of someone looking in from the outside, with wonderment, or bemusement, in the same way that my mother, at that hospital in Connecticut, used to regard me.

But we'd also get out, spending quite a number of afternoons roving through the back courtyards behind his building, climbing fences and high walls, to make our way over to 117th Street, which in those days seemed one of the more elegant blocks in the neighborhood. It was a placid elm-tree-lined street whose Georgian edifices, owned by the university, were remarkably ornate, and as much as we felt that we were encroaching on alien territory, as it were, we occasionally managed, just by nicely asking, to play billiards in one of the sunny front brownstone fraternity house rooms (if that's what they were.) And we'd go on the occasional excursion to a nearby park, though Morningside, even then a Harlem mugger's paradise, remained far less inviting than its cousin by the Hudson, where we would go "exploring" through its winding, tree-laden trails as far north as Grant's tomb.

Always fast on his feet, Richard, dark haired and of a slim and compact build, could run around the block, and quickly, without as much as taking a deep breath or working up a sweat, a remarkable thing, mainly given the fact that he smoked a carton of Winstons every week. I don't know how—or why—his habit started; it was always just there. Of his three brothers, the eldest, Bernie, an army officer fresh out of West Point, probably didn't smoke (I would never see him doing so, at any rate), but I think the next oldest, of my brother's age, and the most burly of them, Johnny, did, and Tommy certainly (Tareytons, as I recall). It simply wasn't a big thing on my block—if it was illegal for adolescents to smoke, you wouldn't have known that from checking out the street. Kids like Tommy, very much a fellow of this earth, could play three-sewer stickball games and go running the makeshift bases with a fuming butt between his lips, and, as a matter of course, a lot of the kids, having no trouble getting ahold of them, smoked while hanging out on the stoops, singing doo-wop, or in the midst of a poker game, on which they would wager either money or cigarettes. Some guys walked around with a pack stuffed up in the upper reaches of their T-shirt sleeve, by the shoulder, or with a cigarette tucked J.D.-style alongside their ear. Cigarettes were just everywhere, that's all, a normal thing, which, however, I never found particularly inviting except when I'd get the occasional yearning to be like everyone else.

In any event, Richard's household became a refuge to me. It was close by, and the family treated me well. His mother played the piano—I first heard Debussy's "Clair de Lune" over there, and one Friday evening, in the days when Catholics still observed such rules, I consumed my first Italian-style red snapper dinner at their table. But I especially loved going there around Christmas, when they'd put up a crèche and a majestic nine-foot pine tree, their living room table always covered with Italian cold cuts from Manganaro's downtown, and other seasonal niceties, like macaroons and brandy-drenched cherries, the holiday atmosphere so cheerful and strong, what with high piles of presents stacked under the evergreen and wreaths on the walls, that our own strictly budgeted Christmases suffered by comparison. We always had lots of food and booze around, of course, but my father wanted to spend only three dollars on a tree, which we'd get down on Amsterdam; and when it came to our presents, my brother and I received only one gift apiece. I don't recall my mother or father ever having any presents of their own; nor did we welcome El Día de los Reyes, Three Kings Day, the way other Latino families were said to—in fact, I only heard reference to that holiday many years later; and if anything, after the revolution, when my parents' thoughts turned to their family in Cuba—my mother receiving her sisters' plaintive letters with guilt and sadness—a kind of maudlin spirit became a part of the holiday. Having said this, I can't complain, for even with a humble tree, there was something wonderful about the way the pine smelled in our house, so sweet that not even cigarette smoke overwhelmed it.

At Richard's, the holiday remained the great event of the family calendar—certainly of his own—and while I suppose they were an affluent family relative to our street, they were quite generous and always allowed me to join in their festivities.

I probably envied my friend—he seemed to always receive the best gifts, purchased down at the old FAO Schwarz: hand puppets from Germany and train sets when he was younger, and, during my adolescence, military board games, like Tri-Tactics or Dover Patrol, and Risk, which we'd play on many an afternoon. On those occasions with Richard, whom I admired and respected, smoking away, it became inevitable that I would try one of those cigarettes myself. I was probably twelve at the time, if that, and while I can't remember having any sense of elation at those first inhalations—did I cough or make faces?—smoking at least a few, mainly Richard's, soon enough became part of my days, and the foundation of a habit that would hold on to me, on and off, for many years.

Did I like them? I seem to have gotten used to their bitter taste, and perhaps on some other level I was thinking about my father, of finding one more way of becoming a little more like him. Though I didn't smoke many at first, they kind of grew on me, and a little weary of my lingering self-image as the frail sick son, it wasn't long before, in addition to *comiendo mucho*—lots of food, tons of it—I began sneaking cigarettes out of the half-filled packs that my father would leave in one of his top dresser drawers. I'd sometimes go down to Morningside Park to smoke, where I was fairly certain that my mother wouldn't see me, and while I never lingered long there, it happened that, on a certain afternoon as I stood along one of its glass-strewn passageways, a couple of stringy Latino teenagers, the sort to wear bandannas around their foreheads, coming out of nowhere, held me up at knifepoint. It was one of those occasions when I wished I had the presence of mind to muster up some Spanish, but I'm fairly certain that no matter what I might have said (*"Pero soy latino como tú"*—"I'm Latino like you") it would have made no difference: They didn't like the way I looked, my blond hair and fairness

alone justification enough for them to hate me without even knowing just who I was; it would happen to me again and again over the
years, if not with Latinos, then with blacks—prejudice, truthfully,
beginning and ending in those days with the color of your skin. I
wasn't stupid, however; I gave them what I had in my pockets—a
few bucks from one of my jobs working at a laundry before school
down on 121st for this nice man named Mr. Gordon, who'd make his
morning deliveries while I watched his shop (and pilfered the loose
change on his shelves), and two of my pop's cigarettes, which I had
in my shirt pocket.

Eventually, my pop figured me out. Not that he put it together by
how many cigarettes were left in his packs—I'd never overdo it—but
because I started feeling too slick for my own good. Coming back
from some afternoon movie on 96th Street one day, I had lit up one
of his Kents only to see my father, peering out a bus window at me
as it passed along the avenue. First he whistled at me, a high low
whistle that he'd call me by, and gesturing with his hand against
his mouth as if he were drawing on a cigarette, he shook his head,
mouthing the word no. Then he pointed his hand toward me—ges-
ticulating the way Latinos do, his index finger stuck out, and going
up and down, meaning I was going to get it. Later, at home, he took
out his belt and reluctantly gave me a beating, as always on the legs
but painful just the same. Then, hearing about what happened, my
mother got into the act, slapping my face that night and looking
strangely at me, as if I were a criminal who had betrayed her, for
weeks afterward. Naturally, it made no difference; I adjusted, telling
myself that, as with other things, I would have to become far more
careful.

Around the same time, a picture began to hang over the living room
couch. My brother had painted it. Having creative aspirations, at
seventeen or so, he had started to make paintings somewhere—not
in our apartment, at any rate. Amazingly enough, he had talked his
Irish girlfriend from uptown, whose brothers and father happened
to be cops, into posing nude for him, that portrait of her, with her
burst of dark hair and nice body reclining against a bluish background, going up on the wall. No one objected, and my mother,
while probably bemused by his rakish ways, seemed to take great
pride in his talent; in fact, that painting would remain there for the

rest of my mother's life—for among other reasons, I think it spoke to her memories of her own cultured father back in Cuba, whose creative blood, she would always say, flowed in my brother's veins.

Of the two of us, José was always the more gifted: Lacking a center, I had a basically infantile mind, and no sense of order; I was lackadaisical in my mode of dress, while he, a more sartorial sort, had the kind of instincts that simply amazed me. He knew how to iron a shirt or a pair of trousers to a sharp crispness, and given the challenge of creating a costume for a Halloween party, he once fashioned a gaucho outfit out of some pieces of felt cloth from which he made a vest and, flattening out an old hat, came up with a new one with jangles around the brim, the final touch a wrapping in velvet cloth around his waist. (He sort of looked like Zorro and was quite handsome in the mirror before which he posed.) He was sharp in a way I would never be, and effortlessly so, though I doubt that he didn't secretly work hard at it. Above all, I'd always thought, even then, of him as being far more Cuban than I, the Spanish he would speak with some of our neighbors seemingly of a level that I, in those days, could not begin to approach. (*"Tú hermano es mucho más cubano,"* my mother would always say.)

Nevertheless, sharp as he could be, he went through some rough times. Going back a few years, once the Catholic high school he had attended closed down, he ended up at George Washington up on 187th Street, a high school where he always had to watch his back (which is to say, people were always kicking one another's asses) and from which by his senior year he had dropped out. (For the record, my parents were not happy about that.) He worked delivering Sunday newspapers, starting at six in the morning, a job I benefited from because, working for tips, I'd deliver the missed issues of the *New York Herald*, the *New York Journal American*, and the *New York Times* around the neighborhood once the calls came in at about nine. (There was also the *Daily News*, which most people also ordered, those Sunday editions with their fabulous four-color comic pages weighing three or four pounds apiece. However, I don't recall ever seeing a Spanish-language newspaper like *El Diario* on those racks.) He'd apparently also worked for a gay mortician for a time, around Washington Heights, whose advances in those parlors of cadavers he fended off. Altogether, though he seemed always to have money in his pocket, my brother remained a restless sort, looking for some distant horizon better than what we seemingly had before us. (A pet peeve of his was to the fact that the name *Basulto* still adorned, as it had for decades, the mailbox and bell.)

Generally, he rarely stayed at home, spending more than a few nights away—where, I don't know; wherever he had been hanging out, perhaps at the homes of friends like the Valez family on 122nd or up on a rooftop on a mat. There came a day when his girlfriend's brothers, dressed in their New York City police officers' blue uniforms, began knocking at our door. They knocked because my brother, in the process of painting their sister nude, or at some other point—perhaps during their teenage outings to the piers under Coney Island's boardwalk—had, in the parlance of the day, "gotten her in trouble." She was pregnant, and her family was not pleased.

My father, coming to the door and probably knowing much more than he let on, claimed, as he faced those burly officers, to have no awareness of my brother's whereabouts. (He spoke a low-toned, generally unaccented English, maybe Spanish-inflected in some ways but always calm.) In any case, after several visits with their officers' hats in hand, they stayed away. One of those nights, when my brother had come home with the air of a fugitive on the run, my father, despite their differences, sat him down in the kitchen and counseled him—an unusual thing in our family—as to his choices. Given the situation, I think it came down to the following: Either marry her or get lost. My brother would always say that my father, without a drink in his gut, rose to the occasion and, truly concerned, advised him well. Not so much to take the high road perhaps, but to consider what would be best for his future. For, as it turned out, my brother, eighteen at the time and with a pregnant girlfriend with a cop family to worry about tracking him down, decided to enlist in the air force, and within a few months, he was gone.

Rick Bragg
b. 1959

From *All Over but the Shoutin'*
(1997)

The middle child in a family with three boys, Rick Bragg grew up in segregated rural Alabama. This story contrasts an act of neighborly kindness with the ills of alcoholism, poverty, and racial bigotry.

I grew up in a house where the word *nigger* was as much a part of the vocabulary as "hey," or "pass the peas." If I was rewriting my life, if I was using this story as a way to make my life slickly perfect, this is the part I would change. But it would be a lie. It is part of me, of who I was, and I guess who I am.

It does no good to try and qualify it, certainly not to the people whom that word slashes like a razor. It does no good to say we didn't know any better or that it was part of our culture or that Yankees just don't understand that, when a Southerner uses it now, he doesn't "mean anything" by it. But if you sit and talk to old black people, the people who recall the time of my childhood, that time in history, they will tell you that there are degrees of meanness in this world, degrees of hatred, degrees of ignorance, and calculating those degrees, over decades, was a means of survival. They will tell you that the depth of that meanness and hatred and ignorance varies from soul to soul, that white Southerners are not the same and symmetrical, like the boards in a white picket fence. They will tell you that the depth of that meanness often depends on what life has done to a person, on the impressions left by brushes with people different from you, on those rare times when the parallel universes came close enough to touch.

To find our own, to find what ultimately shaped and softened my own family, I have to reach back into the darkest and ugliest time of my childhood. To find the good in it we have to peel back layers of bad, the last few months we lived with our daddy, the year we went to sleep every night afraid.

It unfolded against a backdrop of a broader meanness, a racial one. It was a year of burning buses and Klan picnics, and looking down on it from up high was the man they called the "Fighting Judge." [George] Wallace had lost his first run for governor because he claimed he was "out-niggered," and vowed never to lose another race because he seemed soft on segregation. The people and the governor fed off each other, until both grew full on their own doomed ideal. They thought it would last forever.

But in the midst of it, in the middle of the hating and fear, was a simple kindness from the most unexpected place, from people who had no reason, beyond their own common decency, to reach across that fence of hate that so many people worked so hard to build.

The closet door banged open in the fall of 1965 and the old monster was loose among us, again.

Someone had sold my daddy several bottles of aged moonshine of high quality, or so he believed. It was not in ceramic jugs or Mason or Bell jars, but in thin, dark-brown bottles of about a half pint. One night, he drank one straight down, standing up in the kitchen, and another. I cannot remember exactly what happened next, but it ended with Momma slamming the door to our bedroom, to protect us.

The next day I came home from the first grade at Spring Garden Elementary to find her standing over the sink, slowly pouring bottle after bottle of it down the drain.

I was six years old. I was still trying to figure out what nine plus nine was, still trying to color between the lines. But as I watched her, I distinctly remember thinking: "He's gonna kill you, Momma. He's gonna kill you for that."

That night, when he came home, Sam and I, pitiful in our inability to help her, to protect her, stood in the door of the kitchen and watched as he opened the cupboard and reached for his home brew. "Not all of it?" he asked, and she nodded. My momma did not run, did not hide. She stood there like a statue. Then, slowly she took off her glasses.

"Don't hurt my teeth," she said.

I guess the angels were with her. He looked at her, hard, and she nodded her head, slowly. Then he just went over to the Formica table and sat down.

"Margaret," he said, "you couldn't have hurt me no worse if you shot me dead." He got up, after a while, and walked out the door, to find a bottle somewhere else. I didn't know then, like I do now, of the devils that rode his back, flogging him, didn't know that he was free of them sometimes, for weeks, for months, and he lived upright, then, mostly sober. But that when they descended shrieking on him the only place to hide was in the bottom of a bottle. But instead of freeing him, it only fed them.

She never moved until the door banged, and then she just walked kind of stiff-like into her bedroom, and shut the door.

He quit work. He stayed drunk most of the time, instead of weekends, and he yelled at her and told her how sorry he was that he ever married her, what a mistake it was when she brought a passel of brats into his life, cluttering it up. Once, drunk, he tried to cut my hair. My momma stopped him, and he hit her.

And there was nothing, nothing we could do. I would stand beside Sam, a little behind him, because like her he always seemed to be between him and me. Once, I guess because I couldn't stand it anymore, I screamed at him to leave our momma alone, and he got up out of his chair and reached for me, but what might have happened I will never know. Sam launched himself at our daddy like a wildcat, and in my mind's eye I can see him swinging his little balled-up, fists into that grown man, again and again. My daddy grabbed his hands, and then Sam commenced to kicking his shins, or trying to, as my daddy swung him wildly around the room.

I remember that my own fear seemed to break then, and I ran in and grabbed one of his legs above the thigh, and bit him hard, behind the leg in the bend of his knee, and heard him howl. I do not remember him hitting us, only that my momma, one more time, somehow got between us, saving us. Mostly I remember how helpless and weak and useless I was.

It was a cold winter that year, and it seemed that with each passing day of December the temperatures dropped a little more. Once
it got so cold that the small pond near our house froze, which is no
big deal to Yankees but was amazing to us. We skidded rocks over
it, and gingerly stepped out on it, never more than a few inches. But
my little brother, Mark, was fearless at age three.

He was wearing two coats and two pairs of pants, so trussed-up
his arms stuck almost straight out at his sides. As my daddy stood
with his hands in his pockets, smoking, lost in thought, Mark decided to go skating in his baby shoes.

He walked straight out to the edge of the pond and was fine,
laughing, too light to even break the ice, but then one of us, Sam or
me, made the ice crack with a rock or a footfall, and the next thing I
saw was my daddy running, wild-eyed, crazy-looking, snatching up
my little brother and running with him to the house. That night, for
no reason at all beyond the fact he was drunk, he went mean again.
Momma, as always, tried to fend him off even as she herded us out
of harm's way, back into the bedroom. We hid not in the bed but under it, and whispered to each other of how you reckon you can kill a
grown man.

A few days later he left us, with no money, no car, nothing. I
remember my momma sitting at the table, crying. At the time I
thought it was because she missed him, but now I know that had
nothing to do with it.

I remember how the meals got smaller and smaller, plainer and
plainer. The welfare checks, the government cheese and peanut butter and grits and meal had quit when she went back to our daddy, so
there was not even that. Once a week she would bundle us up in our
coats and we would walk the mile or so to the old, gray, unpainted
store, where an elderly man sold us groceries on credit, and then we
would pull them home again in Sam's wagon. She carried Mark, to
keep him from running out into the road, and Sam and I took turns
pulling the wagon. People rode by us and stared, because no one—
no one—walks in the Deep South. You ride, and if you don't have
something to ride in, you must be trash. I remember how the driver
of a pulpwood truck made a regular run up and down the road, and
when he would see us he would throw sticks of chewing gum out the
window, sometimes a whole pack.

Eventually the credit ran out. The milkman came by one day to get his empties and left nothing for us. Weeks went by and we ate what was in the house, until finally I remember nothing but hoe-cakes. Usually, her sisters would have come to our rescue, but her decision to go back to my father had caused hurt, and bad feelings. Out of pride, she wanted to wait as long as she could.

Then she got sick. She lay for days in her bed, dragging herself out just long enough to fix us something to eat, then she would struggle down the path to the outside bathroom, hunched over, and stay out there too long, in the cold. Finally she would struggle back into her bed, and sleep like the dead. We did not know it then, but she was going to have another baby.

We were at rock bottom.

Then one day there was a knock at the door. It was a little boy, the color of bourbon, one of the children who lived down the road. He said his momma had some corn left over and please, ma'am, would we like it.

They must have seen us walking that road. They must have heard how our daddy ran off. They knew. They were poor, very poor, living in unpainted houses that leaned like a drunk on a Saturday night, but for a window in time they had more than us.

It may seem like a little bitty thing, by 1990s reasoning. But this was a time when beatings were common, when it was routine, out of pure meanness, to take a young black man for a ride and leave him cut, broken or worse on the side of some pulpwood road. For sport. For fun. This was a time when townspeople in nearby Anniston clubbed riders and burned the buses of the Freedom Riders. This was a time of horrors, in Birmingham, in the backwoods of Mississippi. This was a time when the whole damn world seemed on fire.

That is why it mattered so.

We had seen our neighbors only from a distance. They drove junk cars and lived in the sharecroppers' shacks, little houses of ancient pine boards, less than a mile from our own. Their children existed beside us in a parallel universe, climbing the same trees, stealing the same apples, swimming in the same creek, but, somehow, always upstream or downstream.

In the few contacts we had with them, as children, we had thrown rocks at them. I knew only one of them by name. He had some kind of brain condition that caused tremendous swelling in his head. The others called him Water Head, and he ran slower than the rest and I bounced a rock off his back. I heard him cry out.

I would like to say that we came together, after the little boy brought us that food, that we learned about and from each other, but that would be a lie. It was rural Alabama in 1965, two separate, distinct states. But at least, we didn't throw no more rocks.

Mary Childers

b. 1952

From *Welfare Brat: A Memoir*
(2005)

> Mary Childers had just turned thirteen when she
> entered a ninth-grade honors class at a Bronx public
> school. She was one of seven children of a single mother
> on public assistance. During the previous summer she
> had worked as a full-time babysitter, having lied about
> her age, and earned enough money to buy a winter coat.

The size of your bust doesn't seem to matter when the dropouts and high school boys in my neighborhood celebrate the beginning of the school year. They huddle in anticipation of girls turning a corner or walking past an alley, and then attack, blasting us in the chest with balloons bulging with cold water. The missiles burst on contact, plastering our blouses against skin, bras and T-shirts. Light-colored blouses wilt into transparency; bra patterns and nipple shapes and shades are exposed. Boys then follow us home rating our headlights and contours as if they are comparing cars. One day I'm called a flat tire and another I'm praised. "Here's one who's built for speed, not comfort." All the girls are supposed to be sporty vehicles the guys ride to some mysterious destination of their own choosing.

If I wear two layers under my blouse to protect my nipples from detection when they perk up in self-defense as the cold hits, I'm hot all day and create unnecessary laundry. Covering myself with my books after an attack only provokes more teasing about how there's nothing much to hide. Changing my route by taking the long way home from school is also chancy, I learn at someone else's expense.

Two girls on my block cut through buildings and across the elementary school recess yard to avoid their hair frizzing from a spritzing. Nine guys ambush them with a full body drenching, the whole time mimicking their cries and ridiculing them for thinking they could get away. When the girls complain at their school, the boys punish all of us.

Positioned on fire escapes and rooftops, they hurl not only balloons, but also tomatoes and, one horrible day, eggs. Even the balloons hurt as they plummet from a third story, thudding on our heads and necks like rocks. The boys tired of ogling breasts and were aiming for serious contact, which they finally achieve when one girl's glasses are broken by an egg. Her big brothers assemble a posse and teach those high school bullies a lesson.

The boys decide to play nicer with us. On Friday after school, a douser I recognize by his acne-ridden face greets me like a friend. He even knows my name. "Hear about the truce, Mary?" He lifts both of his arms and opens his hands as if under instruction from the police. "See, I'm not holding anything."

Walking next to me, he machine-guns instructions about how I should show up at the Shakespeare Avenue triangle park at four p.m. for a game of MM30. He assures me that a girl with my legs will have no trouble outrunning the other girls. Bumping up against my shoulder, he challenges me. "Be there. Don't be square."

I'm not about to admit to being intimidated or ignorant. Mom and Joan haven't heard of a game called MM30 either, but Mom urges me. "You spend too much time with your head in books and your nose in the air. Make friends in the neighborhood."

Soon I'm testing my legs and nerve with a bunch of white kids I've rarely nodded at but have noticed ever since we moved to Shakespeare and then up the hill to Merriam Avenue. One of the leaders, a hunk named George, snaps when I suggest including my friend Paula in the game. "No Jews allowed in our gang."

As the timekeeper, George signals when it's time for the girls to run and hide within a twelve-block area, promising the boys won't pursue us for a full ten minutes. I nudge some girls to range further, but they wave me off and continue ducking behind the library or the pillars of the Noonan Plaza, a six-building high-rise complex with an inner courtyard of broken benches and concrete sculptures. A girl named Cookie and two of her friends bolt with me at first. Cookie's fast and determined as she trills over her shoulder: "No boy will catch me without a fight." She leaves us behind.

The other girls are impressed that I know which buildings have lobbies with clocks and unlocked entryways or back doors. One of them heads for a secret spot she has successfully used for two games. The other tucks herself into the first hiding place I identify, a pile of boxes underneath and on top of a table in the mail corridor of a big building. She's grateful, so I don't resent heading for my second choice, an alley that stretches at an incline between three of the buildings that climb the stairs from the Edward L. Grant Highway to Shakespeare Avenue.

I'm glad I finally sprung for a watch. Heart pounding, I consult it every minute, thinking much more time has elapsed. The boys have only twenty minutes to find us; after that I'm home free. From my vantage point I scope out some of the guys at the top of the hill and scan the bottom. I'm watching the action and hiding at the same time. If someone heads down or up the alley, I'll scurry behind staircases or scramble upstairs in either of the two closest buildings. Even when eighteen minutes of this part of the game have passed, and I've stuck to my station for seven, I'm still sweating. I don't want to get caught. I don't want to get caught. From the way Cookie tore off and the other girl beamed at the secure hiding place I pointed out, I know something bad happens to those girls who don't scatter far enough.

After twenty minutes from our start time, I emerge victorious, but still wary. Figuring I'll play this game again, I conceal my location by skipping all the way down the alley and then sprinting up the stone steps carved into the hill. I bound to the top and cross the street to the park, where I'm disheartened. There are only ten kids there to applaud my great escape, and no one pays me much attention. One girl, who lives a bus ride away, is pissed that she arrived too late to play. "Stupid," she sneers, "you're supposed to get caught." Two of the tardy guys look forlorn. Two others are embarrassed they couldn't find anyone and one girl sulks because no one picked her.

Turns out that the dreaded culminating event is kissing. MM30 stands for Make-out Manhunt 30 minutes. The hide-and-seek part lasts thirty minutes and whatever happens after that is nobody's business. For the next hour sheepish couples slither back to the park or separate a block away. Lots of kids don't reappear; there are dinners waiting for them at home. After he returns, holding hands with a cute girl with big breasts, George presides once again. He's the Master of Ceremonies of Make-out Manhunt 30 minutes. "The turnout is bigger every time. Saturday night should be a blast."

As I wander off with a vague salute to everyone, George acknowledges me. "I hear you got away this time. Comin' back tomorrow night?"

"I'm baby-sitting."

So he turns on me. "Who cares. You're a flat-chested skank anyway. Go home and wash your face."

I slump up the hill. Now realizing my hands are dirty from leaning into filth in the alley, I examine my face in a car mirror and discover stringy hair and a sooty left cheek. I imagined myself as a sleek deer scampering in the hills and hiding from hunters, but I'm a ragamuffin. Next time I play, I'll pocket a handkerchief and a compact.

I forget the mirror, of course, but when I return to the same spot two more times, I inspect where I rest my hands as diligently as I check the time. While climbing the stairs at the end of the game, I poke bobby pins into my scalp to tighten my hair behind my ears after combing it with my hands. The third time, Cookie salutes me for outsmarting the guys. "Two of them were looking for you," she warns, but when I describe my haunt, she congratulates me. "They'll never track you there."

But next time they do. After only eleven minutes, they're on me. One clinches my arms behind my back while the other one kisses my neck and then opens his mouth like a fish about to swallow. It's the guy with the pimples. When his face zooms in and blurs out of focus, I feel faint. Up close, all I can see is bubbles of pus or Clearasil.

I butt his chest with my head, wrench my arms away from his teammate, and sprint straight up the alley, hoping the park is empty. But the kids who are there wave when I run by. The twenty minutes are now up and they must think I scored again and am heading back home.

At school I bump into Cookie's friend I helped to hide, Judith, not at all surprised that she's in the lowest-level class. There's something muted and unfinished about her, something simple that's cute and odd as she sidles up to me and squeals that Cookie ratted me out.

I'm dumbfounded. "Why?"

"She wanted to test your reaction, or something like that." Her head rolls before she finishes what she has revved up to share. "Cookie would crucify me for snitching."

After that, Cookie surprises me again. She grows friendlier, inviting me to hang out with her and her friends any time. She's a deer and a ragamuffin, too. For the first time in my life, I'm exhilarated by belonging.

One Saturday I join Cookie, Judith and the other girl, Amy, in what they call *running*. First we terrorize the three Fanny Farmer stores within roaming distance of the triangle park on Shakespeare. Pretending one of us is buying a box of candy for her mother's birthday, we post ourselves in front of three towers of perfectly wrapped packages. At Cookie's whistle, we simultaneously knock over each carefully balanced display. Walloping our mouths in an Indian cry, we dash out.

I feel giddier than I have my entire life when I prove myself to the tough girls by suggesting our next target: a huge wholesale/retail store of candy bins near the Grand Concourse. I promise shortcuts through the alleys to The Biggest Confectioner in the Bronx. Cookie is the leader; I'm the guide.

I've seen it before and I'm still astonished by the aisles of bins of peppermint, butterscotch, sour cherry drops and chocolate footballs that can be bought by the quarter-pound or more in any assortment desired. "A little of this, a little of that, a lot of that because they are the only candy my husband eats," a lady hums to her skinny friend. My friends are humming, too.

The sales ladies glare at us. They don't see customers, they see grubby, sweaty trouble. What a pleasure it is to surprise but not disappoint them.

Invisibly cupping small amounts of candy, we skip our hands from one bin to another and mix the contaminators around. Then we transfer an assortment from that bin on to the next. We are a coordinated destruction machine. It will cost those sneering ladies hours to sort out the containers.

In sync like a glee club or sisters, when we sense that the sales ladies' suspicions are mounting toward conviction, we saunter out, salivating and snorting: "There's nothing we want here."

Then, staking claim to the Grand Concourse as our territory, we seriously and politely accost men. "Excuse me, sir, I thought you'd want to know . . ." We point to the ground solemnly and say, "Your shoes are untied" to men wearing loafers or "Your slip is showing" to men wearing shoes with laces. Some of them curse; some actually look around their feet and calves until they hear us cackle; several seem to worry about our sanity. Not me. I never before felt so sane and clear with girls who aren't my sisters.

On another day Cookie and the girls she calls her posse lure me into *running* to the Chinese laundry a couple of blocks away. I'm alarmed when they start whirling, yanking carefully folded shirts wrapped in plain brown paper off the shelves lining two walls of the tiny, steamy store. Then they stomp, splitting open the paper and dragging shirts on the floor with their feet. Screaming some imitation of Chinese followed by "Coolie" and "Ching Chong Challywock," they run out when the guy lunges at them with a broom. As he doubles over in the middle of the street, wheezing and coughing, Cookie threatens to grab his broom and whack him. Her friends jerk her away.

They are deliriously happy and ready to proceed to the next Chinese laundry not far away. When I head in a different direction, claiming that I have to take care of my younger siblings, Cookie grimaces. "Later for you, then." Rushing home, I fantasize about returning to the store to help the mam clean up, turning Cookie in to the cops, and spending more time with girls at school in the honors classes.

The reality of my behavior has suddenly become clear: appalling cruelty that could have netted me a deserved J.D. card. The snooty ladies in the candy store had snubbed me when I first went there with pocket money from baby-sitting, but we dished out more comeuppance than they deserved. Friendship and the giddiness of revenge had enclosed me in a fog of fun that made it somehow acceptable to heckle strangers on the street. Just as I have sublime moods, I am capable of reckless, random insolence. In the right company, my spiteful streak colors my personality. I'm as mixed up as those candy bins and as startled as our targets.

commentary for chapter two: **NEIGHBORHOODS**

For the writers in this section, the neighborhood was not merely the background for a tough childhood. They present their neighborhoods as the stage where life's early trials, achievements, and setbacks played out, leading sometimes to life-changing consequences and biting regret. Oscar Hijuelos and Rick Bragg describe how their communities were affected by social change: shifting ethnic makeups and class lines in Hijuelos's case, the civil rights struggle and the white backlash against it in Bragg's. Mary Childers focuses on the edgy interpersonal dynamics between high-school students like herself in the Bronx, with their sexually charged games, peer pressures, and casual cruelties, as well as the autonomy from adults that neighborhood life grants to children.

All three writers show the corrosive effects of ethnic and racial divisions on their neighborhoods' fabric, yet they suggest such divisions are perhaps not as intractable as they seem. Motivated by age-old grudges or "pure poverty-driven anger," black youths from Harlem would challenge Latino and Irish boys in Hijuelos's neighborhood in upper Manhattan to rumbles. Still, he writes, the worst of that violence was finished by the time he was a teenager, when most of the older youths got along and mixed-race couples were common. Race-based violence had faded, at least in his neighborhood, he writes, so much that his family and friends remembered "that gang-era mythology" by enjoying the soundtrack of *West Side Story*.

The theme of racial resentment looms large in Bragg's account from 1965, when Alabama was ablaze with white resistance to the still-tenuous gains of the civil rights movement. Constant, lethal violence by the Klan and white thugs against African Americans creates a tense backdrop to the story. Bragg (who is white) and his mother and brothers are left destitute after their abusive, alcoholic father abandons them. They have little to eat and no car, a particular humiliation since it forces them to walk a mile to buy supplies in a society where to be carless means "you must be trash." A poor black family living nearby takes pity on them and sends over some food, an astonishing act of solidarity. One act of neighborly kindness cannot overcome a society's deepest pathologies, Bragg writes. The two races continued to live in "two separate, distinct states." Yet for the working poor, the story suggests, neighbors can be a lifeline.

Oscar Hijuelos grew up in New York City and Paul Clemens (in chapter 1) in Detroit, but their recollections of rough play with neighborhood boys bear remarkable similarities. Clemens remembered "simple, violent games," while Hijuelos remembered ones where kids beat "the living hell" out of each other. Both writers, in adulthood, describe these games as fun. What is the source of pleasure in such youthful male physicality? Hijuelos ascribes it to "the pent-up *something*" inside of him, and to pride that he, a formerly sickly child, could hold his own. Whatever its individual origins, the desirability of physical toughness is a norm—indeed, a necessity—among people growing up in environments where making a living depends on physical strength and skill.

Hijuelos also remembers how he was disciplined, and here again physicality is the primary instrument of influence. Because they are poor, Oscar's mother worries about how much new eyeglasses and clothes will cost when her son comes home with his glasses broken and his shirt torn up. Somehow, to avoid more unnecessary expense, she has to impress upon her son that he must avoid such rough games. So what does she do? She beats him with a belt, thus exposing him to still another form of violence. Neighborhoods can also offer friendship and solidarity across class lines, as demonstrated by Oscar's friendship with Richard, whose "household became a refuge to me."

All three writers own up to committing cruel, lawless or self-destructive acts in their youths, behavior for which they take responsibility and sometimes express regret. Hijuelos describes his youthful smoking; Bragg speaks with remorse about throwing stones at his black neighbors. These accounts demonstrate how memoir is a moral undertaking, in which the writer looks honestly at his own actions in the past to try to understand and, sometimes, explain them. The memoirist is trying to understand why he did what he did, as an act of self-discovery.

Childers, in that vein, recalls wreaking havoc at candy stores with her girlfriends, knocking over displays and moving products to the wrong containers to annoy the shopkeepers. They invade a Chinese laundry and throw shirts on the floor, taunting the employees with ethnic slurs. These acts might seem more mischief than crime, but Childers sees in them a capacity for brazen challenges to authority that might have earned her a record as a juvenile delinquent had she been caught. The neighborhood thus offers support and companionship for these youths, but it can also reinforce bad behaviors and a taste for mayhem that can have very grown-up consequences.

QUESTIONS FOR DISCUSSION

1. How do the attitudes of Oscar Hijuelos and Mary Childers toward their own neighborhoods shift in the course of these accounts? Do you think the authors changed, or did the neighborhoods change, or some combination of the two?

2. Treating girls and women like objects is a common problem in the eyes of feminists. What is an example of objectification in Mary Childers's account? What were the consequences for girls like her of trying to cope with it?

3. Adolescence is a period when lasting personal characteristics begin to be established. From his memoir what do we learn about Oscar Hijuelos's character development?

4. As parents, the mother and father of Oscar Hijuelos had problems to face: their twelve-year-old son's smoking and their eighteen-year-old son's impending fatherhood. How did they handle those issues?

5. What was the "old monster" let loose in Rick Bragg's family, and how did members of the family attempt to deal with this problem? Is his narrative mainly one of hope or one of despair?

6. Racial and class divisions are deeply intertwined in Rick Bragg's community, but do either of them come to predominate in his account? Does he suggest that those divisions—class and race—can ever be bridged?

chapter three
FRIENDS AND ENEMIES

Michael C. Keith

b. 1948

From *The Next Better Place: Memories of My Misspent Youth* (2003)

Two years after his parents divorced, Michael Keith's mother reluctantly gave permission to his father to take their eleven-year-old son on a journey across the country. The father was an alcoholic who had been sober for only three months, but Michael's mother felt she had enough on her hands with a waitressing job and two younger children to raise. This memoir is the story of Michael's journey with his father from upstate New York to California and their numerous stops along the way, including in Denver, where he attended school. Over a year later, they return to find his mother distraught at the sight of how thin her son has become on the road.

At dinner with friends a few years ago, the conversation turned to the subject of childhood memories. Most of the accounts had to do with joyful events, family outings, and holidays. Occasional stories about the loss of a grandparent or a pet were the exceptions. When it was my turn, I blurted out the first thing that came to mind.

"I didn't crap for nearly two years once," I declared.

"Now that's a heartwarming recollection," quipped someone. "It's true," I responded, adding that when you don't eat . . .

"So you're saying that you were starved as a child?" interrupted the wife of a colleague.

"And you were kept in a windowless basement, right?" said her husband with a playful smirk.

"Just the opposite," I replied. "I was free to roam the wide-open spaces and go pretty much where I wanted. The problem was meals were often few and far between."

"And this was because? . . . "

Before long I was recounting life on the road with my father, including the fact that, despite my now being an academic of some distinction, I hardly ever attended school, missing some grades entirely and never reaching beyond the first weeks of high school.

"God, our childhoods were so boringly normal compared to yours," observed one friend.

"Don't complain," I answered. "Normal is pretty good when you're a kid."

That night sleep was slow in coming and when it did it was anything but restful. My dreams retraced the highways my father and I wandered in vain pursuit of our utopias.

Who was it that said a normal childhood is one not worth living? I'd like to tell that person a story. [. . .]

The Greyhound is on time and to my joy the front seat is empty. I can think of nothing better than this at the moment. It is the beginning of a great day. In less than two hours, after passing through other dusty prairie towns like Quinter, Grainfield, Oakley, Colby, Brewster, Goodland, and Kanorado, I will be in my first honest-to-God western state, with only Utah and Nevada separating me from the Pacific Ocean.

"Hi-yo Silver, away!" I whisper to myself, and begin humming the theme from *The Magnificent Seven* as the bus moves down WaKeeney's deserted main drag.

We have stalled in the Mile High City. Many weeks have passed because my father has lost his taste for thumbing rides and has taken a job as an elevator operator at the Hotel Ames. The strategy behind this layover is to gather enough money to reach Los Angeles in one unbroken leap, but it is almost Labor Day and we have been unable to put aside a cent.

Things cost money, my father snaps when I complain about our lack of progress. The cost of our efficiency room, or light housekeeping studio apartment as it is more glamorously called, off Colfax Avenue and other basic living expenses take up my father's twenty-nine-dollar-a-week paycheck and the occasional tips he earns. We live in the hope that he will get to bellhop a couple of days a week as the manager has promised.

"A few days on the floor and we'll have plenty for tickets. Those guys do okay. That's why they hold on to those gigs. Maybe something will open up at the Brown Palace. They rake it in there."

He has canvassed other hotels for a better-paying job but nothing has panned out. I pass my days wandering the city and going to quarter movie matinees when I have the price of admission. The plan now is for me to attend school when it begins and continue until we are able to get back on the road. So I am registered in the sixth grade at a school in our district. My father has to promise the assistant principal that he will send for my transcripts.

"What do they need records, for Christ's sakes?" he complains later. "You're only a kid. What do they think that place is, Harvard or something?" [...]

My favorite parts of the school day are lunch and geography, but making friends is not easy. A couple of weeks into the semester I am approached in the schoolyard by a kid who says he wants me to be his partner in music, or so I think.

"I choose you for Music," he says, and I say sure, not exactly certain what he means but willing to go along with it if it means gaining a new friend.

When I readily accept his invitation he seems somewhat surprised. I follow him around the building, where a small crowd has gathered.

"How come you picked on Music?" he asks accusingly, and I begin to get an idea of what is happening.

"Music?" I reply, still not clear what he means, and he points to a kid in the crowd whom I remember bumping into in the hallway that morning during the rush of the bell.

"That's Dondi Music. He says you pushed him. How come? Why don't you pick on someone bigger? Like me. Come on—push me, asshole."

A part of me wants to do just that, to knock him clear off his feet, but I can't help imagining the possible grim consequences. He is taller and broader than I am, maybe a seventh- or eighth-grader, and his fists are clenched and ready for action. I know what Gary

Cooper or Alan Ladd would do, but the hero I am in my fantasies resists translation to reality, so I ask to be left alone, swearing I will never bump into Music again. However, that is not good enough for Music's protector and defender, who knows he is about to score an easy victory.

"You chicken? Hey, everybody, he's chicken! Go ahead, I'll let you take the first punch," says Music's friend, holding his arms outstretched from his sides.

Someone in the crowd calls him Doyle and tells him to flatten the bag of bones, meaning me. I have been subjected to similar epithets before. When I reject his offer of first strike, he slaps me in the face. I feel stunned and humiliated, but my resolve to avoid all-out war with him is only deepened. Passivity is my defense. My way to stay alive. Few people shoot an unarmed man, I assure myself.

"Shit!" he shouts, clearly savoring his victory. "You're a friggin' baby. Hey, Music, you could take this little chickenshit yourself. Come on, take a punch, liver lips."

I remain inert in my resolve and shame as he administers yet another stinging blow to my cheek. The crowd of kids laughs and a couple of girls tell him to leave me alone as my eyes begin to mist over. There is no retaliation in me. I am a coward, yellow to the core, and I plan to vanish forever once my conqueror frees me.

"What are you, queer?" he asks, tauntingly pursing his lips and fluttering his eyelashes. "You use lipstick? How come your lips are so girly red, homo?"

He takes my lips between his fingers and pulls and pinches them. For a split second I am close to letting loose on him. Blasting his big beak with my fist. Kicking him in the stomach, and if he doesn't drop to the ground sobbing and pleading for mercy, running away as fast as my legs will carry me.

"You ever pick on my friend again, I'll beat the shit out of you. This was nothing, just a little spanking. You understand?"

Yes, I say, and he shakes his fist at me before marching triumphantly away, his entourage in tow. A kid, whom I figure to be Mexican because of his tan skin and coal-dark hair and eyes, remains behind, and I wonder if there is more trouble in store for me. He says something that I don't understand and then flips his finger at the receding crowd.

"Going to get my brother to kick his ass sometime. He try that on me, maybe I'll use this on him," he says, holding a sleek jackknife and snapping his wrist so that the long blade pops out. "Stiletto. You put some butter right here and it works real good. Comes out faster."

His name is Joey Ramone and he's three months younger than me, we determine. At his suggestion we play hooky the balance of the school day and go down by the railroad tracks where he claims he found a human thumb.

"Didn't have a nail on it either. Maybe it got cut off in a knife fight. Like this." He demonstrates, passing the bright blade of his knife across the knuckle of his thumb.

When it is almost dark we head in our separate directions. Joey has promised to recruit his big brother, Manny, to protect me too, and I no longer feel the need to disappear from the planet. Yet my cowardly behavior back at school leaves a bitter aftertaste in my mouth. I want another chance to show what I'm really made of but at the same time dread getting one.

On my way home I spot Doyle and his cronies and hide until they are long out of sight. If I make a stand it will be with Joey's brother at my side, or someone else able to keep me from being disfigured. The movies do not hire actors with scarred faces, I reason, unless it is for monster pictures. Back in our room I perforate the lid of a can of potatoes with a bottle opener, imagining it is Doyle's fat skull, and while I gulp down the bland contents of my supper I dream of reversing the events of the day, slashing at the air with my spoon.

Monica Wood

b. 1953

From *When We Were the Kennedys: A Memoir from Mexico, Maine*

(2012)

In this passage Monica Wood's father, Albert, an immigrant from Prince Edward Island in Canada, known by his nickname Red, has died suddenly of a heart attack on his way to work in a Maine paper mill. Monica is nine years old. She has an older sister, Anne, who teaches high-school English, and two younger sisters, Cathy and Betty, the latter developmentally disabled. Her neighbors are the Vaillancourts. Mr. Vaillancourt works at the paper mill where Monica's father was foreman.

"What are you reading?"

I look up. It's Denise, standing nearby with her bicycle. We were friends at school but I haven't seen her since school let out.

"Nancy Drew. She's a sleuth."

"I love Nancy Drew." Denise lays her bike on the grass, and in the miraculous way of childhood friendships, this moment—or a moment like it, small and unremarkable—marks our first as best and lifelong friends.

"You have to leave your bike outside the fence," I tell her. Our landlords are fussy about their grass, their driveway, their everything.

Denise moves her bike, then sits on the grass with me. She tilts my book to look at the cover.

"I don't have this one."

"I've already read it," I say. "I'll ask Norma if you can borrow it."

Denise looks at me for a moment; she likes me a lot, but like other children she's a little bit afraid of me because my father died. "You want to come over to my house?"

I look up; I can see her block on Brown Street from here—she, too, lives on the top floor—just over the rooftop of the O'Neills'.

"Okay."

Unbeknownst to Denise—or anyone else—I've begun writing my own mystery, starring a titian-haired girl with no freckles. This character, named Nancy Drew—but not *the* Nancy Drew—will solve *The Mystery of the Missing Man.* I've cracked open a clean pack of Dad's paper, feeling a little like Ferdinand Magellan setting out in his ship. I've set goals: A man will go missing in Chapter I. Cliffhangers will ensue. Then the man will be found. In an act of authorial benevolence, I've exhumed Nancy's mother *(Nancy, dear, you really must try harder to keep out of trouble!)* and retained her "prominent attorney" father, but I've ditched the housekeeper, the boyfriend, and the girl sidekicks. My Nancy will do her sleuthing alone.

I've written two pages full of beginning—Nancy's mother, Nancy's father, Nancy's house, Nancy's yard, Nancy's clothes and car and meals—searching, I suppose (in my book, in every book), for a family with no missing pieces, the family we used to be. When I follow Denise up the stairs of her block, where her beautiful mother and father say *Hello, Monica!*, my eyes sting open. There we are. [...]

We've made it through the Fourth of July. First, too many Dadless days to count; then too many weeks; now I'm counting by months. Two going on three.

I'd rather be at the Vaillancourts, where the landlords are nearly invisible and I've been thoroughly absorbed into the family routines [...] No shoes indoors, dear. No food away from the table, hon. No animals in the house, please.

Mr. Vaillancourt pats my head. He looks me in the eye. He calls me dear. Mrs. Vaillancourt pats my head. She looks me in the eye. She calls me dear. They ask, *How's your mother?* They always ask, *How's your mother?*

Good, thank you. She's very good.

I don't say, *She sleeps a lot.*

I don't say, *In our bed.*

I don't say, *If Anne left I think we would die.*

I don't say, *I'm afraid my mother might be shrinking.*

I don't say, *She does everything the same but she's not here.*

I don't say, *Sometimes I pretend I live here with you.*

I don't ask Mr. and Mrs. Vaillancourt, who have brightened my days like an apology from heaven: *Why did God forget the rest of my family?*

Mum wants to know: *What's it like over there? No shoes, really? Even in summer?* It's as if with Dad gone she's lost her knack for mothering and is featuring how to get it back without having to leave home. I deliver stagy reports in the style of Dad's old PEI neighbor Mrs. McCarn, clearing our kitchen counter of bread wrappers to replicate Denise's mother's pristine kitchen, which, like ours, must be endlessly swabbed against the myriad assaults of children. Mum nods and squints, taking mental notes, intensely interested in how this other, mother-father Catholic family operates. She's grown fond of Denise, a dimpled child with large, trusting eyes and impeccable manners, to whom our household is a revelation of broken rules: cupboards unlatched, the TV on whenever we want, cats parked on tables and chairs, a talking bird lolloping from room to room and landing on mirrors and bedposts and our own heads. Mum takes in only small breaths of comfort in these suffocating weeks, and one of these comforts is Denise, who makes no secret of her wonderment.

But lately, as I head to the Vaillancourts' at afternoon shift change—the better to catch a father coming home in his dusty clothes—Mum says, *Why don't you stay here?* Softly, not sternly. *Stay here,* she says. My insides open to a flood of love and I stay. [...]

I slip over to the Vaillancourts' as often as I can, where Denise and I sit on the whaleback of grass that passes for her front yard, planning stakeouts or refining our code or reading Nancy's next case, Denise trying to puzzle out the plot's secrets in advance. My own secret is that I'm waiting for Mr. Vaillancourt to come home.

I wait for him.

I watch him

I love him.

Every moment in his company feels desperate and vanishing.

"Don't tell me what happens," Denise warns me, looking up from her book. "She's reading volume 9, the one where Nancy saves an orphan who turns out to be an heiress.

"Keep your eye on the guardians, that's all I'm saying."

What I've been reading in the *Times* is also a mystery.

Employees of Oxford Paper Company, goes the United Mine Workers' quarter-page ad, *you owe it to yourself and your future to obtain the GUARANTEES IN WRITING from the UPP officials ... Watch the UPP SQUIRM AND TWIST when you demand in WRITING, guarantees to ensure your FUTURE.*

This sounds like the dramatic talk of Suspicious Characters, so I ask Mr. Vaillancourt what "squirm and twist" means. Mostly I want to hear his heartening voice. His name is Omer, but everyone calls him Oats. When I imagine him climbing the massive machinery—which I do, often—he seems too small for a job like that, too handsome and wavyhaired. I imagine his path having crossed Dad's every day at the gates.

Hello, Red!

Hello, Oats!

There's a contract negotiation coming right up, Mr. Vaillancourt explains; a tough one. Management wants change and the papermakers don't. The United Pulp and Paper Workers union has been signing up members, lobbying to replace the existing union.

"Is that what you wanted to know?" he says, standing by the sink in his coveralls, unpacking his lunch pail. I have followed him inside.

"I guess so."

He looks at me. French, soft-spoken, and young, Mr. Vaillancourt isn't much like Dad, but he goes to work on the morning shift like Dad, wears hard-used boots exactly like Dad's. Are my eyes filling? I don't know what I'm after, but he does. "Your father was still one of us," he says.

My father: promoted to foreman but a union man to the bone. A light blinks on inside me.

Mr. Vaillancourt pats my head. "It's good that you're paying attention."

I nod, yes, yes, I'm paying attention! The Vaillancourts, like everybody else, have a *Times* lying out where anyone can pick it up.

Sometimes I read it over here. On this day there is likely a front-page photo of the Oxford's president, Bill Chisholm—grandson of the first Hugh Chisholm, son of the second Hugh Chisholm, the third Chisholm to make his way in paper. He's handing out a scholarship, or planting a tree, or cutting a ribbon for the new steam plant or power station or grinding room, always in that good dark suit. A Yale man in heavy, bookish eyeglasses, Bill is in his seventh year at the helm, following the four-decade tenure of his father, the great Hugh II, whose legacy still burns high in the breasts of Mexico's fathers. It was Hugh II who'd run the mill when Dad first saw it; Hugh II who'd rightly predicted that the road to riches would be paved with machine-coated paper. Out with the old machines, in with the new, two million bucks here, four million bucks there, big fat plans undimmed by fire or flood or war or Great Depression. While the rest of America had stood in bread lines, Hugh II's papermakers kept their mill running three and four days a week, heeding their president's advice to place their faith in paper.

Smiling out from another front-page picture in the *Times*, shovel in hand, Hugh II's son Bill has no idea—how could he?—that he's presiding over the beginning of the paper industry's long decline, that the current labor tensions presage a change in the Oxford's fundamental character, one as life-altering as a death in the family.

"You keep it up," Mr. Vaillancourt says to me, which is what adults say to overachieving children.

From outside comes the slamming of car doors, Denise's aunties arriving for their summer visit. They move like starlings in flight, arrowing this way, then that way, in unison, trilling and hooting and cackling and hugging everybody more than once and pattering up and down the stairs to fetch overnight bags and presents and hats, bracelets jangling. I huddle like a stunned dormouse as they circle me, skirts aswirl, Mrs. Vaillancourt introducing me as "Denise's little friend." They are so *enchantée* to meet me. How do you do!

I don't say, *Fine, thank you*. In fact, I say nothing at all. I'm struck dumb, as I often am. Despite my lists of words, my perfect marks in spelling, my desperately thumbed dictionary, I have no vocabulary with which to respond to the kindness that pours in from every quarter. This muteness, and its accompanying well of yearning, fills me with dread. Imagine: a childhood burdened by too much kindness.

The aunties clank their coffee cups and laugh like birds and tell the same stories twice and laugh harder the second time and water up over their own deceased father and sing funny songs in French. They've brought kids with them—Denise's cousins—too many, all ages. I stand at the periphery, memorizing names, but there are too many names, too many people.

At the end of this cacophonous afternoon, I linger outside in the quiet before heading home. Denise is back inside, being quizzed on French words or wheedled into a public performance of *"Je Te Trouve Toujours Jolie"* with her siblings and cousins or asked to report on her hopes for fifth grade. I'm in the yard, picking up my sleuthing notebook, looking over at the empty schoolyard with my own hopes for fifth grade, praying that Sister Bernadette has heard about Dad and therefore will refrain from the obligatory first-day Who Is Your Mother Who Is Your Father get-acquainted routine.

All of a sudden, another little flock from the house, not aunties or cousins, just Denise and Mr. Vaillancourt and Denise's baby sister, Jane. He's going to drive us to the Frosty for an ice cream—before supper, which is unheard-of. Maybe he needs a break from the aunties, who tell chancy jokes in French just to see him blush.

So he drives us to the Frosty. We stand in line. He takes out his wallet and says, "Three vanillas for my girls."

Is this what I've been waiting for? I don't know, then I do.

We get back into Mr. Vaillancourt's Plymouth; he waves out the window to this one and that one. Everybody likes Omer. Sometimes he takes his wife dancing. They play cards with people. They put the words *social* and *life* together in a way I've never heard. It means their friends.

Everyone can see me in Mr. Vaillancourt's Plymouth, eating my ice cream in rude, gulpy, hoggish bites. *Lookit me, everybody!* I say to myself. *Lookit me! Lookit lookit, there's a father at the wheel!* When I get back to their house, I hide in the bathroom, patting my eyes with my fists, as if my eyelashes have caught fire. Outside the door the aunties' laughter sounds like expensive glass breaking. Then I press my eyes so hard the sockets will still ache that night, when I'm lying in bed next to Cathy, wishing she had a best friend with a father like Mr. Vaillancourt. But she doesn't, and neither does Betty, and it's beginning to dawn on me that God might not love all His children the same.

Michelle Tea

b. 1971

From *The Chelsea Whistle: A Memoir*

(2002)

Michelle Tea grew up in working-class Chelsea, a city
bordering Boston, where her mother and stepfather
were on the nursing staff at a veterans' old-age home.
Michelle's biological father, whom her mother divorced,
lost his job at the post office because of alcoholism. At
age thirteen, Michelle met Lydia, a runaway.

Me and my friends would roam the Mystic Mall, moving through
the wide corridors, cruising past all the shops, and then we would
need to smoke. There were boxes of cigarettes tucked into the curv-
ing pleather of the Jordache purses that hung horizontal across our
torsos, swinging on our hips. We smoked our cigarettes in the mall
bathroom, deep in the bowels of the mall by the security and business offices, at the end of a long, fluorescent-lit hallway that looked
so employees-only and foreboding that hardly anybody but us went
back there. We would push open the wooden door and settle into
our clubhouse. It was me, Marisol, Tiffany, who was funny, and Vivian, caked in Duran Duran merchandise, who was generally kept
around for Marisol to be mean to. Marisol would steal Vivian's pin,
I (Heart) Nick, and hold it just above the flushing toilet while Vivian howled and hit the tiled wall. We were smoking a communal
pack of Marlboros we'd pool our change to buy. We'd sit on the floor,
tiny square tiles with dust in the cracks, or try to get a perch on the
little metal ledge that ran beneath the long mirror. Me, with my
skinniest ass, would wedge into the long porcelain sink that didn't

work, my butt cupped in the strong porcelain saucer. I loved sitting there, smoking, flicking my ashes in the wet sink beside me like a big white ashtray. I can't tell you how special the smoking was. It was our secret sacrament and I loved the motion of every drag, lifting my hand, sealing my lips around it, the tug of my whole body pulling, and the grand finale of the sexy tough exhale, smoke leaving my lips like a train pulling out of the station of the most boring city in the world, leaving exhaust like a scar on the sky. Smoking does look cool.

We made up lists of the boys we liked, one to ten in order of the seriousness of the crush. Going over with desperate rakes the pathetically small snippets of conversation we'd had with the boy while buying our poster or slush. The bands we were all going to be in. We all wanted to be the singer, though if necessary I'd play drums. We'd be called the Scabs, Black Lace, JailBait. We would not sound anything like Duran Duran, Marisol said with a glare at Vivian. No fag music. Judas Priest and Mötley Crüe. I carved awkward, angular pentagrams into the bathroom door with my house key, digging and digging, making the side of my knuckle deep red and shiny and cramped, and sometimes took a lighter to the painted white ceiling and wrote my initials with dark streaks of heat, scorching my thumb on the hot metal tip.

We found Runaway Lydia in the mall bathroom. It was like finding ET pitching Reese's Pieces against the back of your house, a runaway. Like a gypsy, something mythical from television, which you are not supposed to think is for real unless it's telling you not to use drugs. Girls really ran away. They walked around without parents or school, and they washed their hair in the sink of the bathroom at the back of the mall, contorting their hungry bodies to fit their heads beneath the stream, pumping pearly pink soap from the dispenser to use as shampoo. That's where we found Lydia. It was like we'd walked into the wrong place, we all jumped back when the door swung open and she was there, hunched over, blotting the back of her neck with paper towels. It was like walking into her house, or catching her taking a pee. We all stood stiff and didn't talk, pulled cigarettes from the red box, not touching the lucky cigarette turned upside down in the box, to be smoked last while making a wish. Lydia shifted and looked sore, wringing the mall water from her hair, which was bleached to a deep nicotine yellow and fried from the effort. Still, it was bleached and that was good. We would have all been happy with a head of hair like that, but you couldn't bleach your hair with parents around. You had to be a runaway, and Lydia was. Like a girl in a book. Her jeans were so tight and her legs so skinny you wouldn't think you could find jeans small enough to look like that. Little white T-shirt, dirty like her white sneakers. I wondered briefly if she would beat us up. I always wondered that when I met a girl I didn't know. Sometimes one would want to, but Lydia smiled and bummed a cigarette, asked us our names. She told us right away she was a runaway, she was pretty proud of it and she should have been. It was an amazing feat, shucking off your parents. She lived in an abandoned store in Bellingham Square that was a real pit, she stayed there with her boyfriend who was older, and his friends would come over and they all drank beer together and hung out and it was really fun. I couldn't believe this. It was like a paperback teen novel had opened its pages and sucked me in like little Carolann's closet in *Poltergeist*. I had to be Lydia's friend. If I couldn't be a runaway, then at least I could know one. I could help her. It had to be hard, it had to be so hard. She was so brave and alone, washing her hair in the sink at the mall, she knew how to do all the things you had to do if you ran away. How to take care of herself, at once a grownup and a kid, like any other impossible combination of creatures, a unicorn, or a horse with wings.

I wanted to give Lydia everything I had. Stuff I loved lost all value in the face of having nothing at all like Lydia. Lydia needed things. Shoes, I gave her my cracked leather ones with the run-down heels and bows at my toes. She loved them. I gave her some shirts and she wanted more, wanted blankets and jackets but I couldn't give her those. What about food? How did runaways eat? Well, her boyfriend fed her, he sold drugs. I smuggled cans of stuff from my pantry shelves, I told her where I lived and she came to my door. *Do you have a can opener?* she asked. I gave her the can opener from the drawer in the kitchen. Lydia was such a secret. My mother would kill me. She was like a pet I knew I couldn't have, I had to feed and take care of her in this sneaky way, and like the stray animal I dreamed of someday finding and keeping, I never lost the fear that Lydia might bite. A girl who ran away from home was certainly capable of anything. I never asked her why she left. It was pointless, we all wanted to go. To be gone, to climb aboard our lives like a bus and leave. I wouldn't have picked Chelsea, I would have gone to New York or at least Boston, but Chelsea is where Lydia went. It was hard to imagine a place that made Chelsea look like a good place to run to.

Once, Lydia came to my door when my family was home. She had her boyfriend with her, and he was a man and that was a shock. He was much older than Lydia, who was a little older than me but not so much that she wasn't still a kid. I panicked at my mother finding this man at the door for me, hickey-necked runaway Lydia in tow. He nodded at me and smiled, seemed nervous or at least uncomfortable. Lydia did the talking. *Can we have some food? We're pretty hungry.* I Can't, I whispered, My Parents Are Here. *Really?* she asked. *Not even nothing?* Hold On. I shut the door and went into the kitchen. There was my mom smoking endless cigarettes with whoever, Will, grandparents, my aunt next door, cousins upstairs—there were always a million people in my house, filling it up with smoke, getting the shakes on milky cups of Tetley, talking shit about everybody. I really liked it. I'm pretty social, I liked sitting at the table doing my homework, soaking up the smoke and the gossip, offering my own jibe here and there, my grandmother biting her lower lip and shaking her head, saying *Listen to you. Is she a hot ticket? Aren't you a hot shit. Do your homework.* I went into the pantry and gathered some snacks. *Whatcha doin' Shell?* Nothing. I grabbed Popsicles from the freezer, took it all back into the living room, where the front door was. The television blared. Out in the hallway were Lydia and the boyfriend. Here, I said quickly, Take These. The junkiest food. They were happy to have it. Eat The Popsicles, They'll Melt, I said. I wanted to give them instructions, like I had done something very complicated for them, because I really had, and it didn't show in the stale, half-empty bags of Doritos and Wise potato chips with the owl on the package. *Thanks, Michelle,* Lydia said, gathering the stuff in her arms. *Bye,* the guy nodded. They left my house and I went back to the television.

I went into Boston with Lydia and her boyfriend, whose name was something like Mike. Lydia never went into Boston, which I thought was incredible because she was a runaway and could go anywhere she wanted, but she just hung around Chelsea. I was taking them on a field trip. Boston Is So Cool, I promised them. I still wasn't allowed to go into the city, I had to sneak on and off the bus and tell my mother I was at the mall. I had a pin on my Jordache bag that said "My Mother Thinks I'm at the Movies." My mother didn't think it was funny. *You're a pip, Shell.* Lydia lit up a cigarette and smoked it right there on the sidewalk and I broke out in a sweat. Someone's Going To See You, I hissed. *Who?* Lydia laughed. There was no one to yell at Lydia for smoking. I couldn't imagine a freedom like that. It was almost too much. I knew I would get in trouble just for standing next to the smoking runaway Lydia, not to mention her grown-up boyfriend. We rode the bus into Boston and I took them to this great funky shop at Faneuil Hall that I went to so much I started to know the people who worked there, really cool older people who lived in Boston and were maybe punk-rock. I thought they were punk-rock. They had weird hair. I wanted to be their friend so bad, I wanted to show them all to Lydia but she didn't really care. She stole a bunch of stuff, pencils with shimmery stars, erasers shaped like frogs, scratch 'n' sniff stickers that smelled like pickles and chocolate. I was so mad at her for it. This wasn't the mall, it was Boston, the real world, where there were people who I wanted to like me, and if they caught Lydia stealing stuff, they'd never let me in again and I'd be trapped in Chelsea forever, smoking at the back of the mall. Lydia, Don't Steal From There, I said. I felt like she'd stolen from me. *Just a couple pencils,* she shrugged. Her boyfriend didn't say anything. He was a pretty quiet guy. Lydia gave him a sticker that smelled like pizza. The way I thought, it was like all the things I knew were great were one, not separate. Punk rock and runaways, if you were a runaway you were punk and all the realest punks would be runaways. But Lydia was just this fucked-up girl.

I saw her years later, at a party this kid Kenneth had at his parents' house while they were gone. I went to vocational high school with Kenneth. All these metal boys, with long hair static from the hair dryer, were at the party, Metallica loud on the stereo. Lots of pot and beer and Kenneth's favorite, cream soda with Captain Morgan's spiced rum, delicious like candy, overwhelmingly sweet. There were hardly any girls there, just me and a couple of my friends, death-rock kids who lived outside Chelsea. I'd convinced them it would be weird and fun to go to a metal party in my town, I promised no one would beat us up. Was it fun? I got drunk, that was always fun. I smoked some heavy-metal pot that made my vision go weird, my head sick and spinny, and I walked out into the hallway to get some air. There was runaway Lydia, crying. She didn't look much different, better bleach in her hair, and those little Stevie Nicks boots with laces and a tiny heel. Same tight skinny jeans, blue eyeliner making trails down her cheeks. Hey! I told her who I was, she remembered me, stopped crying for a minute. *Do you got a cigarette?* We sat down on the stairs to smoke. Are You Okay? *Those fucking assholes*, she said, wiping the runny blue from her face, pulling furiously on her cigarette. *I passed out at a party here last week and they all ate me out. I just found out, I didn't even know, they just told me.* Who? I said, incredulous. *Chris*, she spat. *Andrew, Matt, Kenneth. Kenneth's okay, because we're going out, but . . .* He Let Them Do That? This was unbelievable to me. I had thought they were nice guys, they'd been nice to me, stuck up for me at school when jocks called me "freak" and threw food in my gigantic goth hairdo. I felt like an idiot for having trusted them. *Kenneth was fucked up*, Lydia said. *They were all fucked up. Fucking assholes!* She smoked more, pulling hard on her skinny white cigarette, her hands chapped pink and shaking as she held it to her lips. That's Awful, I said to her. That's Wrong, That's Really Wrong. She nodded, tears fell off her face and turned into dark spots on her jeans. Chris came to the top of the stairs. This pudgy kid with long, orange flyaway hair, freckles. *Lydia, I'm sorry*, he started. His voice was too large for the words, he was drunk, swaying at the top of the stairs. *Fucking asshole!* Lydia yelled, *Fuck you!* I just looked at him. I really hadn't thought they would do something like that. They were just kids like me, outsiders, only they listened to heavy metal and not the Smiths. If everything I believed in was one, then outsiders—metalheads and punks and skaters and goths—stuck up for girls, and boys who stuck up for girls were outsiders, metalheads and punkers, gothboys and skateboarders. It just made sense to me. My fragile philosophy dissolved beneath Lydia's weeping, and I felt a stab of despair—was there any way to figure out which boys were good, which ones bad? All my little experiments were failing. If rockers and punkers, goths and skaters, could be rapists, then they might as well be jocks, preppies, redneck normals. What made them different, made them outsiders, what did their fashions stand for? Nothing. Costumes. A different way to look intimidating and do the same things frat boys did. They did that to runaway Lydia. Was she still a runaway? If you never go home, are you a runaway forever, even when you're all grown up? Do you grow up and get a home and stop washing your hair at the bathroom at the mall? Lydia continued to cry, and my brain kept spinning, with marijuana and awful revelation. Chris stood like an idiot at the top of the stairs, and then he turned around and went back to the party.

commentary for chapter 3: **FRIENDS AND ENEMIES**

Stories in this section focus on how children whose lives have been marked by family disarray or tragedy can find refuge in friendship. All children need friends, of course, but these stories suggest the outsized importance of companionship for young children or teenagers when their home life is difficult or, in Monica Wood's case, has been struck by the loss of the family breadwinner. Friends can even offer a kind of substitute family when parents are unable or unwilling to provide.

Hitchhiking and taking Greyhounds cross-country, Michael Keith and his alcoholic father wash up in Denver. There the boy wanders alone through the city for days until, in September, he starts sixth grade and is soon bullied and punched by a schoolyard tough. At first he adopts an attitude of defensive passivity, but another boy, Joey Ramone, steps in to protect him. Joey packs a stiletto and has a big brother who will protect him too. What are Joey's motives for defending the new boy? We never find out for sure, but the narrative suggests a certain class solidarity between them, a shared understanding of the dregs of society that unites them in friendship, at least temporarily. Joey hangs out by the railroad tracks where, he says, he once found a human thumb, and he is clearly very experienced in using that knife. When they play hooky together that afternoon, Michael gains the companionship of someone whose strength he can identify with, thereby feeling stronger himself. In friendship he finds a measure of security that his father, struggling to earn money to continue their journey, was unable to give.

Like Michael, nine-year-old Monica Wood felt vulnerable. In the weeks after her father's heart attack on his way to work at a Maine paper mill, she sensed that other children were "a little bit afraid

of me because my father died." A friend from school named Denise Vaillancourt reaches out to her and, both avid readers, they delight in puzzling out plots in books together about the girl detec-
tive Nancy Drew. Denise's parents also show warmth and decency
to Monica. Their friendship helps Monica emerge from the shock
left by her father's death, but decades later she writes that so much
kindness can become almost too much for a bereaved girl to bear.
"Imagine: a childhood burdened by too much kindness," she writes,
suggesting that no friendship, no matter how sincere, can completely erase the grief of losing a beloved parent.

The friendship between teenagers Michelle Tea and Lydia (whose
last name we are never told) is more complicated because Lydia was
no ordinary schoolmate or neighbor. Lydia's family background remains mysterious, and on the surface she appears to have little in
common with Michelle, thirteen, a popular girl with a clique of
friends. They encounter Lydia in the basement restroom of a mall
in Chelsea, an industrial city near Boston. Despite their differences,
Michelle is compelled to befriend this homeless, feral-seeming girl
who wears dirty T-shirts and washes her hair in the restroom sink.
What is Lydia's appeal? Michelle is fascinated by her independence
and street smarts. Lydia was "so brave and alone [. . .] she knew
how to do all the things you had to do if you ran away."

Yet Michelle's feelings about Lydia are riddled with the ambivalence that reflects the fundamental dilemma of adolescence: how to
find a pathway between natural dependence on family and a drive
to break free and rebel against authority, as Lydia had done. Michelle chafes at her mother's injunctions again traveling to Boston,
smoking cigarettes, and dyeing her hair. She identifies with Lydia
who had broken out of the prison of parental constraints. Yet Michelle has strong attachments to home. Her relationship with Lydia
could be seen as a compromise solution to the mixed feelings she
has about home: both tied to it and struggling to break free. "If I
couldn't be a runaway," she writes, "then at least I could know one."

QUESTIONS FOR DISCUSSION

1. Bullying is central to Michael Keith's story. What features are es-
   sential to the concept of bullying and how do they play out in his

narrative? What are Michael's defenses against attack and are they effective? If so, how?

2. What physical and sensory details does Michelle Tea include to help us picture her and her friends in their "clubhouse" at the mall? What are the senses that these images evoke?

3. How does Monica Wood structure her narrative about her relationship with the Vaillancourts so that we understand that period's social context and the threat of deindustrialization to the mill town where she lives?

4. We expect parents to nurture children, but Monica Wood's mother is so stricken herself by the death of her husband that she's limited in how much she can comfort her daughters. How does young Monica accept responsibility for their mutual problem and help her mother? How does Monica deal with her own grief?

chapter four
RELIGION

Joe Queenan
b. 1950

From *Closing Time: A Memoir*
(2009)

Joe Queenan's father was laid off from an office job and spent the rest of his working life doing manual labor and sometimes receiving public assistance. Young Joe aspired to the priesthood at an early age and so was willing to accept an unusual call to service from the Mother Superior at the parochial school in Philadelphia that he attended.

My first direct involvement in official Church ritual occurred when I was ten years old. A hoot and a holler up the road from the housing project stood Ravenhill Academy, the ritzy private school where Grace Kelly received her top-of-the-line education and, presumably, replaced her Philadelphia accent with something more plummy. Ravenhill was run by a mysterious order of nuns based, so the story went, in the Philippines. The Religious of the Assumption had actually started out in France, but their numbers included quite a few Filipinos, which is how the rumor of a Manila connection reached my ears. They wore phantasmagoric maroon and yellow habits, but instead of concealing their heads inside starched lampshades the way most nuns did, they topped off the ensemble with headdresses that looked like top-quality dishcloths. The Filipino nuns were giggly and bouncy and spoke preposterous English. At that point in my life, they were the most exotic people I had ever met, challenged for visual glitz only by the Mummers. Until our paths crossed, I had no idea that people with dark skins were even allowed to be Brides of Christ.

One day toward the end of fifth grade, Mother Superior waddled into our classroom at Saint Bridget's seeking volunteers to serve mass for the nuns at Ravenhill during the summer. This was an unusual request, because altar boys were typically not allowed to serve mass until they were in seventh grade. For reasons that later became clear, no one in the upper grades had put in dibs for the assignment. So I nabbed it. Paradise, as Christ once put it, was a mansion filled with many rooms, and accepting this assignment was my chance to get in on the ground floor.

No sooner had I signed on the dotted line than the downside of the enterprise manifested itself. Masses were served at 7:00 a.m. and 8:30 a.m. every day of the week save Sunday, when the services were held somewhat later. This meant that I had to go to bed every night at eight o'clock in order to get up in time to serve mass the following morning. It meant that the summer was wrecked. It meant no late evening baseball, no tag, no foraging for bumblebees, no masquerading as Zorro. I had been hoodwinked. I had been had.

Ravenhill Academy was about a mile from my home, but to get there, I had to walk all the way to the back of the project; tiptoe across a vast, deserted, overgrown plot known as the Jungle; then walk on the shoulder of an out-of-the-way road up to the private school. The road had no sidewalk on either side; it was mostly used as a truck bypass. The nuns would not have permitted me to take this assignment, nor would my parents have agreed to it, unless I was accompanied by another boy. By custom, if not by edict, two altar boys were needed to serve mass: one to hold the cruets, the other to pour ablutions over the priest's fingers, but mostly to provide visual symmetry for the congregation. In a pinch, you could get away with a single altar boy, but only in an emergency, as the sight of one adolescent serving mass all by himself looked unprofessional. And so Jackie Godman was recruited for the assignment.

Jackie Godman lived directly across the path from my house. His mother was a smidgen plump, with a smushed-in face that gave her the appearance of a charwoman in a Dickens novel, hemmed in by a phalanx of wee nippers who refused to part with a precious morsel of information for less than a guinea. Jackie's father was an intense

American Indian. He had long black hair and piercing eyes, and did not say much, but every so often the screen door would burst open and Jackie would come rocketing out into the front yard with his father in hot pursuit, usually with a belt flailing. In our family, this sort of behavior was viewed as poor form, as the Irish-Catholic code of conduct stipulated that children should always be beaten in private, and beaten mercilessly, but preferably with the windows closed, if only to keep up appearances. It was an unassailable tenet of our family credo that no matter how bad our father's behavior was, other children's fathers were worse. Especially stupid goddamn Indians.

Whenever Mr. Godman would explode out of his house and chase Jackie down the street, my father would quip that our neighbor was "on the warpath." We never knew what tribe Mr. Godman belonged to, nor what he did for a living, though it was bruited about that he, like most Indians of that era, worked as a steeplejack. This was because Indians, as everyone knew, had no fear of heights, since heights did not exist in pre-Columbian culture. None of us ever knew if the ethnic myths we were ceaselessly retailed were true, but as adults invariably coated them with a patina of plausibility, gullible children generally accepted them as gospel truth.

Jackie was the only one of my friends who I knew for a fact was beaten by his father. He, on the other hand, never found out what transpired inside my home, as I deemed the whole subject too shameful to discuss. Though we were friends for years, we never talked about our fathers, not even to compare how much we disliked them. I have no idea what we talked about back then. Nor do I recall what byzantine arguments I marshaled to hornswoggle him into a summer of diocesan penal servitude. Unlike me, Jackie had no clerical aspirations; why he became an altar boy in the first place was never made clear. He was not a cerebral sort, not a reader, nor terribly communicative. But he was sturdy and reliable, and somehow I managed to talk him into getting up every morning for three months straight an hour before sunrise to serve mass for the nuns who had taught Grace Kelly all the things that the daughter of a construction tycoon needed to know in order to pass herself off as a femme fatale Cary Grant simply could not live without—thereby punching her ticket out of Philadelphia. I also suspect that we were enticed by the very elegance of the institution, which made such a sharp contrast with the banality and obviousness of the housing project. Or at least I was.

By the time I grew up, few parents would have allowed their children to make a daybreak pilgrimage on a deserted road, no matter how majestic the enterprise. But people didn't think that way back then. School House Lane was not entirely untraveled in the morning; there were always a few delivery trucks whizzing by. My father made me swear that I would walk up the side of the road facing traffic, because to do otherwise was to invite death. But Jackie and I decided that if we walked up that side of the road, it would be impossible to get rides from passing truckers. Though we had been warned not to accept lifts from strangers, we ignored this counsel, because the road was steep, because the truckers we met seemed to be salt-of-the-earth types, and because little boys only fear danger they can see.

The principal structure at Ravenhill Academy was an imperious gray brick building that sat a hundred yards or so back from the road. In my memories, it resembles Salisbury Cathedral, sulking there in indolent repose, reticent, confident, fully cognizant of its all-encompassing, quasi-arcadian magnificence. It was ringed by lovely, manicured grounds, speckled with trees and flowers; but we never roamed around the property, because we had no interest in scenery and felt uncomfortable in places where we did not fit in. Inside the main structure was a beautiful chapel where we served two masses every morning. The chapel may have been neo-Gothic or postmedieval or Romanesque; it looked like something you would see in Europe.

The chapel bells I recall in much greater detail. Up until then, I had attended services where the altar boys were equipped with tiny silver bells that had a single clapper inside. These bells emitted a tinny, noncommittal sound, as if a telephone were ringing three rooms down the hall. But the ponderous objects we found waiting for us on the altar steps at Ravenhill Academy were chunky, eye-catching chimes the size of teakettles. They were massive and blaring and imbued with a just-add-water orientalism I found intoxicating. The elaborate devices had four separate compartments, each filled with a cluster of ringers that, when rattled, suggested that the czar was arriving with a retinue of 350 sleighs. Years after the fact, I cannot remember one single thing about the priests who served mass each morning, nor what beatitudes the chapel's stained-glass windows may have depicted, but I have never forgotten those amazing bells. They were wonderful playthings, and I loved to make them sing out, having always been a sucker for affordable exoticism, particularly at the municipal level. Whenever I rattled those chimes, I felt transported to Samarkand or Constantinople or Oz.

The best thing about that summer at Ravenhill Academy was breakfast. Every morning after the first service, one of the diminutive Filipino nuns would scurry into the sacristy to bring us a tray containing orange juice, raisin toast, and coffee. Children did not drink coffee in those days—I am not sure they do now—but once I overcame my initial disgust at the acrid taste, I drained those urns to the dregs. After the second mass, another pint-sized nun would appear with a second tray, overflowing with pancakes, sausage, and bacon, or eggs, scrapple, and home fries, or some kind of delicious pastry, always accompanied by more coffee and more orange juice. Breakfasts at home mostly consisted of off-brand cornflakes. These were the best breakfasts I have ever tasted, rivaled only by a few crack-of-dawn, belt-loosening repasts in Limerick and Kilkenny. It is impossible to put into words how much those meals meant to us. They made it easier to go to bed in the early evening, easier to drag ourselves out of bed in the dead of night. They gave us something to look forward to every day. They made us feel like princes.

One morning halfway through August, one of the little nuns told us that we did not need to come serve mass the following morning. We could sleep late, kick back, relax. It was our only day off that summer, and I am sure we enjoyed the respite. That night my aunt Rita, who had a reputation as a gossip, phoned my mother, two years her junior. Aunt Rita was occasionally sent to reasonably priced, well-maintained institutions to recuperate from seasonal nervous breakdowns that were, apparently, the high point of her marriage. My mother always referred to her as "high-strung," but the smart money said she was crazy. She was married to the dullest man in the history of *Homo erectus*, a postman said to have achieved the only perfect entry-exam score in the history of the United States Post Office, even though everyone knew that he was the sole author of this rumor.

The Lynches, whose dour, roly-poly son no one liked, rarely visited the housing project, so if Rita was taking time to call my mother, it was probably to stir up trouble. We did not have a phone most of the time we lived in the project; if relatives needed to reach us, they would call the Dengels' house next door. Because of this, the Dengels always knew what my mother referred to as "all our business."

My sisters and I viewed the Dengels as ambulatory fossils, though they were probably only in their fifties at the time. Even by the standards of marked-down humanity that flourished in the project, they looked a trifle shopworn. Mr. Dengel was a short, stubby, serious man with a stooped back, who wore his trousers up around his chest like an unhappy dwarf treading water in a pair of 46-long waders. He drove a puke-green Studebaker, the first unapologetically hideous car I can ever recall seeing on the streets of Philadelphia. He himself was uncompromisingly ugly; he looked like Richard Nixon's Scandinavian cousin Blingen the Troll.

His wife was a chain-smoker who used to perch her jumbo-sized buttocks against a rail at the foot of our cul-de-sac and run her mouth all day long. I never saw Mrs. Dengel wear a dress; she always left the house cosseted in a loose shift called a muumuu. For all intents and purposes, she spent her entire adult life lounging in her pajamas. My mother did not approve of her, as she was vulgar and a smoker and forever had her hair up in curlers and talked like Lauren Bacall. My father liked her well enough but always maintained that the childless Dengels were closet gentry, the kinds of well-heeled individuals who did not have to live in a housing project but did so because they were cheap. Mr. Dengel's not having a job reinforced this perception.

Anyone who could support himself without going to work every day my father suspected of being closet gentry, a sponger who sucked at the public's copious teat. The Dengels lived next to us for four years, and we were never once in their house, nor they in ours. They did not care much for children. This was during the Sputnik era, when America was terrified that the Russians might catch us off guard during the World Series or the season opener of *The Honeymooners* and drop the H-bomb. The Dengels looked kind of foreign, as he, in particular, was quite the hatchet face and she was no bathing beauty herself. A lot of people in our cul-de-sac thought the Dengels were communist spies, though why they would have gone underground to gather information about losers like us was any-body's guess.

Whatever their relationship with the Soviets, the Dengels did have a phone, and, so long as we did not overdo it, they would al-low us to receive calls in case of an emergency. The night of my un-expected furlough from Ravenhill Academy, Aunt Rita called to get all the details about that morning's service, having heard on the ra-dio that the new archbishop had celebrated mass there. And so he had, assisted by a pair of eighth-graders handpicked for this most blessed event. When my mother told me this, I refused to believe it. Or let us say that, while I had no trouble believing that the priests at Saint Bridget's had stabbed us in the back, I would not accept that the sweet little Filipino nuns were complicit in such treachery. They knew that I had my heart set on being a priest; they knew that my life was short on surprises; they knew how much a once-in-a-lifetime chance to serve mass for the archbishop would have meant to me.

When Jackie and I resumed our duties the next day, I asked the tiniest, youngest nun about the service the day before. Her English was impenetrable; she had no idea why we had been given the day off; she did not understand the question; it was not her fault. We had no way of finding out whose fault it was. It was all some sort of mix-up; lines had gotten crossed somewhere; these things hap-pened. As usual, she brought us juice and coffee and raisin toast af-ter the early mass, then a hearty breakfast after the later service. We left without eating that day, and perhaps even the next day. We were angry, humiliated, disappointed, ashamed. We would have loved to vent our fury on someone, but it was hard to hold a grudge against these cherubic creatures in their divine little costumes, and those breakfast banquets were unimaginably tasty; so by the end of the week we had lost our nerve, swallowed our pride, and gone back to enjoying our early-morning smorgasbords. After all, we adored the little nuns, and they adored us.

It would be nice to say that we never ate breakfast again after realizing that we had been betrayed, or that the meals never tasted half as good. But this was not the case. Poor people have dignity, but not much of it, least of all children. We continued to serve mass at Ravenhill Academy every day for the next three weeks. We dutifully honored our commitment. Then the summer came to an end, and we returned to school. I never went back to Ravenhill Academy, and I doubt that Jackie Godman ever did, either. The wonderful little nun, as always, brought us breakfast that final day, and, as always, we ate it. But when we left that morning, we did not say thank you and we did not say goodbye. At the very beginning of the summer, our parents had warned us about accepting treats from strangers. And now we had learned our lesson.

Michael Patrick MacDonald
b. 1966

From *All Souls: A Family Story from Southie*
(1999)

Michael Patrick MacDonald had eight older siblings
and two younger ones, from four different fathers. In
1974, the neighborhood where his family lived, South
Boston, erupted in protest against busing that had been
ordered by a federal judge to achieve racial integration in the Boston public schools. White students from
South Boston were bused to black Roxbury and black
students from Roxbury were bused to South Boston
("Southie" to its proud residents). Both neighborhoods
were among the city's poorest. The busing led to months
of violent resistance in South Boston and a school boy-
cott by thousands of students. The MacDonalds, like
all their neighbors, deeply resented busing. MacDonald
himself described it as "liberals targeting" his neighborhood for their "experiment." Southie was still recovering
from the disruption caused by busing when it was hit
by a drug epidemic. Drugs were distributed seemingly
everywhere by the neighborhood's own master criminal
Whitey Bulger. Michael's older brother Davey was mentally ill and suicidal when, in 1979, he fell off the roof of
the family's housing project and died. Two years later,
tragedy struck again, this time involving his older sister
Kathy, nineteen. When her boyfriend knocked on the
door to bring the news, it was fifteen-year-old Michael
who answered.

"Kathy went off of the roof," Richie Amoroso yelled when I opened the door. He was out of breath and looked scared, holding onto his head with both hands. I had heard the fire engines going down Patterson Way, but was trying to pay no attention. I didn't know Kathy was lying in a pool of blood down the street. "She crashed onto her head," a woman's voice outside echoed right through me. There was no way I was going to believe this. This couldn't happen twice. Ma came out of the back room, where she'd been keeping to herself since Davey died, retreating whenever she didn't have the energy to be all smiles for the world to see that she was okay after losing her son. She'd heard what Richie had just said at the door, and she held onto a wall, because her knees were buckling under her. Her back arched. Her face looked as if she was being beaten on her back with baseball bats. The house was dark except for the flashing red lights from the fire trucks outside. The little kids came out, asking questions. Stevie, who was five, asked, "Is she gonna die?" Ma straightened up then. She could never let her babies see her fall apart.

Later on, Kathy was in critical condition in the intensive care unit at City Hospital. Ma said she'd be fine. But I didn't believe her—that's what she'd said about Davey the night he died. I don't think any of us slept. When I got out of bed in the morning, I called the hospital for patient information. They said Kathy was on the "danger list." I spoke to a doctor who told me her brain was still bleeding, and that they were working to stop the hemorrhage. I lied and said I was eighteen so that he'd give me all the details; and he did, but mostly in language I'd never heard before. He talked about contusions and neuro this and neuro that. Mary had come over from her apartment in the Old Harbor Project, and since she was going to nursing school, I handed the phone to her. "She's not feeling anything," Mary told me after hanging up. Kathy was in a coma.

The doctor said Kathy's system was loaded with Valium, speed, and cocaine on the night she fell. Ma went through Kathy's pocketbook that a neighbor found up on the roof, and came across bottles of yellow pills and some coke. The pills were prescribed to Kathy by a doctor who lived up on "Pill Hill," a section toward City Point where quite a few doctors had offices. Ma said she knew people who got phony prescriptions up on Pill Hill, but she was shocked that this doctor would be prescribing to kids since, as she said, he was "as sensible looking as the day is long."

All we knew about Kathy's fall was that she'd been up on the roof with Richie Amoroso, on top of the building where she'd been staying with her new friend, Joanie. The neighbors listening at their windows that night said they'd heard Richie and Kathy fighting over drugs, and that Kathy had accused Richie of stealing her Vals. They said Richie had taken the keys to Kathy's apartment too. And some neighbors said they thought Richie Amoroso pushed Kathy off the roof in the struggle that broke out.

Every day we called the hospital, and it turned into months of hearing the same thing: "Danger list," the voice would say before hanging up on me, as if they were sick of me calling. But I was relieved, after every call, not to be told she was dead. Every day through the winter months of 1981, we woke up to continue our watch. Some nights I couldn't sleep at all, thinking I'd wake up to bad news. No doctor or nurse could tell us whether Kathy would live or die. The nurses said they didn't want to give us too much hope, when she could die at any moment, and I thought they were cold to say such useless words. They did tell us early on, though, that the longer Kathy stayed in a coma, the worse her brain damage; and that it was unlikely she'd ever be the same again.

We all took turns visiting Kathy in the intensive care unit, but it seemed I was there around the clock, in the surgical mask and gloves they made me put on so I wouldn't pass on any germs to her. I should've been at Boston Latin High School, but I couldn't sit through class, knowing Kathy might die at any moment. I thought that if I kept talking to Kathy while she was in the coma, it might get her brain working and she'd come back to life. The nurses never asked why I wasn't in school, and every morning Ma saw me leave the house with my huge stack of ancient history and Latin books, not knowing that I was going to the City Hospital. Our telephone was disconnected in those days for not paying the bill, so the school could never call Ma. And I ripped up any mail that would come from Latin. I was relieved that the telephone was out, except that I kept thinking no one would be able to reach us when Kathy died. So whenever I couldn't be at Kathy's bedside, I'd go out to the phone booth at least once an hour to call patient information.

One of our neighbors who was a nurse at City Hospital came by the house every day, to give Ma updates about Kathy and to offer some hope that Kathy would get through this. Karen was always sneaking by Kathy's bedside, checking on her vital statistics even though it wasn't her floor at the City Hospital. Karen said Kathy was a fighter, and that she must really have the will to live, because she was baffling the doctors, overcoming every threat of death that came her way. Karen Young was one of the people in the neighborhood who came and went from Old Colony each day, never getting caught up in the action on the streets. She was always smiling, and some of the younger kids bragged that they knew her whenever they saw her going off to work in her nurse's uniform. One of her brothers, Charlie, hung out with Kevin [the writer's older brother] in the back room. One time I'd walked in on them, weighing white powder on scales and snorting lines. But Karen seemed different. That's why the neighborhood went into a dark and silent state of shock a year later, on the day she was strangled to death by her boyfriend. I remember having seen Karen and her boyfriend the day before her murder, and thinking it might be possible to live a normal life in the Old Colony Project.

I saw all the comings and goings from the room where Kathy lay in a coma. It was like being at a wake, with everyone stopping by with flowers and a card to pay respects over the body. Kathy was listed in "stable condition," but she just lay there with her eyes sealed shut and tubes connecting her to machines. No one knew what to do, the way we never knew what to do around the bodies that we were seeing more and more of those days at Jackie O'Brien's Funeral Parlor. "Should we pray?" "Should we talk to her?" "Can she hear us?"

Early in the day, I was the only one up there. Then Ma would come in the afternoon, and ask me to leave the room so that she could be alone to yell into Kathy's ear and try to wake her up. "Kathy always hated like hell to be woken up in the morning," she laughed. Ma was all smiles when she showed up, like everything was normal. Then, after spending some time alone with Kathy, she looked like she'd been crying, but she still forced a smile when she left to pick up the little kids from nursery school. Ma always told me not to stay too long, and every day she'd say she had "a good feeling" that Kathy would be coming out of the coma.

All the aunts, Ma's four sisters, came in regularly to visit Kathy. My Aunt Mary Kelly would come bursting into Kathy's room to tell her that the hostages in Iran had been freed, or to give other updates, like that Ronald Reagan was doing a great job running the country. But all she got in return was the beeping from the machines that told us Kathy was still alive. My Aunt Leena looked around the room at some of the cards Kathy was receiving and made conversation about Kathy's nice friends. "Ohhh, who's this one from?" she asked about a poem written to Kathy; "my Irish Colleen" it called her. "Oh, just some guy," I said. I didn't have the heart to tell her it was from a convicted bank robber doing time in a federal prison.

Kathy's friends didn't come in much. Most of them were usually too busy getting high on Patterson Way and East 8th Street, the way Kathy would have been if she hadn't crashed onto the sidewalk. Ma said they didn't come around much because they couldn't deal with the pain of seeing Kathy like that. She'd been a beautiful girl, hard to remember now, with half her hair shaved off, infections all over her face, tubes going in and out of her, and the machine that beeped every second. I had a hard time seeing her like this too, I thought, but isn't that what Southie loyalty is all about? Kathy had been such a popular girl, and I wondered why more people didn't seem to care. Some of her friends did come, though, and sometimes I'd walk in to find them blessing themselves or holding Kathy's hands and crying, or talking away and laughing as if she was alive and well.

Timmy Baldwin was one who came in all the time. He wanted to be alone with Kathy, just like Ma. And he always brought flowers. Timmy was known to be a tough kid in Southie—we all knew about his beating someone over the head with a crowbar once when he was high, and about the time he was all messed up and shot a sawed-off shotgun from the project rooftop, yelling, "Look out below!" But I got to see his soft side, like at Kathy's bedside, and remembered the times he'd appeared out of nowhere when I was having a problem with older kids in the neighborhood. "What do you want, a beatin'?" he'd say to them. "Do you know who this is? He's a MacDonald!" pointing at me like I was some kind of royalty in the Old Colony Housing Project. I knew the Timmy who was loyal and watching our backs, like you were supposed to do in Southie. When Kathy dated Timmy, I thought they'd get married someday, and I'd have my own personal bodyguard for a brother-in-law. They'd broken up before Kathy went off the roof, but here was Timmy, still loyal to Kathy and to the MacDonald family. Timmy was both tough and loyal, like everything we wanted to believe about Southie. [. . .]

Kevin came to the hospital with Okie O'Connor. Kevin and Okie were best friends, and it was Okie who made sure the two took time out from their busy day to visit Kathy. Ma always raved about how polite Okie was, carrying her bundles and answering all her questions with a "Yes, Mrs. MacDonald" or a "No, Mrs. MacDonald." Frankie [another older brother] and Kevin said that Okie was a comedian, keeping them laughing all the time. But Frank was worried about Okie's coke use. Still, no one imagined he'd be found, two years after I saw him talking to Kathy in her coma, hanging from a rope in his parents' basement, dead by the age of nineteen. Kevin and Frankie broke into Jackie O'Brien's Funeral Parlor in the middle of the night to stay awake by Okie in his casket. Jackie O'Brien was going to press charges to get them to pay for the back door they broke, but Okie's father had no problem with what the kids had done to show their loyalty, and said he would pay for the door himself. [...]

But then I only knew my own family's pain. First Davey, and now Kathy. We were too closed in on ourselves to know that we were only part of a bigger bloodbath spilling into the streets of the neighborhood we'd thought was heaven on earth. [...] No one took the time to make all the connections. Most of us were too busy picking up the broken pieces of our families. And those who hadn't been hit yet protected themselves by seeing our young dead or wounded as somehow deserving their fate.

Frankie came in to the City Hospital and watched Kathy with anger in his eyes and fists clenched. One time he put a holy medal in her hands and left in tears. That day he walked up to Richie Amoroso on Dorchester Street and gave him a beating that landed Richie in the hospital. Frankie wasn't usually a troublemaker now that he was winning titles in boxing rings all over New England. But he said he was tired of waiting on the cops to investigate Kathy's fall. All the same neighbors who said they'd seen and heard the fight between Kathy and Richie that night, the coldest night of the year, never answered the door when Ma and Frankie showed up with detectives looking for a statement. Ma saw their peepholes go dark, though, from their eyes looking through, so we all knew they were just minding their own business. We knew that minding your own business was the rule in Southie, but it was different for us now that we wanted some answers about Kathy being in a coma. Frankie chose street justice, with no one talking and the cops giving up so easily. But Amoroso was back out on the streets in no time, and people were already starting to ask less often about how Kathy was doing in the hospital.

I started to get to know who Kathy was while she was in the coma. I felt guilty because I knew it was a little late. One day when she went back on the critical list, I was sure she'd finally die. She was only nineteen, and she'd have to be buried in the extra spot we had next to Davey. I went into her bedroom to prepare. Kathy had never wanted me snooping in her room, so I thought I'd probably find drugs or maybe even evidence of witchcraft from her friendship with Julie Meaney. I was looking for any explanation for what had happened to her life. But instead I found out all the things Kathy felt about herself, all the photos and letters she's saved through her teenage years, all the insecurities of a girl in poems that played up how "K-O-O-L" she was. She'd kept every one of her school pictures, even the ones of her as a chubby fourth grader with hand-me-down clothes, photographs over which she's scrawled FAT, or else scribbled out the face completely. In her teenage years, Kathy had become thinner, prettier, and she wore sexy stolen designer clothes and put on faces that looked like she was the baddest. "K is for Kool," Kathy wrote in a jingle that spelled out the meaning of the letters of her name. Her other poems were about her friends and how cool her whole crew was. In letters to herself, Kathy wrote about how worried she was about girlfriends like Julie Meaney and Doreen Riordan, and how much she loved Southie. Her doodles on paper said all the stuff we saw written on the walls of the neighborhood: SOUTHIE FOREVER, IRISH POWER, HELL NO WE WON'T GO, RESIST, NEVER, and KATHY # ONE.

Then there was the scrawl WHITEY RULES. I wasn't sure if Kathy was talking about white people being the best, or about Whitey himself, who some said was bringing up the finest cocaine from Florida these days. I already felt myself missing Kathy, but I didn't want to think about that. I gathered up all her secret belongings and got ready for another funeral.

The next day Grandpa met me at the City Hospital. He said he had some holy water from Fatima, where the Blessed Mother was said to have appeared before three children in 1917. He said I'd have to help him throw the water onto Kathy when the nurses weren't looking. Kathy was on the danger list again. Infections were taking over her body, and she had pneumonia—there was no way the nurses would let us dump water on her. But this was holy water I figured, so I went along with him. I was willing to try anything at this point.

The nurses caught Grandpa after he'd managed to pull the jug from out of his baggy trousers and pour it all over Kathy's head, hands, and feet. Grandpa was shaking and in tears, and he told one nurse to go fuck herself when she came in screaming and trying to pull the old-fashioned jug from his hands. More nurses came running in when they heard the fighting. They started to gang up on him, but Grandpa was too strong for them. He kept on reciting the Rosary and telling the nurses in his Irish brogue to shut their fucking mouths. The hospital johnny that they made him wear over his clothes into Kathy's sanitized room was hanging now from his two wrists, and he kept pulling it up over his shoulders, in between throwing more holy water and fighting nurses. The shower cap they'd made him put on over his hair was now barely hanging onto the back of his head. "Kathy, if you can hear me now, move your arm!" Grandpa yelled. And she did. We both looked at each other. After that he just took a deep breath and relaxed. "Now," he said, "are ye right so?" That's what he said when he meant, "Are you ready?" I said I was, and we left the nurses still screaming.

We walked out into the first signs of spring after one of the coldest winters I remember, and the whole way home Grandpa had tears in his eyes, but the brightest smile. He said he had "a good feeling" now that Kathy would be coming out of it. He asked me if I had a good feeling too, and I said I did. But I think I had a good feeling mostly because for the first time in my life I saw how much Grandpa really did care about us, and how much pain he felt for Ma. Even though he could never tell her that.

All winter long, we'd been yelling into Kathy's ears, asking her to move a foot or an arm if she could hear us. Sometimes she twitched, but the day Grandpa threw the holy water on her was the first time she'd clearly heard us, and she'd slowly lifted her limp arm and held it there. The following week, on Easter Sunday morning, Ma got the call. "Kathy woke up!" she screamed, banging on the door to the bedroom where I was sleeping. When we all went in to see Kathy, she was lying there looking at us with her two eyes open, and she smiled. She tried to say "Ma." Her lips said it but she still couldn't talk. It just sounded like air.

Kathy had to start all over again, they told us. The doctors didn't know if she would ever walk again; she had extensive nerve damage that couldn't be repaired. Half her body was almost useless, the right side, which they said was controlled by the left side of her brain, which had hit the sidewalk. When she came home to Old Colony, a crowd had gathered to cheer her arrival out of a handicapped van. Kathy was in a wheelchair. Her mind seemed to be all there, though. She was having speech therapy, and getting a little bit of her voice back. She had chewed off a good bit of her tongue in the coma, so it was hard to make out what she was saying. But she could keep up a conversation and she knew who everyone was.

Within a year Kathy took her first steps, at first with a walker, then with a cane. She dragged her right side when she walked. Before long she was dragging her right side around Old Colony, to all of her old haunts. But more and more her walks were up toward Jackie O'Brien's to attend her friends' wakes. More and more often I found myself sitting at the window, noticing how clean-cut all the teenagers in the neighborhood looked, with ties on and wet hair slicked back like Catholic school kids, gathering out on Patterson Way for the three-block journey up Dorchester Street to the funeral parlor. You wouldn't even recognize some of the roughest ones among them. Kathy, Kevin, and Frankie put on their best clothes too. Kathy followed at the back of the crowd, with a few others who walked with canes or were wheeled in chairs. It was becoming another one of our Southie traditions, these groups of spiffed-up kids gathering to see their friends in a casket; and Ma found herself wondering which one would be next.

bell hooks

b. 1952

From *Bone Black: Memories of Girlhood*
(1996)

Born Gloria Watkins to a working-class black family in rural Kentucky, bell hooks adopted the pen name of her great-grandmother and eschewed capital letters because they are "about ego" and a book's substance is what should matter. As a rebellious and bookish child with asthma, she felt isolated within her family of six girls and one boy. A teenager in the early days of school integration, she was chosen for "smart" classes with white students and had white friends, but walking through rows of national guardsmen on her way to classes made her think of school as "a place where we come face to face with racism." Her religious mother bought her a book of Bible stories that her daughter took house to house, reading to invalids and shut-ins, which she saw as Christian missionary work.

Slowly I have become involved in campus ministry. Leaders in the crusade for christ in our town do radical political work as well for they dare to cross the barriers between white and black. They hold integrated meetings. They embrace everyone. They live the meaning that we are all one. I have become involved slowly because my faith is not as strong as theirs. I am not strongly enough a believer in sin. In fact I do not believe in it at all, evil yes but sin no. And god, I am a true true believer in all gods.

To cure my asthma they have a laying on of hands. It is a hot summer night. We are all together on a farm outside town listening to the crickets. We are all kneeling. Everyone whose hand can reach touches me or something of mine. Although my breathing continues to move in and out in a painful way those hands are blessing me, holding me in a sweeter love than that we experience one to one. They pray that god's love, which is all expansive, will take us all in, will heal us all, but especially will heal the asthma. I do not believe in cause and effect. My asthma attacks continue. It is not a lack of faith. I believe in the power of the hands. I believe in the miraculous. And the miracle will come later. Though I have lost touch with the many hands, it is the power of that night that makes all other nights of healing possible.

To strengthen our ties with one another we go to a retreat. It is only after the white grown-ups, respected in the community, have called to plead my cause for me that mama allows me to go. She restricts my movements constantly for fear that these new experiences are ruining me, making me disconsolate. This is the new word they use to describe me. I give it to them. I learn it at church when we are singing. Come ye disconsolate wherever ye languish, come to the mercy fervently kneel, here bring your wounded heart, hear tell your anguish, earth has no sorrow that heaven cannot heal. I am not crazy, I tell them. I am disconsolate. I show them in the dictionary that it means dejected, deprived of consolation. Whatever it is, they are sick of it. They are waiting for it to go away. They do not understand that I am also waiting for it to go away.

Here among the faithful I can reveal that I am anguished in spirit. They understand the primacy of the spirit. When we sing together, eat, and join hands I feel there is solace, that this is a mercy seat where I can rest. The group is led by the energy of a middle-aged white woman. She and I take a walk together to get more in touch with one another. We talk about the healing power of love. I want to take the sincerity of our talk, our faith, and cover the world with it like icing on a cake. I want to understand why the healing does not spread outward. I want to know why if the healing is real it does not touch us in the places where we live. At home they are concerned about this new passion for the group, for god. They want to make sure that the god that is talked about, worshiped and prayed to, is the god of the old and new testament and not the god of this rewritten paperback Bible.

To us the Catholic church is a mystery. We know there is strong prejudice against Catholics among the white folks in this town. Black folks say religion is all the same. The Catholic church is one of the few white churches black people have joined with no protest. Black folks say the few that join do so just for show. We children come to believe that the one difference between the Catholic church and our Baptist church is the degree of show. Catholicism is more showy—with the robes, the candles, and all that singing and praying in a language most people cannot understand. We go there only once for an interfaith Christmas service. We are impressed by the show even though we do not feel moved in spirit, we do not feel the hand of god pressing against our heart when the priest speaks. We are fascinated by the idea of confession, especially me. We want to ask the Catholics at school what confession is like but we don't because we know better.

When I become active in the campus crusade for christ, I meet and talk to Catholics for the first time. We attend a retreat where believers come from all around to join together. Banners on every wall say The Way Is One But The Paths Are Many. We are Methodist, Baptist, Lutheran, Catholic, Episcopalian. There are only a few of us who are not white. We retreat to a place in the hills. It is early spring and everywhere flowers bloom. There is a glory everywhere in nature that seems to echo the exuberance in the voice of the true believers, the true crusaders. I am still filled with doubt. I am glad to be at the retreat, to escape the tensions of home, the feeling that I stand on the edge of a cliff about to fall off. I know that many people come to god to be rescued, to be taken from the cliff and placed on solid ground. I come to god and yet remain at the edge of the cliff. I have not been rescued. For comfort I read over and over the story of John the Baptist wandering in the wilderness. I too linger in the wilderness wanting desperately to find my way.

We are to hear a talk from the Catholic priest who is here. It is the opening session of the retreat. He is wearing clothes that are a slate gray, dark but not black. It is hard for me to imagine him wearing black, since I have been told all my life that black is a woman's color.

He is lean and without the plump smug flesh that so often identifies the men called by god. When he speaks I feel as though we have suddenly entered a room where only he and I are present. This feeling disturbs me. I look around me to make sure that everyone is still there. They are staring straight ahead. They, too, have entered that room. With me his voice is soft-spoken, gentle. He tells me that he understands the aloneness that I feel, that he sees me poised on the edge of a cliff.

For the first time in my life I hear someone say that there is nothing wrong with feeling alone, that he, too, has been at the edge, has felt the fear of drowning, of being moved toward death without consciously contemplating suicide. I do not ask him how he knows, how he feels with me this pain in my heart. When the talk ends, when we are alone, he repeats again and again the words that are a net catching the body falling from a tall place. When I weep and sob all over the slate gray clothing he tells me that the young woman standing on the cliff, alone and afraid to live, is only suspended in a moment of hesitation, that she will overcome her fear and leap into life—that she will bring with her the treasures that are her being: the beauty, the courage, the wisdom. He tells me to let that young woman into my heart, to begin to love her so that she can live and live and go on living. [. . .]

Loneliness brings me to the edge of what I know. My soul is dark like the inner world of the cave—bone black. I have been drowning in that blackness. Like quicksand it sucks me in and keeps me there in the space of all my pain. I never say out loud that I could die in this space of loneliness, of outsiderness. I never say out loud I want to kill myself—to go away from all this. I never tell anyone how much I want to belong. The priest I met saw me standing on the edge of a cliff about to jump off and pulled me back. It was not a real cliff, just the one inside myself. Before anyone goes to that real place where we leap to our death, the dying has to be imagined. And so he finds me there in that bone black place within myself where I am dreaming my escape.

He sends a student to spend time with me at the retreat. She gives me Rilke's *Letters to a Young Poet*. I am drowning and his words come to rescue me. He helps to make sense of the pain I feel.

Now it is Rilke who speaks to me and urges me to go into myself and find the deeps into which my life takes rise. At last I am not alone. I have been seen.

I read poems. I write. That is my destiny. Standing on the edge of the cliff about to fall into the abyss, I remember who I am. I am a young poet, a writer. I am here to make words. I have the power to pull myself back from death—to keep myself alive.

Now when they tell me I am crazy, that if I keep reading all those books I will end up crazy, locked away in the asylum where no one will visit me—now when they tell me this I am not so afraid. Rilke gives meaning to the wilderness of spirit I am living in. His book is a world I enter and find myself. He tells me that everything terrible is really something helpless that wants help from us. I read *Letters to a Young Poet* over and over. I am drowning and it is the raft that takes me safely to the shore. [. . .]

At night when everyone is silent and everything is still, I lie in the darkness of my windowless room, the place where they exile me from the community of their heart, and search the unmoving blackness to see if I can find my way home. I tell myself stories, write poems, record my dreams. In my journal I write—I belong in this place of words. This is my home. This dark, bone black inner cave where I am making a world for myself.

commentary for chapter four: RELIGION

The readings in this section focus on the way religion offered hope, direction, and a measure of solace at times of loneliness or despair for these writers when they were young. Faith could be a source of beauty and mystery, a force that could put them into contact with something much greater than themselves, or it could lead to some of life's early disappointments. By the time he was ten, Joe Queenan had resolved to become a priest but soon hit a stinging setback. Michael Patrick MacDonald was a teenager when he saw his grandfather use holy water to try to revive the author's comatose sister. For bell hooks, spiritual guidance proved a lifeline at a time of despair in adolescence.

Physical expressions of religious belief—cathedral architecture, images of saints, a priest's vestments—can bring awe and wonder into the drab lives of poor families. Queenan escaped the humdrum world of the housing project where he lived every time he entered the elegant Catholic academy where he served as an altar boy. The hefty chapel bells he rang during mass amazed him and had an exoticism that he never forgot. For Baptist bell hooks, Catholicism was a "showy" religion with its robes and candles, and she was fascinated by the rite of confession.

Yet these stories suggest that, for young people, the power of religion lay not just in its spectacle and mysticism but in the people who were its practitioners. Queenan adored the nuns at the chapel where he served mass, confident they adored him and his altar-boy partner too. Just as leaders of the church contributed to the strength of his commitment to religious service, they played a decisive role in crushing his spirit when he and his friend were passed over to serve mass to a visiting archbishop. Church higher-ups, not the adorable nuns, had their own reasons for choosing other boys for that honor. Childhood is a time when no matter how good one tries to be, grown-ups are in charge and make the decisions. Adults may be totally oblivious to the pain they are inflicting on powerless children.

The Catholic priest who ministered to teenage bell hooks at an ecumenical retreat pulled her back "from the edge of a cliff," the cliff that was inside herself. That cathartic encounter led to a transformative experience for the author, when the priest sent a student to spend time with her. The student introduced young Gloria (her given name) to Rainer Maria Rilke's *Letters to a Young Poet*, which she read over and over until they became the raft that saved her from drowning psychologically and helped her discover her calling as a writer.

MacDonald's story focuses on faith as an act of desperation. His sister Kathy had been in a coma all winter and was not responding to treatment. His grandfather, a devout Irish immigrant, pulled out a jug and tossed holy water from the sacred site of Fatima, where the Virgin Mary was said to have appeared, all over comatose Kathy. He recited the Rosary while pouring, alarming the hospital nurses and turning his actions into a kind of Catholic religious ceremony. When Kathy lifted her arm, the grandfather was overjoyed to have worked what looked like divine intervention. In Michael's eyes, however, what counted was Grandpa's compassion. More than showing the power of religious faith, he had shown how much he cared about their family at a time of crisis.

QUESTIONS FOR DISCUSSION

1. How would you describe Joe Queenan's attitude toward his neighborhood? How does his use of language convey his attitude toward his neighbors and relatives? What is the significance of the actress Grace Kelly in his description?
2. What do we learn about the characteristics and problems of South Boston in Michael Patrick MacDonald's account?
3. How does MacDonald's relationship with his sister Kathy evolve in the course of this account? When he examined her possessions in her bedroom, what did he learn?

4. What were the social and psychological problems that young bell hooks was facing? How did religious participation in its various forms help her cope with them?
5. At the end of these accounts, are the three writers firmer in their faiths than at the beginning, or do they grow more skeptical of religion?

chapter five

SCHOOL AND COLLEGE

Russell Baker

1925–2019

From *Growing Up*

(1982)

Russell Baker's father, a stonemason, died suddenly of a heart attack when the boy was five. He and his mother went to live with her relatives in Belleville, New Jersey, where they found a welcoming, if transient, home. His mother later remarried and they moved again to live with his stepfather, a railway worker, in Baltimore. There, Russell entered a special program for fast learners at a public high school.

The only thing that truly interested me was writing, and I knew that sixteen-year-olds did not come out of high school and become writers. I thought of writing as something to be done only by the rich. It was so obviously not real work, not a job at which you could earn a living. Still, I had begun to think of myself as a writer. It was the only thing for which I seemed to have the smallest talent, and, silly though it sounded when I told people I'd like to be a writer, it gave me a way of thinking about myself which satisfied my need to have an identity.

The notion of becoming a writer had flickered off and on in my head since the Belleville days, but it wasn't until my third year in high school that the possibility took hold. Until then I'd been bored by everything associated with English courses. I found English grammar dull and baffling. I hated the assignments to turn out "compositions," and went at them like heavy labor, turning out leaden and lackluster paragraphs that were agonies for teachers to read and for me to write. The classics thrust on me to read seemed as deadening as chloroform.

When our class was assigned to Mr. Fleagle for third-year English I anticipated another grim year in that dreariest of subjects. Mr. Fleagle was notorious among city students for dullness and inability to inspire. He was said to be stuffy, dull, and hopelessly out of date. To me he looked to be sixty or seventy and prim to a fault. He wore primly severe eyeglasses, his wavy hair was primly cut and primly combed. He wore prim vested suits with neckties blocked primly against the collar buttons of his primly starched white shirts. He had a primly pointed jaw, a primly straight nose and a prim manner of speaking that was so correct, so gentlemanly, that he seemed a comic antique.

I anticipated a listless, unfruitful year with Mr. Fleagle and for a long time was not disappointed. We read *Macbeth*. Mr. Fleagle loved *Macbeth* and wanted us to love it too, but he lacked the gift of infecting others with his own passion. He tried to convey the murderous ferocity of Lady Macbeth one day by reading aloud the passage that concludes

> *. . . I have given suck, and know*
> *How tender 'tis to love the babe that milks me.*
> *I would, while it was smiling in my face,*
> *Have plucked my nipple from his boneless gums. . . .*

The idea of prim Mr. Fleagle plucking his nipple from boneless gums was too much for the class. We burst into gasps of irrepressible snickering. Mr. Fleagle stopped.

"There is nothing funny, boys, about giving suck to a babe. It is the—the very essence of motherhood, don't you see."

He constantly sprinkled his sentences with "don't you see." It wasn't a question but an exclamation of mild surprise at our ignorance. "Your pronoun needs an antecedent, don't you see," he would say, very primly. "The purpose of the Porter's scene, boys, is to provide comic relief from the horror, don't you see."

Late in the year we tackled the informal essay. "The essay, don't you see, is the . . ." My mind went numb. Of all forms of writing, none seemed so boring as the essay. Naturally we would have to write informal essays. Mr. Fleagle distributed a homework sheet offering us a choice of topics. None was quite so simpleminded as "What I Did on My Summer Vacation," but most seemed to be almost as dull. I took the list home and dawdled until the night before the essay was due. Sprawled on the sofa, I finally faced up to the grim task, took the list out of my notebook, and scanned it. The topic on which my eye stopped was "The Art of Eating Spaghetti."

This title produced an extraordinary sequence of mental images. Surging up out of the depths of memory came a vivid recollection of a night in Belleville when all of us were seated around the supper table—Uncle Allen, my mother, Uncle Charlie, Doris, Uncle Hal—and Aunt Pat served spaghetti for supper. Spaghetti was an exotic treat in those days. Neither Doris nor I had ever eaten spaghetti, and none of the adults had enough experience to be good at it. All the good humor of Uncle Allen's house reawoke in my mind as I recalled the laughing arguments we had that night, about the socially respectable method for moving spaghetti from plate to mouth.

Suddenly I wanted to write about that, about the warmth and good feeling of it, but I wanted to put it down simply for my own joy, not for Mr. Fleagle. It was a moment I wanted to recapture and hold for myself. I wanted to relive the pleasure of an evening at New Street. To write it as I wanted, however, would violate all the rules of formal composition I'd learned in school, and Mr. Fleagle would surely give it a failing grade. Never mind. I would write something else for Mr. Fleagle after I had written this thing for myself.

When I finished it the night was half gone and there was no time left to compose a proper, respectable essay for Mr. Fleagle. There was no choice next morning but to turn in my private reminiscence of Belleville. Two days passed before Mr. Fleagle returned the graded papers, and he returned everyone's but mine. I was bracing myself for a command to report to Mr. Fleagle immediately after school for discipline when I saw him lift my paper from his desk and rap for the class's attention.

"Now, boys," he said, "I want to read you an essay. This is titled, 'The Art of Eating Spaghetti.'"

And he started to read. My words! He was reading *my words* out loud to the entire class. What's more, the entire class was listening. Listening attentively. Then somebody laughed, then the entire class was laughing, and not in contempt and ridicule, but with open-hearted enjoyment. Even Mr. Fleagle stopped two or three times to repress a small prim smile.

I did my best to avoid showing pleasure, but what I was feeling was pure ecstasy at this startling demonstration that my words had the power to make people laugh. In the eleventh grade, at the eleventh hour as it were, I had discovered a calling. It was the happiest moment of my entire school career. When Mr. Fleagle finished he put the final seal on my happiness by saying, "Now that, boys, is an essay, don't you see. It's—don't you see—it's of the very essence of the essay, don't you see. Congratulations, Mr. Baker."

For the first time, light shone on a possibility. It wasn't a very heartening possibility, to be sure. Writing couldn't lead to a job after high school, and it was hardly honest work, but Mr. Fleagle had opened a door for me. After that I ranked Mr. Fleagle among the finest teachers in the school.

My mother was almost as delighted as I when I showed her Mr. Fleagle's A-Plus and described my triumph. Hadn't she always said I had a talent for writing? "Now if you work hard at it, Buddy, you can make something of yourself."

Esmeralda Santiago
b. 1948

From *When I Was Puerto Rican*
(1993)

Esmeralda Santiago was thirteen when she moved
with her mother, recently separated from her father,
from rural Puerto Rico to Brooklyn, where Esmeralda's
maternal grandmother, known as Tata, and Tata's friend
Don Julio lived. Shortly afterward, they were joined by
several younger siblings and eventually by Francisco,
her mother's partner. Esmeralda had been a diligent
student in their village, Macún, in Puerto Rico, but her
English was very heavily accented when she enrolled in
New York City's public schools.

The first day of school Mami walked me to a stone building that
loomed over Graham Avenue, its concrete yard enclosed by an iron
fence with spikes at the top. The front steps were wide but shallow
and led up to a set of heavy double doors that slammed shut behind us as we walked down the shiny corridor. I clutched my eighth-
grade report card filled with A's and B's, and Mami had my birth
certificate. At the front office we were met by Mr. Grant, a droopy
gentleman with glasses and a kind smile who spoke no Spanish. He
gave Mami a form to fill out. I knew most of the words in the square
we were to fill in NAME, ADDRESS (CITY, STATE), and OCCUPA-
TION. We gave it to Mr. Grant, who reviewed it, looked at my birth
certificate, studied my report card, then wrote on the top of the form
"7-18."

Don Julio had told me that if students didn't speak English, the schools in Brooklyn would keep them back one grade until they learned it.

"Seven gray?" I asked Mr. Grant, pointing at his big numbers, and he nodded.

"I no guan seven gray. I eight gray. I teeneyer."

"You don't speak English," he said. "You have to go to seventh grade while you're learning."

"I have A's in school Puerto Rico. I lern good. I no seven gray girl."

Mami stared at me, not understanding but knowing I was being rude to an adult.

"What's going on?" she asked me in Spanish. I told her they wanted to send me back one grade and I would not have it. This was probably the first rebellious act she had seen from me outside my usual mouthiness within the family.

"Negi, leave it alone. Those are the rules," she said, a warning in her voice.

"I don't care what their rules say," I answered. "I'm not going back to seventh grade. I can do the work. I'm not stupid."

Mami looked at Mr. Grant, who stared at her as if expecting her to do something about me. She smiled and shrugged her shoulders.

"Meester Grant," I said, seizing the moment, "I go eight gray six mons. Eef I no lern inglish, I go seven gray. Okay?"

"That's not the way we do things here," he said, hesitating.

"I good studen. I lern queek. You see notes." I pointed to the A's in my report card. "I pass seven gray."

So we made a deal.

"You have until Christmas," he said. "I'll be checking on your progress." He scratched out "7-18" and wrote in "8-23." He wrote something on a piece of paper, sealed it inside an envelope, and gave it to me. "Your teacher is Miss Brown. Take this note upstairs to her. Your mother can go," he said and disappeared into his office.

"Wow!" Mami said, "you can speak English!"

I was so proud of myself, I almost burst. In Puerto Rico if I'd been that pushy, I would have been called *mal educada* [poorly educated, rude] by the Mr. Grant equivalent and sent home with a note to my mother. But here it was my teacher who was getting the note, I got what I wanted, and my mother was sent home.

"I can find my way after school," I said to Mami. "You don't have to come get me."

"Are you sure?"

"Don't worry," I said. "I'll be all right."

I walked down the black-tiled hallway, past many doors that were half glass, each one labelled with a room number in neat black lettering. Other students stared at me, tried to get my attention, or pointedly ignored me. I kept walking as if I knew where I was going, heading for the sign that said STAIRS with an arrow pointing up. When I reached the end of the hall and looked back, Mami was still standing at the front door watching me, a worried expression on her face. I waved, and she waved back. I started up the stairs, my stomach churning into tight knots. All of a sudden, I was afraid that I was about to make a fool of myself and end up in seventh grade in the middle of the school year. Having to fall back would be worse than just accepting my fate now and hopping forward if I proved to be as good a student as I had convinced Mr. Grant I was. "What have I done?" I kicked myself with the back of my right shoe, much to the surprise of the fellow walking behind me, who laughed uproariously, as if I had meant it as a joke.

Miss Brown's was the learning disabled class, where the administration sent kids with all sorts of problems, none of which, from what I could see, had anything to do with their ability to learn but more with their willingness to do so. They were an unruly group. Those who came to class, anyway. Half of them never showed up, or, when they did, they slept through the lesson or nodded off in the middle of Miss Brown's carefully parsed sentences.

We were outcasts in a school where the smartest eighth graders were in the 8-1 homeroom, each subsequent drop in number indicating one notch less smarts. If your class was in the low double digits, (8-10 for instance), you were smart, but not a pinhead. Once you got into the teens, your intelligence was in question, especially as the numbers rose to the high teens. And then there were the twenties. I was in 8-23, where the dumbest, most undesirable people were placed. My class was, in some ways, the equivalent of seventh grade, perhaps even sixth or fifth.

Miss Brown, the homeroom teacher, who also taught English composition, was a young black woman who wore sweat pads under her arms. The strings holding them in place sometimes slipped outside the short sleeves of her well-pressed white shirts, and she had to turn her back to us in order to adjust them. She was very pretty, with almond eyes and a hairdo that was flat and straight at the top of her head then dipped into tight curls at the ends. Her fingers were well manicured, the nails painted pale pink with white tips. She taught English composition as if every one cared about it, which I found appealing.

After the first week she moved me from the back of the room to the front seat by her desk, and after that, it felt as if she were teaching me alone. We never spoke, except when I went up to the blackboard.

"Esmeralda," she called in a musical voice, "would you please come up and mark the prepositional phrase?"

In her class, I learned to recognize the structure of the English language, and to draft the parts of a sentence by the position of words relative to pronouns and prepositions without knowing exactly what the whole thing meant.

The school was huge and noisy. There was a social order that, at first, I didn't understand but kept bumping into. Girls and boys who wore matching cardigans walked down the halls hand in hand, sometimes stopping behind lockers to kiss and fondle each other. They were *Americanos* and belonged in the homerooms in the low numbers.

Another group of girls wore heavy makeup, hitched their skirts above their knees, opened one extra button on their blouses, and teased their hair into enormous bouffants held solid with spray. In the morning, they took over the girls' bathroom, where they dragged on cigarettes as they did their hair until the air was unbreathable, thick with smoke and hair spray. The one time I entered the bathroom before classes they chased me out with insults and rough shoves.

Those bold girls with hair and makeup and short skirts, I soon found out, were Italian. The Italians all sat together on one side of the cafeteria, the blacks on another. The two groups hated each other more than they hated Puerto Ricans. At least once a week there was a fight between an Italian and a *moreno*, either in the bathroom, in the school yard, or in an abandoned lot near the school, a no-man's-land that divided their neighborhoods and kept them apart on weekends.

The black girls had their own style. Not for them the big, pouffy hair of the Italians. Their hair was straightened, curled at the tips like Miss Brown's, or pulled up into a twist at the back with wispy curls and straw straight bangs over Cleopatra eyes. Their skirts were also short, except it didn't look like they hitched them up when their mothers weren't looking. They came that way. They had strong, shapely legs and wore knee socks with heavy lace-up shoes that became lethal weapons in fights.

It was rumored that the Italians carried knives, even the girls, and that the *morenos* had brass knuckles in their pockets and steel toes in their heavy shoes. I stayed away from both groups, afraid that if I befriended an Italian, I'd get beat up by a *morena*, or vice versa.

There were two kinds of Puerto Ricans in school: the newly arrived, like myself, and the ones born in Brooklyn of Puerto Rican parents. The two types didn't mix. The Brooklyn Puerto Ricans spoke English, and often no Spanish at all. To them, Puerto Rico was the place where their grandparents lived, a place they visited on school and summer vacations, a place which they complained was backward and mosquito-ridden. Those of us for whom Puerto Rico was still a recent memory were also split into two groups: the ones who longed for the island and the ones who wanted to forget it as soon as possible.

I felt disloyal for wanting to learn English, for liking pizza, for studying the girls with big hair and trying out their styles at home, locked in the bathroom where no one could watch. I practiced walking with the peculiar little hop of the *morenas*, but felt as if I were limping.

I didn't feel comfortable with the newly arrived Puerto Ricans who stuck together in suspicious little groups, criticizing everyone, afraid of everything. And I was not accepted by the Brooklyn Puerto Ricans, who held the secret of coolness. They walked the halls between the Italians and the *morenos*, neither one nor the other, but looking and acting like a combination of both, depending on the texture of their hair, the shade of their skin, their makeup, and the way they walked down the hall. [. . .]

Every day after school I went to the library and took out as many children's books as I was allowed. I figured that if American children learned English through books, so could I, even if I was starting later. I studied the bright illustrations and learned the words for the unfamiliar objects of our new life in the United States: A for Apple, B for Bear, C for Cabbage. As my vocabulary grew, I moved to large-print chapter books. Mami bought me an English-English dictionary because that way, when I looked up a word I would be learning others.

By my fourth month in Brooklyn, I could read and write English much better than I could speak it, and at midterms I stunned the teachers by scoring high in English, History, and Social Studies. During the January assembly, Mr. Grant announced the names of the kids who had received high marks in each class. My name was called out three times. I became a different person to the other eighth graders. I was still in 8-23, but they knew, and I knew, that I didn't belong there. [. . .]

"Tomorrow," Mami said, "you're not going to school. I need you to come with me to the welfare office."

"Ay, Mami, can't you take Delsa? [the writer's younger sister]"

"No, I can't."

When Mami was laid off, we had to go on welfare. She took me with her because she needed someone to translate. Six months after we landed in Brooklyn, I spoke enough English to explain our situation.

"My mother she no spik inglish. My mother she look for work evree day, and nothin. My mother she say she don't want her children suffer. My mother she say she want work bot she lay off. My mother she only need help a leetle while."

I was always afraid that if I said something wrong, if I mispronounced a word or used the wrong tense, the social workers would say no, and we might be evicted from our apartment, or the electricity would be shut off, or we'd freeze to death because Mami couldn't pay for heating fuel.

The welfare office was in a brick building with wire covering the windows. The waiting room was always packed with people, and the person at the front desk never knew when we would be helped or where the social workers were. It was a place where you went and waited for hours, with nothing to do but sit and stare at the green walls. Once there, you couldn't even go out to get a bite to eat, because your name might be called any time, and if you were gone, you'd lose your turn and have to come back the next day.

On the way there, Mami bought the paper, and I brought along the thickest library book I could find. The first couple of hours usually went by fast, since there were forms to fill out and interesting conversations going on around us as the women told each other their stories. There were never any men, just tired-looking women, some with their children, as if bringing children there would make the social workers talk to them.

Mami dressed nicely for the welfare office and insisted that I do too.

"We're not going there looking like beggars," she said, and while we waited she kept reminding me to sit up, to stay alert, to look as neat and dignified as the women on the other side of the partition, phones at their ears, pens poised over the forms handed to them by the receptionist with the dour expression who wouldn't smile if her life depended on it.

Occasionally there were fights. Women beat up on the clerks who refused them help, or who made them wait in line for days, or who wouldn't see them at all after they'd waited for hours. Once Mami punched a social worker who was rude to her.

They treat us like animals," she cried after she'd been restrained. "Don't they care that we're human beings, just like them?"

Her makeup streaked, her hair dishevelled, she left the welfare office with her back slumped and her eyes cast down and furtive. I was sure everyone on the bus knew that we had spent the day in the welfare office and that Mami had just hit a social worker. That night as she told Tata and Don Julio what had happened, Mami made it sound like it was a joke, no big deal. I added my own exaggerated details of how many people had to restrain her, without any mention of how frightened I'd been, and how ashamed I'd felt when she lost control in front of everybody.

Often I would be asked to translate for other women at the welfare office, since Mami told everyone I spoke good English. Their stories were no different from Mami's. They needed just a little help until they could find a job again.

Every once in a while I could tell that the people I translated for were lying.

"What do you think?" they'd ask. "Should I say my husband has disappeared, or that he's a *sinvergüenza* [shameless person] who refuses to help with the kids?"

Women with accents that weren't Puerto Rican claimed they were so that they could reap the benefits of American citizenship. A woman I was translating for once said, "These *gringos* don't know the difference anyway. To them we're all spiks."

I didn't know what to do. To tell the interviewer that I knew the woman was lying seemed worse than translating what the woman said as accurately as I could and letting the interviewer figure it out. But I worried that if people from other countries passed as Puerto Ricans in order to cheat the government, it reflected badly on us.

I never knew if my translations helped, but once an old *jíbara* [rural Puerto Rican] took my hands in hers and kissed them, which made me feel like the best person in the world. [. . .]

While Francisco was still alive, we had moved to Ellery Street. That meant I had to change schools, so Mami walked me to P.S. 33, where I would attend ninth grade. The first week I was there I was given a series of tests that showed that even though I couldn't speak English very well, I read and wrote it at the tenth-grade level. So they put me in 9-3, with the smart kids.

One morning, Mr. Barone, a guidance counsellor, called me to his office. He was short, with a big head and large hazel eyes under shapely eyebrows. His nose was long and round at the tip. He dressed in browns and yellows and often perched his tortoiseshell glasses on his forehead, as if he had another set of eyes up there.

"So," he pushed his glasses up, "what do you want to be when you grow up?"

"I don't know."

He shuffled through some papers. "Let's see here . . . you're fourteen, is that right?"

"Yes, sir."

"And you've never thought about what you want to be?"

When I was very young, I wanted to be a *jíbara*. When I was older, I wanted to be a cartographer, then a topographer. But since we'd come to Brooklyn, I'd not thought about the future much.

"No, sir."

He pulled his glasses down to where they belonged and shuffled through the papers again.

"Do you have any hobbies?" I didn't know what he meant.

"Hobbies, hobbies," he flailed his hands, as if he were juggling, "things you like to do after school."

"Ah, yes." I tried to imagine what I did at home that might qualify as a hobby. "I like to read."

He seemed disappointed. "Yes, we know that about you." He pulled out a paper and stared at it. "One of the tests we gave you was an aptitude test. It tells us what kinds of things you might be good at. The tests show that you would be good at helping people. Do you like to help people?"

I was afraid to contradict the tests. "Yes, sir."

"There's a high school we can send you where you can study biology and chemistry which will prepare you for a career in nursing."

I screwed up my face. He consulted the papers again.

"You would also do well in communications. Teaching maybe."

I remembered Miss Brown standing in front of a classroom full of rowdy teenagers, some of them taller than she was.

"I don't like to teach."

Mr. Barone pushed his glasses up again and leaned over the stack of papers on his desk. "Why don't you think about it and get back to me," he said, closing the folder with my name across the top. He put his hand flat on it, as if squeezing something out. "You're a smart girl, Esmeralda. Let's try to get you into an academic school so that you have a shot at college." [. . .]

A few days later, Mr. Barone called me back to his office.

"Well?" Tiny green flecks burned around the black pupils of his hazel eyes.

The night before, Mami had called us into the living room. On the television "fifty of America's most beautiful girls" paraded in ruffled tulle dresses before a tinsel waterfall.

"Aren't they lovely?" Mami murmured, as the girls, escorted by boys in uniforms, floated by the camera, twirled, and disappeared behind a screen to the strains of a waltz and an announcer's dramatic voice calling their names, ages, and states. Mami sat mesmerized through the whole pageant.

"I'd like to be a model," I said to Mr. Barone.

He stared at me, pulled his glasses down from his forehead, looked at the papers inside the folder with my name on it, and glared. "A model?" His voice was gruff, as if he were more comfortable yelling at people than talking to them.

"I want to be on television."

"Oh, then you want to be an actress," in a tone that said this was only a slight improvement over my first career choice. We stared at one another for a few seconds. He pushed his glasses up to his forehead again and reached for a book on the shelf in back of him. "I only know of one school that trains actresses, but we've never sent them a student from here."

Performing Arts, the write-up said, was an academic, as opposed to a vocational, public school that trained students wishing to pursue a career in theater, music, and dance.

"It says here that you have to audition." He stood up and held the book closer to the faint gray light coming through the narrow window high on his wall. "Have you ever performed in front of an audience?

"I was announcer in my school show in Puerto Rico," I said. "And I recite poetry. There, not here."

He closed the book and held it against his chest. His right index finger thumped a rhythm on his lower lip. "Let me call them and find out exactly what you need to do. Then we can talk some more."

I left his office strangely happy, confident that something good had just happened, not knowing exactly what.

"I'm not afraid ... I'm not afraid ... I'm not afraid." Every day I walked home from school repeating those words. The broad streets and sidewalks that had impressed me so on the first day we had arrived had become as familiar as the dirt road from Macún to the highway. Only my curiosity about the people who lived behind these walls ended where the façades of the buildings opened into dark hallways or locked doors. Nothing good, I imagined, could be happening inside if so many locks had to be breached to go in or step out.

It was on these tense walks home from school that I decided I had to get out of Brooklyn. Mami had chosen this as our home, and just like every other time we'd moved, I'd had to go along with her because I was a child who had no choice. But I wasn't willing to go along with her on this one.

"How can people live like this?" I shrieked once, desperate to run across a field, to feel grass under my feet instead of pavement.

"Like what?" Mami asked, looking around our apartment, the kitchen and living room crisscrossed with sagging lines of drying diapers and bedclothes.

"Everyone on top of each other. No room to do anything. No air."

"Do you want to go back to Macún, to live like savages, with no electricity, no toilets . . ."

"At least you could step outside every day without somebody trying to kill you."

"Ay, Negi, stop exaggerating!"

"I hate my life!" I yelled.

"Then do something about it," she yelled back.

Until Mr. Barone showed me the listing for Performing Arts High School, I hadn't known what to do.

"The auditions are in less than a month. You have to learn a monologue, which you will perform in front of a panel. If you do well, and your grades here are good, you might get into the school."

Mr. Barone took charge of preparing me for my audition to Performing Arts. He selected a speech from *The Silver Cord*, a play by Sidney Howard, first performed in 1926, but whose action took place in a New York drawing room circa 1905.

"Mr. Gatti, the English teacher," he said, "will coach you. . . . And Mrs. Johnson will talk to you about what to wear and things like that."

I was to play Christina, a young married woman confronting her mother-in-law. I learned the monologue phonetically from Mr. Gatti. It opened with "You belong to a type that's very common in this country, Mrs. Phelps—a type of self-centered, self-pitying, son-devouring tigress; with unmentionable proclivities suppressed on the side."

"We don't have time to study the meaning of every word," Mr. Gatti said. "Just make sure you pronounce every word correctly."

Mrs. Johnson, who taught Home Economics, called me to her office.

"Is that how you enter a room?" she asked the minute I came in. "Try again, only this time, don't barge in. Step in slowly, head up, back straight, a nice smile on your face. That's it." I took a deep breath and waited. "Now sit. No, not like that. Don't just plop down. Float down to the chair with your knees together." She demonstrated, and I copied her. "That's better. What do you do with your hands? No, don't hold your chin like that; it's not ladylike. Put your hands on your lap, and leave them there. Don't use them so much when you talk."

I sat stiff as a cutout while Mrs. Johnson and Mr. Barone asked me questions they thought the panel at Performing Arts would ask.

"Where are you from?"

"Puerto Rico."

"No," Mrs. Johnson said, "Porto Rico. Keep your r's soft. Try again."

"Do you have any hobbies?" Mr. Barone asked. Now I knew what to answer.

"I enjoy dancing and the movies."

"Why do you want to come to this school?"

Mrs. Johnson and Mr. Barone had worked on my answer if this question should come up.

"I would like to study at Performing Arts because of its academic program and so that I may be trained as an actress."

"Very good, very good!" Mr. Barone rubbed his hands together, twinkled his eyes at Mrs. Johnson. "I think we have a shot at this."

"Remember," Mrs. Johnson said, "when you shop for your audition dress, look for something very simple in dark colors."

Mami bought me a red plaid wool jumper with a crisp white shirt, my first pair of stockings, and penny loafers. The night before, she rolled up my hair in pink curlers that cut into my scalp and made it hard to sleep. For the occasion, I was allowed to wear eye makeup and a little lipstick.

"You look so grown up!" Mami said, her voice sad but happy, as I twirled in front of her and Tata.

"*Toda una señorita,*" Tata said, her eyes misty.

We set out for the audition on an overcast January morning heavy with the threat of snow.

"Why couldn't you choose a school close to home?" Mami grumbled as we got on the train to Manhattan. I worried that even if I were accepted, she wouldn't let me go because it was so far from home, one hour each way by subway. But in spite of her complaints, she was proud that I was good enough to be considered for such a famous school. And she actually seemed excited that I would be leaving the neighborhood.

"You'll be exposed to a different class of people," she assured me, and I felt the force of her ambition without knowing exactly what she meant.

Three women sat behind a long table in a classroom where the desks and chairs had been pushed against a wall. As I entered l held my head up and smiled, and then I floated down to the chair in front of them, clasped my hands on my lap, and smiled some more.

"Good morning," said the tall one with hair the color of sand. She was big boned and solid, with intense blue eyes, a generous mouth, and soothing hands with short fingernails. She was dressed in shades of beige from head to toe and wore no makeup and no jewelry except for the gold chain that held her glasses just above her full bosom. Her voice was rich, modulated, each word pronounced as if she were inventing it.

Next to her sat a very small woman with very high heels. Her cropped hair was pouffed around her face, with bangs brushing the tips of her long false lashes, her huge dark brown eyes were thickly lined in black all around, and her small mouth was carefully drawn in and painted cerise. Her suntanned face turned toward me with the innocent curiosity of a lively baby. She was dressed in black, with many gold chains around her neck, big earrings, several bracelets, and large stone rings on the fingers of both hands.

The third woman was tall, small boned, thin, but shapely. Her dark hair was pulled flat against her skull into a knot in back of her head. Her face was all angles and light, with fawnlike dark brown eyes, a straight nose, full lips painted just a shade pinker than their natural color. Silky forest green cuffs peeked out from the sleeves of her burgundy suit. Diamond studs winked from perfect earlobes.

I had dreamed of this moment for several weeks. More than anything, I wanted to impress the panel with my talent, so that I would be accepted into Performing Arts and leave Brooklyn every day. And, I hoped, one day I would never go back.

But the moment I faced these three impeccably groomed women,

I forgot my English and Mrs. Johnson's lessons on how to behave like a lady. In the agony of trying to answer their barely comprehensible questions, I jabbed my hands here and there, forming words with my fingers because the words refused to leave my mouth.

"Why don't you let us hear your monologue now?" the woman with the dangling glasses asked softly.

I stood up abruptly, and my chair clattered onto its side two feet from where I stood. I picked it up, wishing with all my strength that a thunderbolt would strike me dead to ashes on the spot.

"It's all right," she said. "Take a breath. We know you're nervous."

I closed my eyes and breathed deeply, walked to the middle of the room, and began my monologue.

"Ju bee lonh 2 a type dats berry cómo in dis kuntree, Meessees Felps. A type off selfcent red self pee tee in sun de boring tie gress wid on men shon ah ball pro klee bee tees on de side."

In spite of Mr. Gatti's reminders that I should speak slowly and enunciate every word, even if I didn't understand it, I recited my three-minute monologue in one minute flat.

The small woman's long lashes seemed to have grown with amazement. The elegant woman's serene face twitched with controlled laughter. The tall one dressed in beige smiled sweetly.

"Thank you, dear," she said. "Could you wait outside for a few moments?"

I resisted the urge to curtsy. The long hallway had narrow wainscotting halfway up to the high ceiling. Single bulb lamps hung from long cords, creating yellow puddles of light on the polished brown linoleum tile. A couple of girls my age sat on straight chairs next to their mothers, waiting their turn. They looked up as I came out and the door shut behind me. Mami stood up from her chair at the end of the hall. She looked as scared as I felt.

"What happened?"

"Nothing," I mumbled, afraid that if I began telling her about it, I would break into tears in front of the other people, whose eyes followed me and Mami as we walked to the EXIT sign. "I have to wait here a minute."

"Did they say anything?"

"No. I'm just supposed to wait."

We leaned against the wall. Across from us there was a bulletin board with newspaper clippings about former students. On the rag-ged edge, a neat person had printed in blue ink, "P.A." and the year the actor, dancer, or musician had graduated. I closed my eyes and tried to picture myself on that bulletin board, with "P.A. '66" across the top.

The door at the end of the hall opened, and the woman in beige poked her head out.

"Esmeralda?"

"*Sí*, I mean, here." I raised my hand.

She led me into the room. There was another girl in there, whom she introduced as Bonnie, a junior at the school.

"Do you know what a pantomime is?" the woman asked. I nodded. "You and Bonnie are sisters decorating a Christmas tree."

Bonnie looked a lot like Juanita Marín, whom I had last seen in Macún four years earlier. We decided where the invisible Christmas tree would be, and we sat on the floor and pretended we were taking decorations out of boxes and hanging them on the branches.

My family had never had a Christmas tree, but I remembered how once I had helped Papi wind colored lights around the eggplant bush that divided our land from Doña Ana's. We started at the bottom and wound the wire with tiny red bulbs around and around until we ran out; then Papi plugged another cord to it and we kept going until the branches hung heavy with light and the bush looked like it was on fire.

Before long I had forgotten where I was, and that the tree didn't exist and Bonnie was not my sister. She pretended to hand me a very delicate ball, and just before I took it, she made like it fell to the ground and shattered. I was petrified that Mami would come in and yell at us for breaking her favorite decoration. Just as I began to pick up the tiny fragments of nonexistent crystal, a voice broke in. "Thank you."

Bonnie got up, smiled, and went out.

The elegant woman stretched her hand out for me to shake. "We will notify your school in a few weeks. It was very nice to meet you."

I shook hands all around then backed out of the room in a fog, silent, as if the pantomime had taken my voice and the urge to speak.

On the way home Mami kept asking what had happened, and I kept mumbling, "Nothing. Nothing happened," ashamed that, after all the hours of practice with Mrs. Johnson, Mr. Barone, and Mr. Gatti, after the expense of new clothes and shoes, after Mami had to take a day off from work to take me into Manhattan, after all that, I had failed the audition and would never, ever, get out of Brooklyn. [...]

A decade after my graduation from Performing Arts, I visited the school. I was by then living in Boston, a scholarship student at Harvard University. The tall, elegant woman of my audition had become my mentor through my three years there. Since my graduation, she had married the school principal.

"I remember your audition," she said, her chiseled face dreamy, her lips toying with a smile that she seemed, still, to have to control.

I had forgotten the skinny brown girl with the curled hair, wool jumper, and lively hands. But she hadn't. She told me that the panel had had to ask me to leave so that they could laugh, because it was so funny to see a fourteen-year-old Puerto Rican girl jabbering out a monologue about a possessive mother-inlaw at the turn of the century, the words incomprehensible because they went by so fast.

"We admired," she said, "the courage it took to stand in front of us and do what you did."

"So you mean I didn't get into the school because of my talent, but because I had chutzpah?" We both laughed.

Vivian Gornick
b. 1935

From *Fierce Attachments: A Memoir*
(1987)

Vivian Gornick's mother was ten when she emigrated from Ukraine to the Bronx with her Yiddish-speaking parents. Gornick's father worked in New York's garment district; her mother worked briefly but quit because of objections from her husband. When he died at age fifty-one, the father left behind thirteen-year-old Vivian and her older brother. The mother took a dreary clerical job and never fully recovered from grief over the death of her husband, saying that "love was the most important thing in a woman's life." For seventeen-year-old Vivian, the most important thing in life was education.

As thousands before me have said, "For us it was City College or nothing." I enjoyed the solidarity those words invoked but rejected the implied deprivation. At City College I sat talking in a basement cafeteria until ten or eleven at night with a half dozen others who also never wanted to go home to Brooklyn or the Bronx, and here in the cafeteria my education took root. Here I learned that Faulkner was America, Dickens was politics, Marx was sex, Jane Austen the idea of culture, that I came from a ghetto and D. H. Lawrence was a visionary. Here my love of literature named itself, and amazement over the life of the mind blossomed. I discovered that people were transformed by ideas, and that intellectual conversation was immensely erotic.

We never stopped talking. Perhaps because we did very little else (restricted by sexual fear and working-class economics, we didn't go to the theater and we didn't make love), but certainly we talked so much because most of us had been reading in bottled-up silence from the age of six on and City College was our great release. It was not from the faculty that City drew its reputation for intellectual goodness, it was from its students, it was from us. Not that we were intellectually distinguished, we weren't; but our hungry energy vitalized the place. The idea of intellectual life burned in us. While we pursued ideas we felt known, to ourselves and to one another. The world made sense, there was ground beneath our feet, a place in the universe to stand. City College made conscious in me inner cohesion as a first value.

I think my mother was very quickly of two minds about me and City, although she had wanted me to go to school, no question about that, had been energized by the determination that I do so (instructed me in the middle of her first year of widowhood to enter the academic not the commercial course of high-school study), and was even embattled when it became something of an issue in the family.

"Where is it written that a working-class widow's daughter should to go college?" one of my uncles said to her, drinking coffee at our kitchen table on a Saturday morning in my senior year in high school.

"Here it is written," she had replied, tapping the table hard with her middle finger. "Right here it is written. The girl goes to college."

"Why?" he had pursued.

"Because I say so."

"But why? What do you think will come of it?"

"I don't know. I only know she's clever, she deserves an education, and she's going to get one. This is America. The girls are not cows in the field only waiting for a bull to mate with." I stared at her. Where had *that* come from? My father had been dead only five years, she was in full widowhood swing.

The moment was filled with conflict and bravado. She felt the words she spoke but she did not mean them. She didn't even know what she meant by an education. When she discovered at my graduation that I wasn't a teacher she acted as though she'd been swindled. In her mind a girl child went in one door marked college and came out another marked teacher.

"You mean you're not a teacher?" she said to me, eyes widening as her two strong hands held my diploma down on the kitchen table.

"No," I said.

"What have you been doing there all these years?" she asked quietly.

"Reading novels," I replied.

She marveled silently at my chutzpah.

But it wasn't really a matter of what I could or could not do with the degree. We were people who knew how to stay alive, she never doubted I would find a way. No, what drove her, and divided us, was me thinking. She hadn't understood that going to school meant I would start thinking: coherently and out loud. She was by taken by violent surprise. My sentences got longer within a month of those first classes. Longer, more complicated, formed by words whose meaning she did not always know. I had never before spoken a word she didn't know. Or made a sentence whose logic she couldn't follow. Or attempted an opinion that grew out of an abstraction. It made her crazy. Her face began to take on a look of animal cunning when I started a sentence that could not possibly be concluded before three clauses had hit the air. Cunning sparked anger, anger flamed into rage. "What are you talking about?" she would shout at me. "What *are* you talking about? Speak English, please! We all understand English in this house. Speak it!"

Her response stunned me. I didn't get it. Wasn't she pleased that I could say something she didn't understand? Wasn't that what it was all about? I was the advance guard. I was going to take her into the new world. All she had to do was adore what I was becoming, and here she was refusing. I'd speak my new sentences, and she would turn on me as though I'd performed a vile act right there at the kitchen table.

She, of course, was as confused as I. She didn't know why she was angry, and if she'd been told she was angry she would have denied it, would have found a way to persuade both herself and any interested listener that she was proud I was in school, only why did I have to be such a showoff? Was that what going to college was all about? Now, take Mr. Lewis, the insurance agent, an educated man if ever there was one, got a degree from City College in 1929, 1929 mind you, and never made you feel stupid, always spoke in simple sentences, but later you thought about what he had said. That's the way an educated person should talk. Here's this snotnose kid coming into the kitchen with all these big words, sentences you can't make head or tail of . . .

I was seventeen, she was fifty. I had not yet come into my own as a qualifying belligerent but I was a respectable contender and she, naturally, was at the top of her game. The lines were drawn, and we did not fail one another. Each of us rose repeatedly to the bait the other one tossed out. Our storms shook the apartment: paint blistered on the wall, linoleum cracked on the floor, glass shivered in the window frame. We barely kept our hands off one another, and more than once we approached disaster.

One Saturday afternoon she was lying on the couch. I was reading in a nearby chair. Idly she asked, "What are you reading?" Idly I replied, "A comparative history of the idea of love over the last three hundred years." She looked at me for a moment. "That's ridiculous," she said slowly. "Love is love. It's the same everywhere, all the time. What's to compare?" "That's absolutely not true," I shot back. "You don't know what you're talking about. It's only an idea, Ma. That's all love is. Just an idea. You think it's a function of the mysterious immutable being, but it's not! There is, in fact, no such thing as the mysterious immutable being . . ." Her legs were off the couch so fast I didn't see them go down. She made fists of her hands, closed her eyes tight, and howled, "I'll kill you-u-u! Snake in my bosom, I'll kill you. How dare you talk to me that way?" And then she was coming at me. She was small and chunky. So was I. But I had thirty years on her. I was out of the chair faster than her arm could make contact, and running, running through the apartment, racing for the bathroom, the only room with a lock on it. The top half of the bathroom door was a panel of frosted glass. She arrived just as I turned the lock, and couldn't put the brakes on. She drove her fist through the glass, reaching for me. Blood, screams, shattered glass on both sides of the door. I thought that afternoon, One of us is going to die of this attachment. [. . .]

My mother and I are walking past the Plaza Hotel [in Manhattan] at noon, on our way to eat lunch in the park. Gathered around

the fountain in front of the hotel a swarm of people: sitting, standing, strolling out to the sidewalk to buy shish kebab, soda, pretzels,
falafel, egg roll, and hot dogs. They are eating out of tinfoil, drinking out of plastic, being entertained by street performers who pass
the hat: break dancers, mimes, string quartets. One of the street
performers not passing the hat is a fundamentalist preacher pacing back and forth in front of the fountain, thundering at individual
people: "You are going straight to hell! Not tomorrow, not tonight,
right now!" He makes the mistake of stopping my mother. She dis-
misses him with a brusque "What's *your* problem?" (she can't spare
the time for this one), and keeps walking.

I laugh. I'm exhilarated today. Today *I'm* a street performer. I've
always admired the guts, the skill, the command of the one who
plays successfully to the passing New York crowd. Last night I spoke
at a large public meeting in the city: on the barricades for radical
feminism, also not passing the hat. I spoke easily and well, and I
had the crowd in my hand. Sometimes I don't, but last night I did.
Last night all the skill I've acquired at this sort of thing was there at
my command, and I knew it. It was the knowing it that made me
clear-headed, lucid, expansive and expressive. The crowd was being
stirred. I felt it, and then I had confirmed what I felt.

My mother was in the audience. I didn't see her afterward, because I was surrounded and carried off. Today, right now, is our first
meeting since I walked onstage last night. She is smiling at me now,
laughing with me at the pleasure of the day, the crowd, New York
acting out all over the place. I am properly expectant. She is about
to tell me how wonderful I was last night. She opens her mouth to
speak.

"Guess who I dreamed about last night," she says to me. "Sophie
Schwartzman!"

I am startled, taken off balance. This I had not expected. "Sophie
Schwartzman?" I say. But beneath my surprise a kernel of dread begins growing in the bright bright day.

Sophie Schwartzman had lived in our building for some years,
and she and Mama had been friends. After the Schwartzmans moved
to another neighborhood in the Bronx our two families had continued to meet because the women liked each other. The Schwartzmans had three children: Seymour, Miriam, and Frances. Seymour
became a famous composer who changed his name to Malcolm

Wood. Miriam grew up to become her mother. Frances, a pretty girl with "ambitions," married a rich man. Sophie has been dead a good ten years now. I haven't seen any of her children in more than twenty years.

"I dreamed I was in Sophie's house," my mother says, crossing Fifty-ninth Street. "Frances came in. She had written a book. She asked me to read it. I did, and I wasn't so enthusiastic. She became very angry. She screamed at her mother, 'Never let her come here again.' I felt so bad! I was sick at heart. I said, 'Sophie. What is this? You mean after all these years I can't come here anymore?'" My mother turns to me as we reach the sidewalk and, with a huge smile on her face, says, "But then it was so wonderful! I woke up, and it was only a dream."

My feet seem to have lead weights in them. I struggle to put one in front of the other. My mother doesn't notice that I have slowed up. She is absorbed by her own amazing narrative.

"You dreamed this last night, Ma?"

"Yes."

"After I spoke?"

"Well, yes, of course. Not *right* after. When I got home and went to sleep."

We enter the park, find a bench, sit down, take out our sandwiches. We do not speak. We have each fallen into reverie. After a while my mother says, "Imagine dreaming about Sophie Schwartzman after all these years."

commentary for chapter five: SCHOOL AND COLLEGE

Memoirists in this section depict a wide range of experiences related to education. They range from raw ethnic tension at Esmeralda Santiago's high school, a restrained atmosphere in Russell Baker's English class for fast learners, and the vibrant exchange of intellectual ideas at Vivian Gornick's college. Their educational settings might have differed but these exceptionally smart students all had a lesson to learn. Baker and Santiago had to learn to trust their intuition about how to put their brains to work, and Gornick had to learn psychological sensitivity. All three accounts point to the vital importance of public education and dedicated teachers in enabling youths from working-class families to succeed.

With great verbal aptitudes, these three laid the groundwork in school for later careers as professional writers. Yet these readings emphasize not how they found their talent but rather how they started to gain the psychological maturity and self-confidence needed to apply their talents and make their way in the world. Baker needed to outgrow his misperceptions of what teachers wanted in compositions and instead trust his own inclinations about how to write a good essay. He decided to follow his instincts and write about happy evenings in his extended family, producing a narrative that delighted his fellow students and his teacher. Santiago also learned to appreciate authenticity. She had tried to impress teachers at an audition to enroll at a performing-arts school by speaking aristocratic English, but failed miserably. She succeeded instead when she drew upon personal experience to mime the decorating of a bush with Christmas ornaments in her native Puerto Rico.

The passages by Santiago and Gornick explore the fraught relationship between bright, studious children and often uncomprehending mothers in poor, urban households. Their mothers are ambitious for their daughters, but it is a qualified ambition. When Santiago prepares for her audition, her mother seems proud that her daughter might attend an elite school but worries that it is far from home and adds, perhaps as a note of caution, "You'll be exposed to a different class of people." Gornick's memoir about the fraught relationship with her mother is called *Fierce Attachments*, suggesting intense ambivalence. Her widowed mother advocated for young Vivian to enter an academic track at high school, where students are prepared for college, although it was rare for female children of working-class immigrants to go to college then. Yet when Gornick started expressing abstract thoughts and talking with polysyllabic words, her mother changed from supportive to critical. Gornick wanted to reveal a new world to her mother with the knowledge she gained at City College. Instead, her mother berated the daughter for being a know-it-all who aspired to a station superior to the mother's own, culminating in a bloody standoff. The account shows how tensions can arise at home not just when children fail but when they succeed, and how those among the first in their family to attend college can stir intense resentment.

The episode at the end of the Gornick reading, which occurred decades later, reveals the ongoing tension between an achieving daughter and an aging mother bereft of husband and career. The mother told her daughter about a dream she had had in which she had offended a friend by criticizing a book that her friend's daughter had written (Gornick had by then written several books). It was a seemingly innocuous story, except that it occurred the day after Gornick had given a successful lecture in front of a large New York crowd. Her mother was present at the speech. Gornick hoped her mother might share her impressions of it, but instead the mother recounted the dream that she had that night. Gornick knows enough about Freudian analysis to understand the dream and its implications. While nobody is so old that they would not appreciate praise from a parent, Gornick sees that her intelligent mother's lack of a career keeps her from appreciating her daughter's intellectual achievements and that she even resents them. Such are the Oedipal strains between generations.

QUESTIONS FOR DISCUSSION

1. Russell Baker and Esmeralda Santiago describe in detail the appearance, demeanor, and verbal quirks of their teachers. These details help bring the student's experience to life, but do you think the details also serve a thematic purpose and give the episodes meaning? If so, how?

2. Both Baker and Santiago prepared presentations: he an essay and she a monologue. How audiences received those presentations had a big impact on their lives. From those experiences, what message might young Russell have learned about writing, and what might Esmeralda have learned about performing? Are the lessons similar and are they useful for how to develop one's talent?

3. What inferences can you draw from Santiago's visit to the welfare office about poverty and how it is handled by government agencies?

4. Vivian Gornick's mother criticized her daughter for using abstractions and polysyllabic vocabulary, but praised their insurance agent, a college graduate, for speaking in simple, intelligible sentences. What do these characterizations of speech—complex versus simple—imply about the purposes and focus of higher education?

chapter six

JOBS

Luis J. Rodriguez
b. 1954

From *Always Running: La Vida Loca: Gang Days in L.A.*
(1993)

At age two Luis Rodriguez moved from Mexico to Los Angeles with his parents and three half-siblings. His father was well educated in Mexico but spoke poor English and for many years found only manual labor. His mother, who had an Indian father and "native features," got work cleaning factories. Later, Luis's father was hired as a laboratory custodian and his mother became a seamstress.

"You have to work, to help us out here," Mama said. "You're a big man now. There's got to be something you can do."

We had just moved to South San Gabriel. I was nine years old—a good working age, as far as my mother was concerned; she had picked cotton at the age of nine in South Texas. But looking for work at nine is not easy in a city. We weren't fruit pickers, which were often children as young as three. In a city, a child had to find people to work for—cleaning up for them, doing deliveries or tending lawns. I did a little bit of everything. Mowing lawns with [my brother] Rano, picking up boxes and cleaning out people's garages. I even did housework like my mother had done when we were younger. I vacuumed, wiped windows, scrubbed floors on my knees and used tooth brushes to clean the edges. The homes I went to were in Alhambra, a mostly white area then with some homes sporting swimming pools. I learned how to vacuum the bottom of the pools, and how to use the pumps and the chemicals to keep them clean.

My brother also worked, finally landing a job as a newspaper boy. In those days, it meant delivering papers door-to-door on bikes. At the age of 12, I started working a paper route too. I found an old beat-up ten-speed and delivered around our neighborhood, tossing a local daily called The Post-Advocate. Every day after school, our crew manager dropped off bundles of unfolded newspapers and bags of rubber-bands. On rainy days we used plastic covers.

We had to fold all the papers, place the rubber bands or plastic over them and then stuff them into double cloth bags we draped over the handle bars. Our hands and faces got blackened with newsprint. We had a list of subscribers and we had to make sure they received their newspapers in or around their porches. This was the trick of the trade.

Fíjese [check this out]: I got good at it. It was the first important accomplishment I remember as a child. I couldn't exactly talk with any coherency, or do sports, or show any talent for anything. But, man, I could deliver newspapers! I got so good, I built up a route system which at its peak included four different routes. I received awards. I won recognition in the Copley Newspaper magazine (Copley owned the Post-Advocate then). The routes wound around city blocks for several miles and often took until after midnight to complete. On that old ten-speed, I pedaled through street, alley, boulevard and back road, past vicious dogs and hobo nests, past the *vatos* [guys] who chased me for my bike or change. But I made my deliveries, always on time. On the mark.

Selling the newspaper was the other trick. On weekends, the crew manager would take his den of newspaper boys and drop us off in various neighborhoods to sell subscriptions, what we called "starts." Mainly he had us cover the well-groomed suburban streets because he figured they were more likely to buy subscriptions. Man, I was lousy at it. Door after door slammed in my face. We had free gifts—pot holders, TV trays, things to hang on the wall. But where people had money, this had little effect. They usually received the bigger papers like the Los Angeles Times or the Herald-Examiner. The Herald-Examiner deliverers, in fact, often sneered at us because they took in more pay and the better clientele.

One day the crew manager, at a point of desperation, dropped me off in the Hills.

"Go up this road," he said, sounding unhopeful of my prospects. "I'll meet you down below in about an hour."

I climbed up a sidewalkless street and entered the foliage which shielded the shacks and houses on stilts and cars being worked on. I walked up a cluttered dirt driveway. Children played in and around a mud puddle without shoes. Mexican music burst out of a kitchen window. The porches were old, unpainted, sunken wood planks. I knocked on a torn-screen door nearly off its hinges. A round woman peered from inside. Instead of sofas or end tables, crates furnished her bare living room. There were palm-leaf crosses tacked on cracked sheet rock.

"*¿Qué traes tú?*" she inquired. [What's up with you?]

I didn't believe I'd sell any subscriptions—most of these people didn't even know English. But as soon as I talked about the free gifts, they signed up. So simple. Shack to shack. Off-hinged door after off-hinged door. I tried to explain they were required to pay a monthly fee. But here they were, watching *telenovelas* on beat-up TV sets, those who had them, their children running around in rags and bare feet, and still they ordered the Post-Advocate for the free gifts. In time they'd never pay. They'd never be part of anyone's route. But I got the starts. I became the hero for the day. The crew manager patted my back and announced to everyone the record number of subscriptions I obtained.

The people of the Hills vindicated me.

Work took other turns. At age thirteen, I was hired at a car wash with my brother. We were the cleanup crew. We came to work in the evening after the undocumented guys finished washing cars and had gone home. Rano and I swept, mopped, and picked up around the small office, waiting area and parking lot. We picked up all the dirty rags and threw them into massive washing machines. Then near the end of the evening, we hooked up a monstrous hose and watered down the place. Rano, who was 16, actually washed cars during the day and learned to drive almost every make and model.

"You should have seen the Mustang I pulled out today," he said, excited.

"Oh, listen," he'd tap my arm. "Then there was this Firebird!"

I came along to help him in the evening to make more money

for the family. Everything we made went to Mama—and we always needed more.

But soon after I started working there, I picked up a foot fungus. I often worked in sneakers and I couldn't help but get them soaked every night in the soap and water we used to hose down everything. Terrible flowery lesions sprang up on the soles of my feet and through my toes. I also had an ingrown toenail that produced a painful redness on my left toe, forcing me to place steaming hot towels on it every night to lower the swelling.

A foot doctor prescribed medication, but nothing lessened the sores. And surgery on my toe was out of the question. I couldn't even go to gym classes, which I missed for the rest of junior high.

One day, the sores worsened and I refused to get out of bed. My mother dabbed ointments on them but they were of no use. Then Tío Kiko came over. He examined the sores, staring intently at the petals that seemed to be growing from my feet. Tío Kiko knew a little of the Mexican healing arts, the use of herbs and incantations from old Indian traditions used to treat most ailments. In desperation, Mama asked her brother for help.

"This will hurt you," Tío Kiko told me in Spanish. "But be brave. It will be over soon."

He pulled up a chair and directed my mother's hand.

They sliced each of the milky sores. Blood and pus streamed out. I screamed. I didn't believe in witchcraft or chants or herbs. I felt I would die. Tío Kiko had boiled water and put together some herbs he had brought from a *botánica* [herbal medicine shop]. Mama covered each open wound with leaves and concoctions as Tío Kiko prayed over my feet.

Was there a God for feet? Would the proper words be strung together to wake it from its sleep? Would the magic of the herbs, the spirit evoked, seep into the sores and bring the feet back to me? These were the questions.

Days passed. I lay in bed as the daily rituals worked their wonder. The sores started to disappear. Soon I hobbled around in slippers. Even the ingrown toenail slid back into a somewhat normal shape. Tío Kiko, this border priest, this master of snake and siren, did what the Anglo doctors could not. Who knows if it's real magic? There was another kind of magic which made me feel special, to look at my Indian-descended mother and uncle and believe in the power of civilizations long since written off, long since demeaned and trampled. Jesus Christ was a brown man. A Mexican Indian. A *curandero* [folk healer]. Not a stringy blond-haired, blue-eyed icon. He was like me, like my Tío Kiko. He lived in the earth, got drunk, inhabited the leaves and herbs, not a sanitized doctor's office—or a church of spires and colored glass and elaborate carvings. He lived in my feet, and with the proper calls and enticements, made them whole again. This is the Christ I wanted to believe in.

Maya Angelou

1928–2014

From *I Know Why the Caged Bird Sings*
(1969)

Born as Marguerite Johnson, Maya Angelou was raised
mainly in rural Arkansas in the 1930s by her grandmother. In adolescence Angelou lived in San Francisco
with her mother and her mother's successive male partners and, later, in Los Angeles with her father and his
girlfriend. When she was fifteen, her father took her
to Mexico for what she believed would be a vacation.
When he got drunk and passed out, she took his car
and drove, with no previous lessons, across the Mexican countryside with her father asleep in the backseat.
They made their way back to Los Angeles, where, after a
bloody confrontation with her father's girlfriend, Angelou left for good. She wandered the streets until she
found a junkyard and settled inside an empty car for
several days, having been befriended by homeless young
people. After a few weeks, she returned to San Francisco to live with her mother, who assumed young Maya
would attend high school, but she had another idea.

In the offices of the Market Street Railway Company, the receptionist seemed as surprised to see me there as I was surprised to find the
interior dingy and the décor drab. Somehow I had expected waxed
surfaces and carpeted floors. If I had met no resistance, I might
have decided against working for such a poor-mouth-looking concern. As it was, I explained that I had come to see about a job. She

asked, was I sent by an agency, and when I replied that I was not, she told me they were only accepting applicants from agencies.

The classified pages of the morning papers had listed advertisements for motorettes and conductorettes and I reminded her of that. She gave me a face full of astonishment that my suspicious nature would not accept.

"I am applying for the job listed in this morning's *Chronicle* and I'd like to be presented to your personnel manager." While I spoke in supercilious accents, and looked at the room as if I had an oil well in my own backyard, my armpits were being pricked by millions of hot pointed needles. She saw her escape and dived into it.

"He's out. He's out for the day. You might call tomorrow and if he's in, I'm sure you can see him." Then she swiveled her chair around on its rusty screws and with that I was supposed to be dismissed.

"May I ask his name?"

She half turned, acting surprised to find me still there. "His name? Whose name?"

"Your personnel manager."

We were firmly joined in the hypocrisy to play out the scene.

"The personnel manager? Oh, he's Mr. Cooper, but I'm not sure you'll find him here tomorrow. He's . . . Oh, but you can try."

"Thank you."

"You're welcome."

And I was out of the musty room and into the even mustier lobby. In the street I saw the receptionist and myself going faithfully through paces that were stale with familiarity, although I had never encountered that kind of situation before and, probably, neither had she. We were like actors who, knowing the play by heart, were still able to cry afresh over the old tragedies and laugh spontaneously at the comic situations.

The miserable little encounter had nothing to do with me, the me of me, any more than it had to do with that silly clerk. The incident was a recurring dream, concocted years before by stupid whites and it eternally came back to haunt us all. The secretary and I were like Hamlet and Laertes in the final scene, where, because of harm done by one ancestor to another, we were bound to duel to the death. Also because the play must end somewhere.

I went further than forgiving the clerk, I accepted her as a fellow victim of the same puppeteer.

On the streetcar, I put my fare into the box and the conductorette looked at me with the usual hard eyes of white contempt. "Move into the car, please move on in the car." She patted her money changer.

Her Southern nasal accent sliced my meditation and I looked deep into my thoughts. All lies, all comfortable lies. The receptionist was not innocent and neither was I. The whole charade we had played out in that crummy waiting room had directly to do with me, Black, and her, white.

I wouldn't move into the streetcar but stood on the ledge over the conductor, glaring. My mind shouted so energetically that the announcement made my veins stand out, and my mouth tighten into a prune.

I WOULD HAVE THE JOB. I WOULD BE A CONDUCTORETTE AND SLING A FULL MONEY CHANGER FROM MY BELT. I WOULD.

The next three weeks were a honeycomb of determination with apertures for the days to go in and out. The Negro organizations to whom I appealed for support bounced me back and forth like a shuttlecock on a badminton court. Why did I insist on that particular job? Openings were going begging that paid nearly twice the money. The minor officials with whom I was able to win an audience thought me mad. Possibly I was.

Downtown San Francisco became alien and cold, and the streets I had loved in a personal familiarity were unknown lanes that twisted with malicious intent. Old buildings, whose gray rococo façades housed my memories of the Forty-Niners, and Diamond Lil, Robert Service, Sutter and Jack London, were then imposing structures viciously joined to keep me out. My trips to the streetcar office were of the frequency of a person on salary. The struggle expanded. I was no longer in conflict only with the Market Street Railway but with the marble lobby of the building which housed its offices, and elevators and their operators.

During this period of strain Mother and I began our first steps on the long path toward mutual adult admiration. She never asked for reports and I didn't offer any details. But every morning she made breakfast, gave me carfare and lunch money, as if I were going to work. She comprehended the perversity of life, that in the struggle lies the joy. That I was no glory seeker was obvious to her, and that I had to exhaust every possibility before giving in was also clear.

On my way out of the house one morning she said, "Life is going to give you just what you put in it. Put your whole heart in everything you do, and pray, then you can wait." Another time she reminded me that "God helps those who help themselves." She had a store of aphorisms which she dished out as the occasion demanded. Strangely, as bored as I was with her clichés, her inflection gave them something new, and set me thinking for a little while at least.

Later when asked how I got my job, I was never able to say exactly. I only knew that one day, which was tiresomely like all the others before it, I sat in the Railway office, ostensibly waiting to be interviewed. The receptionist called me to her desk and shuffled a bundle of papers to me. They were job application forms. She said they had to be filled in triplicate. I had little time to wonder if I had won or not, for the standard questions reminded me of the necessity for dexterous lying. How old was I? List my previous jobs, starting from the last held and go backward to the first. How much money did I earn, and why did I leave the position? Give two references (not relatives).

Sitting at a side table my mind and I wove a cat's ladder of near truths and total lies. I kept my face blank (an old art) and wrote quickly the fable of Marguerite Johnson, aged nineteen, former companion and driver for Mrs. Annie Henderson (a White Lady) in Stamps, Arkansas.

I was given blood tests, aptitude tests, physical coordination tests, and Rorschachs, then on a blissful day I was hired as the first Negro on the San Francisco streetcars.

Mother gave the money to have my blue serge suit tailored, and I learned to fill out work cards, operate the money changer and punch transfers. The time crowded together and at an End of Days I was swinging on the back of the rackety trolley, smiling sweetly and persuading my charges to "step forward in the car, please."

For one whole semester the streetcars and I shimmied up and scooted down the sheer hills of San Francisco. I lost some of my need for the Black ghetto's shielding-sponge quality, as I clanged and cleared my way down Market Street, with its honky-tonk homes for homeless sailors, past the quiet retreat of Golden Gate Park and along closed undwelled-in-looking dwellings of the Sunset District.

My work shifts were split so haphazardly that it was easy to believe that my superiors had chosen them maliciously. Upon mentioning my suspicions to Mother, she said, "Don't worry about it:

You ask for what you want and you pay for what you get. And I'm going to show you that it ain't no trouble when you pack double."

She stayed awake to drive me out to the car barn at four-thirty in the mornings, or to pick me up when I was relieved just before dawn. Her awareness of life's perils convinced her that while I would be safe on the public conveyances, she "wasn't about to trust a taxi driver with her baby."

When the spring classes began, I resumed my commitment with formal education. I was so much wiser and older, so much more independent, with a bank account and clothes that I had bought for myself, that I was sure that I had learned and earned the magic formula which would make me a part of the gay life my contemporaries led.

Not a bit of it. Within weeks, I realized that my schoolmates and I were on paths moving diametrically away from each other. They were concerned and excited over the approaching football games, but I had in my immediate past raced a car down a dark and foreign Mexican mountain. They concentrated great interest on who was worthy of being student body president, and when the metal bands would be removed from their teeth, while I remembered sleeping for a month in a wrecked automobile and conducting a streetcar in the uneven hours of the morning.

Without willing it, I had gone from being ignorant of being ignorant to being aware of being aware. And the worst part of my awareness was that I didn't know what I was aware of. I knew I knew very little, but I was certain that the things I had yet to learn wouldn't be taught to me at George Washington High School.

I began to cut classes, to walk in Golden Gate Park or wander along the shiny counter of the Emporium Department Store. When Mother discovered that I was playing truant, she told me that if I didn't want to go to school one day, if there were no tests being held, and if my school work was up to standard, all I had to do was tell her and I could stay home. She said that she didn't want some white woman calling her up to tell her something about her child that she didn't know. And she didn't want to be put in the position of lying to a white woman because I wasn't woman enough to speak up. That put an end to my truancy, but nothing appeared to lighten the long gloomy day that going to school became.

To be left alone on the tightrope of youthful unknowing is to experience the excruciating beauty of full freedom and the threat of eternal indecision. Few, if any, survive their teens. Most surrender to the vague but murderous pressure of adult conformity. It becomes easier to die and avoid conflicts than to maintain a constant battle with the superior forces of maturity.

E. Lynn Harris

1955–2009

From *What Becomes of the Brokenhearted: A Memoir*
(2003)

When Lynn Harris, an African American male, graduated from the University of Arkansas more than twenty family members attended the ceremony. Although his extended family on his mother's side was large and supportive, his early years were marred by his biological father's abandonment and his stepfather's physical abuse. With this background, he had to work hard to overcome what he saw later as a critical lack of self-confidence to succeed in his job as a computer salesman.

I had never planned a career in sales, especially in the highly technical arena of computers. I thought about going to law school, mainly because I thought it would bring me the middle-class life I craved. [...]

I had been lucky when it came to grades at the university.

Several semesters, in many classes, my grades would hover between A's and B's, but because many professors knew who I was from my campus activities they would give me the benefit of the doubt; if I had an 88 or 89 average, say, which was usually a B, I would get an A-, which still translated to four points. One summer session, I was expecting to finish with a 3.00 average but ended up with a perfect 4.00. I had developed the gift of gab that would help me with my grades and would later help me with my sales career.

IBM had recruited me because of my grades and accomplishments, and because I had scored the highest of any minority student
on their technical aptitude test. The white recruiter told me in disbelief, "In all my years of giving this test, I've never seen a Negro student score this high."

I think I scored high on the test because I didn't feel pressure
to do well after the recruiter had told me during our initial interview that he didn't think I would do well because of my liberal arts
background, but that I should take the test anyway. Before the test,
he had told me he would recommend me to IBM Office Products,
which sold typewriters and didn't require a technical aptitude. IBM
salary offers were almost double what journalism graduates were
being offered, and I thought I could work for a couple of years, save
some money, and then go east for law school or journalism school.

Deep down I know I really took the job because of the reactions
of my peers and professors when they found out I had been offered
a job by IBM. They were all impressed, with many telling me I'd be
foolish to turn down such an opportunity, and I, with my low self-
esteem, was impressed that they were impressed.

Still, it amazes me when I think back on getting a job with
IBM, a company very concerned with image. For my final interview with the branch manager, I wore a black open-collar shirt with
a gold chain around my neck. My suit was a well-worn navy blue
double-knit number with a matching vest. In addition, I had one of
the largest Afros ever known to man, which I would braid nightly to
ensure height and bounce.

On my first day at IBM, my fashion fiasco continued when I wore
a modest Sears & Roebuck gray pin-striped suit that had a certain
shine to it, with a pink shirt and a brown and blue clip-on tie. I
didn't know how to tie a regular tie.

My first manager, Leon Creed, a well-dressed black man, called
me into his office after our first lunch meeting. Leon was fair-
skinned and had green eyes and straight auburn-colored hair, and
I didn't realize he was African American until he told me he had attended Howard University. Then I took a closer look at him and realized that he was black.

"Lynn, have you ever heard of Brooks Brothers?" he asked.

"No sir, I haven't," I said.

Leon told me he was giving me an advance on my first month's salary and suggested I take the afternoon to go to a store called Brooks Brothers and see a man whose name he wrote down on a card. "Tell him I sent you, and don't leave until you've spent every penny," he instructed.

As I was leaving his office excited about my new wardrobe, Leon had one more piece of advice. "Lynn, when you leave Brooks Brothers, burn that suit," he said, and smiled.

On my first day at IBM, I had my first dress-for-success lesson. The first of many lessons I would learn.

"My name is Lynn Harris, Dallas branch, and I don't know what in the hell I'm doing here," I joked in a classroom designed like those found in many Ivy League law schools. My fellow classmates warmed me with their laughter, but I was serious. What had I gotten myself into?

I was in Endicott, New York, for my first IBM training class, and on the first morning we were instructed to give our name, the office where we worked, and our academic background. Everyone who preceded me proudly announced impressive educational résumés from some of the country's top universities. In addition, the majority had advanced degrees, and those who didn't had backgrounds in engineering. I was one of three African Americans in a class of forty-six.

One of the conditions of employment with IBM was the successful completion of a sixteen-month training program, which was considered tougher than most MBA programs. I was suddenly ashamed of my University of Arkansas degree and my family background once again. Failure loomed as a real possibility in a situation where I desperately wanted to succeed. Now it didn't matter what my college GPA had been or what I had scored on an aptitude test. IBM was not playing. A valuable lesson about competition in the real world was on tap for me in this quiet, upstate community.

A score of seventy-five was required to pass the course. I didn't think making a seventy-five would be difficult, even though the material was extremely difficult. The memorization skills I had acquired in college were not going to help here.

I studied with every free moment I had for the first test. I scored seventy-three. I made a lot of dumb mistakes, partly because I didn't know how to use a calculator correctly. In college I had had only one math course, something called Math for Liberal Arts Students. I think they just wanted to make sure students could add and subtract.

After my exam came back, I called my boss, and he already knew I had failed the test. He was supportive and told me he knew I could do it. Some of my classmates were actually afraid that their scores in the low nineties would disappoint their managers. All Leon, my manager, wanted me to do was pass the course, so all I needed was a seventy-seven on the next exam since they average the two scores. I assured Leon that I would make that and more. In many ways, I wanted to do well not only for myself, but for Leon. He was the first black sales manager in Dallas, and he and his wife Susan had quickly become my surrogate family and among the few friends I had in Dallas.

The next week I studied harder than I ever had in my life. I felt it was next to impossible for me to fail the second exam. Afterward I was so confident that I called Leon and assured him that I had passed with flying colors. He told me he was happy that I was so confident, but if I failed, it wasn't the end of the world. I ended the conversation by saying, "Don't worry. I aced the test!"

Leon responded, "Well, well, no matter what, you'll be just fine."

When my second exam came back, I was devastated by my score: seventy-four. Again I had made dumb mistakes. I stared at my test paper and was stunned that I had failed a class I had worked so hard to pass. My classmates around me bragged about their scores, but no one asked me what I had made. I guess they could tell from my stone-faced daze. After everyone had left the classroom for a celebration, I remained seated at my desk as tears started to run down my face uncontrollably. Not only had I failed, but I had let Leon down and embarrassed my race in front of my white Ivy League-confident classmates. I felt lower than low.

Right before I left Endicott, my adviser told they were recommending that I keep my position and suggested I repeat the two-week class. At first I said no. I had never failed at something for which I worked so hard. Besides, I knew the material. My adviser went on to tell me that I had an excellent attitude, was a hard worker, and got along well with others. She went on to say that one day I would look back on this class and laugh.

I was not in a jovial mood at the class going-away party or on the plane trip back to Dallas. When I got back to my new apartment on that Friday night, I collapsed on my rented bedroom furniture and didn't wake up until early Sunday morning. I was physically and emotionally drained. I wanted to quit and return to the safe haven of Fayetteville, but first I had to show all those rich white boys and girls I was just as smart as they were.

It would have been easy to walk away and look into law school, since I had just turned twenty-one years old. I felt lonely and I missed Mason [a former boyfriend]. Then I thought about some of the people at the university who were surprised that IBM had offered me a job. I knew that a lot of people felt African Americans, as we were now calling ourselves, weren't qualified when we achieved certain positions. Maybe I wasn't qualified for this highly technical field, but I felt I had at least tried—if not for me, then at least for people, like my family, who thought I could do anything.

When I reported to work on Monday, everyone in the office knew I had failed the class, and that included the garage attendant. I don't know this to be true, but it's how I felt when I entered the building on Turtle Creek Drive. I walked meekly to my desk in the sales pit area and awaited my review meeting with Leon. One of the black service engineers told me that the first black sales trainee in my office had flunked out of the program and I was the first black trainee since he had been fired some five years before. Like I needed to hear that, I thought. I held my head down low as I walked into Leon's office right before noon.

I was surprised that Leon appeared to be in a very upbeat mood. He asked me what I had learned in the class, and I started spouting all the technical information I had learned. He looked at me and said, "That's not what I'm talking about." He then repeated his question. I was silent, because I didn't know what Leon wanted me to say. I felt like a little boy desperately trying to think of an excuse to avoid a whipping I knew I was due.

Leon then gave me a lecture on how I had not allowed any room for failure, so when it happened I let it overwhelm me. He told me that I had to allow room in my life for both failure and success and treat them the same. What he said made sense. He was not telling me I had to look for failure, but just to recognize and prepare for it as a possibility. It was something I had never considered.

Leon became more than a manager to me. He was almost like a father or a big brother. When I made mistakes, he would point them
out. Like how a black man hoping to make it in corporate America
had to give up some things once considered important.

I had cut my huge Afro that I had sported for several years and
was wearing my hair in what was called a short 'Fro. In the South
jheri curls were just appearing on the hair horizon. One Friday
when I jumped into my barber's chair to get a trim, she suggested I
try a jheri curl. I was game, despite the fact that most of the women
I knew hated jheri curls on men and called men who wore them
"bamas," a term short for Alabamas, which meant real country. She
convinced me that she could make my curls look natural and people
would think it was my natural hair. Never mind the fact that they
had never seen curls on my head before.

When she finished, I thought I looked good! Damn, I looked
great. When I went to happy hour later that evening, some people
whom I was familiar with were all asking me what I had done to my
hair. I would pat it gently and smile as if to say, *It looks good, don't
it?* I spent a great deal of the weekend looking in the mirror and
spraying my special activator to keep my curls glistening.

On Monday I arrived at work still under the impression that I
looked fabulous. My white coworkers knew something was different
but seemed afraid to ask. I took my seat at my desk, which was lo-
cated on the front row, directly in front of the branch manager's office.

The branch manager was a dead ringer for a young Ronald Reagan. He walked by my desk and did a double take when he spoke
to me. A few minutes later my phone rang, and Leon asked me to
come into his office for a minute. I walked into his office, and before I took my seat, Leon asked me, "Lynn, what did you do to your
hair?"

"I got a jheri curl," I said proudly as I touched my greasy, satu-
rated curls. Leon had a blank expression on his face. A few seconds
later he said, "Lynn, the haircut has got to go." When I asked him
why, he said that my haircut wouldn't work in this type of environment. When I demanded to know why, he told me he wasn't going
to argue with me but that his supervisor had called him and asked
what in the hell I had done to my hair. When I asked him if the

branch manager told the white boys what to do with their hair, he said, "I'm not telling you that you have to get your hair cut. But I will say that this is one of your first big career decisions."

I looked at Leon with his naturally curly hair. He didn't understand, I thought. Was the IBM management trying to make me like them? I had changed my dress. I laughed at their corny jokes over lunch. I even answered some of my coworkers' dumb questions about what it was like being black when they had had a few drinks. Now they were trying to tell me what to do with my hair. I told Leon I wouldn't do it, and he suggested I take the rest of the day to think about it.

After I left the office, my anger continued and all I could think about was finding a good lawyer and suing IBM for discrimination. I called one of my new friends, Ken Baker, who worked for Southwestern Bell in a management position, and told him what had happened.

When he didn't take my side and agreed with Leon, I began to rethink my position. Maybe Ken and Leon had a point. If I was going to work in corporate America, then I was going to have to play by their rules. I had played by the rules of my fraternity and other organizations while I was in college, and this was pretty much the same thing, like some kind of uniform.

I thought about it for a couple more hours and then I ran to my car and returned to the scene of the hair crime. When I got there I discovered that my regular barber was taking the day off, and I was relieved. She had seemed so proud of her efforts. I jumped into the first empty chair and instructed the barber to cut it off. "When I returned to work the next day, Leon gave me a pleasing smile, winked at me, and said, "I think your future at IBM is going to be just fine." [...]

Things were getting better at IBM, and in the training program, I was making some treasured friendships with people I had nothing in common with. I was one of the few students whom some of the top students would help with assignments, maybe because they didn't see me as a threat for challenging them for the top spot when it came to class scores.

At times I secretly envied and despised them for their seemingly perfect lives. Everything seemed to come so easy for them, like understanding the right type of clothing and managing money. Once, one of the smartest ladies from my class, Suzanne Procter, a Harvard MBA, had a dinner party in her New York City East Side apartment, and she invited me because I was real tight with one of the best-looking white guys in the class, a former Princeton baseball player, Paul Pecka, whom I affectionately called Princeton Paul. Her apartment was like a page out of *Architectural Digest* and the dinner party was one of the most elegant I had ever attended at that point in my life.

In my final IBM training class, one based totally on sales calls and presentations, I finished near the top of my class. The applause I heard when I received one of five baseballs given to students who had received a superior rating on a sales call or presentation eased a great deal of the hurt and embarrassment I had felt at the beginning of my IBM career. I had proved that I could compete in this highly technical field. Yet I never considered if being a top salesman at IBM was something I really wanted to do.

commentary for chapter six: **JOBS**

Jobs often bring young people their first taste of independence, responsibility, and income. In this section, by contrast, the writers express ambivalent views about their early experiences with working life in stories that describe exploitation, racial barriers, and, in the case of Luis Rodriguez, physical hazard.

The stories are emotionally complex and nuanced. All three writers remember finding satisfaction and a measure of pride in their childhood or early adulthood jobs. A sense of accomplishment and even triumph suffuses Maya Angelou's narration of how she landed a job as San Francisco's first African American streetcar driver. E. Lynn Harris finds a mentor and, after swallowing setbacks and racial indignities, a willingness to accept failure along with success in his rocky first weeks as one of the first African American salesmen at an IBM branch office. Yet in all three accounts, there is a lingering sense of regret at the sacrifices they were forced to make, or the hurdles they surmounted, that more privileged youths would not face in order to earn money.

Child labor was ingrained in Rodriguez's family history; his mother had picked cotton as a girl, and he started work cleaning houses at the age of nine. His father was forced to take mostly menial jobs despite having studied biology in Mexico. An early experience with working life begins on a promising note, as Rodriguez takes enthusiastically to his job delivering newspapers from a bicycle in his Los Angeles neighborhood. He has to dodge street toughs and dogs, but he wins recognition for his dedication. Work takes a darker turn later at a carwash. The workers are not given protective footwear, and Rodriguez develops a fungus so severe he is unable to walk. His uncle applies a folk remedy to the lesions, which seems to cure them (an account that recalls Michael Patrick MacDonald's sprinkling of holy water, in chapter 4). The story suggests how easily child workers can be deprived of basic protections and that the labor exploitation endured by his parents continues into the next generation.

In Angelou's account, we see the author while still a teenager going day after day to the Market Street Railway Company, determined to get a job as a "conductorette." When she finally succeeds, she is given overnight or very early morning shifts—the worst time slots, which she believed her superiors gave her maliciously. The satisfaction of gaining a job she badly wanted is thus tempered by the discrimination she faces for being young and black. Yet she perseveres, encouraged by her mother. When Angelou goes back to school the following spring, she finds that she has matured so much that she has little in common with her classmates. School, she feels, has little left to teach her. Through her story we see the transformative power of a job as part of the passage into adulthood.

All three stories feature adults who help young people cope with the pressures of working, yet the assistance rendered is often ethically ambiguous. The mother's advice might stiffen Angelou's resolve, but is the mother, in effect, advising her to take a job for which she is too young and easily exploited? We see this ambiguity more strongly in Harris's relationship with his manager and beloved mentor Leon Creed. When Harris arrives for work with a hairstyle popular among African American men, Creed tells him to change it immediately. Harris initially resists and even mulls suing the company, but relents and shows up the next day with a more conservative coif. Is Creed's advice good or bad, sensible and well-intentioned or intrusive and degrading? The story could be read either way. Angelou, Harris, and Rodriguez do not give us tidy morality plays. They present shaded, realistic stories of the compromises we make in early working life.

QUESTIONS FOR DISCUSSION

1. In each of the narratives in this section an older adult intervened to provide support. What was the work problem for the young person and what interactions between the older adult and the younger person brought about a solution? Do you see any downsides to the older helpers' interventions? If so, what are they?

2. In the last paragraph of her reading, Maya Angelou says that "few, if any, survive their teens." What does she mean by that statement, and how does it relate to the experiences she describes? Do you agree with that statement and, if so, why?

3. In his account of working as an IBM sales trainee, E. Lynn Harris puts great emphasis on his clothes and hairstyles. Why? How did those elements of his appearance affect his early working life, and how do they relate to the writer's larger themes?

4. Luis Rodriguez's uncle used folk remedies to help young Luis overcome a serious foot infection. By describing this experience in detail, what ideas is the author expressing about work, family, and tradition?

chapter seven
ABUSE

Mary Karr

b. 1955

From *The Liars' Club: A Memoir*

(1995)

Mary Karr's mother, a former art student, had had multiple previous marriages, including to "Yankee husbands." Mary's father, an oil worker with "raw good looks," hung his wife's paintings around their house in their east Texas town and made shelves to hold her collection of art books. At the time of the events in this reading, he is not working because the Gulf Oil plant that employs him is on strike. Mary's seventh birthday, with her older sister Lecia, started out with the promise of a lasagna dinner, whose smell Mary loved "better than breath itself," and ended in disaster.

There were a lot of nights that winter when Lecia and I sat watching Mother drink. [. . .] [The] worst of all were the nights when Daddy was home, and Mother put on the blues.

My birthday was such a night. Esther Phillips was moaning out "Misery" from the turntable: "Put no headstone on my grave. / All my life I been a slave. . . ." Those lyrics should have tipped me off to all that was coming. But Mother was baking me a lasagna, which smell I loved better than breath itself. I was also caught up playing with an old pair of army binoculars Daddy had given me that morning.

I stepped through the back screen door and held them up to my eyes. Through our fence slats, I could make out Mickey Heinz sitting on his fat knees next door, running his dump truck through the dirt. I could never see Mickey without a wince. I had once gotten him to smoke a cigarette made out of Nestlé's Quik we'd rolled up in tissue paper. It burnt his tongue. In fact, he'd blistered it so bad that he'd run to show it to his mother, not considering how she and all his people belonged to one of those no-drinking, no-smoking, no-dancing churches. Mrs. Heinz whipped his butt bad with a hairbrush. We listened to the whole thing squatting right underneath the Heinzes' bathroom window—the whap-whap of that plastic brush on Mickey's blubbery little ass, him howling like a banshee.

That January morning, I watched Mickey through my birthday binoculars. I was halfway thinking maybe I'd trot over to his yard and get him to hide his eyes for hide-and-seek, then just go home and watch him look for me till he started snubbing. I had almost talked myself into doing this when I heard Daddy's truck lunge into the garage.

I turned my glasses to the garage door and made out his big silver hard hat bobbing toward me. (Mercury's helmet always put me in mind of that hard hat, for some reason—minus the wings, of course.) "How's the birthday, Pokey?" he said. Then his hard hat left my field of vision. A second later his work boot scuffed the concrete step beside me. I lowered the glasses and looked up and said fine.

Except for the late-night visits he always made to double-tuck the covers under my chin, I hadn't seen him much that January. The union's contract with Gulf Oil had run out, and he'd been out on strike all month, along with everybody else in the county. When he wasn't walking the picket line, he went shrimping or duck hunting—anything to put food on the table. Nights, he hung out at the union hall waiting for any news about the talks to trickle back. Like Mother, he'd become the sort of stranger I longed for a glimpse of without ever expecting to see up close.

But that morning he'd given me the binoculars and a new Archie comic all wrapped up before he headed off to the line. The sweetness of it had drawn tears from some deep sour place way behind my eyes. "Shit, don't cry, Pokey," he said with a wry grin. He'd finally promised to come home for supper and cake that evening if I'd stop crying so's to break his heart.

Anyway, I'd been waiting on the back step the better part of the afternoon, holding back a floodgate of talk for him. When his shadow finally fell on me, I started to prattle about how I'd gone to Beaumont with Mother and Lecia that morning to buy my birthday dress.

It was a black crepe dress—the first black dress I'd owned. Just sitting in it made me feel like a movie star, I'd told him. We'd had hell finding a kid's dress in black. But Mother had driven us all over the county. (Finding that dress, in fact, was about the first event other than an occasional meal that she'd gotten up for since coming back from the funeral [of her mother].) We'd at last settled on an A-line dress that had a big white clown collar hanging all loose and drapy, with three bona fide rhinestone buttons down the front. The dress had been "cut on the bias," according to the saleslady. Lecia took one look and said where's the funeral, but I was already prissing in front of the three-part mirror. When I spun around, both dress and collar fanned out sideways in fluttery ripples. Mother thought I looked like the ballet dancer in my Japanese music box. She rolled her eyes and said, "What the hell," when she handed the saleslady her charge plate. Not ten minutes later, she also bought Lecia a chemistry set from the toy department. On the way home, we'd stopped for shrimp rémoulade at Al's Seafood, where Mother made quick work of two vodka martinis, to celebrate.

Daddy said the dress looked pretty while he wiped his feet. But he wasn't even looking my way. He was being double-careful to worry all the mud off his boots and onto the black welcome mat. Then he slipped into the house.

Suddenly it dawned on me that I wasn't supposed to tell Daddy we'd charged stuff on Mother's plates—the shrimp and the chemistry set and all, not to mention my dress, which cost sixty-three dollars. Nobody said it was secret. But he wasn't drawing any pay, a fact he harped on more or less constantly. The image of him thumping the morning paper and talking about how Gulf Oil was crying to chicken-shit the working man out of a decent meal came to me. Not two days before he'd taken a box of canned goods and our outgrown clothes to the union hall. Kids in the big Catholic families were going hungry, he'd said. It didn't take a rocket scientist to figure out that what we'd done that day—Mother, Lecia, and I—crossed some unspoken line between good times and bad behavior. I also knew that the black dress I had on crossed another line between an outfit and a get-up. I felt like a witch in church. And I kept feeling that way till the black dress was dangling on its hanger, and I was back in blue jeans.

Later, I was on the rug undressing Barbie for the umpteenth time when my parents' mad voices floated back to me. Lecia was next to me, trying to pin her Barbie's straw-colored hair into a French twist with a bobby pin. I couldn't make out the words but the gist was plain. Mother roared and slammed kitchen cupboards. The screen banging closed finally signaled Daddy's walking out. By this time, Daddy had adopted that mean dog Nipper, and he came out from under the house, yipping and lunging against his chain. Daddy's boots scuffed down the steps. The screen banged again, and I heard what I quickly figured out was the glass lasagna casserole shattering on the patio after him. "It's her birthday, you sonofabitch," Mother yelled. Lecia just wound that French twist into a tight coil and said, "Tape Ten, Reel One Thousand: Happy Goddamn Birthday."

Out in the kitchen, Mother stood at the sink, holding both wrists under running water. You could see a big splotch of red under her sharp cheekbone, like somebody had dabbed mad on her face with a paintbrush. "You want some aspirin?" she said to me, and I said no, thanks. Outside, Nipper was going yip yip yip. Mother tossed a handful of baby aspirin in her mouth, then dipped her head under the faucet to wash them down. She took the German chocolate cake down from the top of the fridge. "We can have this cake for supper," she said. Lecia came in, bringing a warm space up close behind me. I told Mother that she could take the dress back, it was no big deal. "No I can't," she said. Then she started planting candles in the muddy top of the cake. The house still smelled of lasagna and of the fresh coconut she'd split and carved and grated for the cake. "Forget about the dress, for Christ's sake," she said.

I went outside, where Mickey was still visible in slices through the fence slats. He was sitting in the dirt like a plaster lawn figurine. He'd heard it all, of course. You could count on Mickey to run tattling to the whole neighborhood that mother had called Daddy an SOB. I took a minute to wish his kneeling figure harm before picking my way around the glass and splattered lasagna.

In the garage, I could at first see the ruby end of Daddy's cigarette and nothing else. After a second, my eyes adjusted. Then I could make out his white T-shirt and the glint of the bottle he lifted to his lips. "Daddy?" I said.

"Just go in the house," he said. The cigarette brightened for a moment as he drew on it. "It don't make a shit," he said. Then a minute later, "I'm sorry."

"It's okay." Outside the locusts started whirring in their husks. That was the only sound till I heard somewhere in the high trees outside what I took for a bat screech. "That a bat?"

"Go in the house, Pokey," he said. Then he said, almost like an afterthought, "Why don't you go on in and ask your mother if she wants to head over to Bridge City for some barbecue crabs." Back in the house, the shattered lasagna dish sat in a dustpan on the sink's edge. Mother was touching the last match to the last candle when I came in. The black fan sweeping past us made the candles fade and brighten on her face. Lecia's face next to hers was as blank as a shovel. She said, go on and make a wish, you little turd. I squinted my eyes as hard as I could and wished silently to go and live some other where forever, with a brand-new family like on *Leave It to Beaver*. Then I sucked up as much air as I could get and blew the whole house dark.

I don't remember our family driving across the Orange Bridge to get to the Bridge City café that evening. Nor do I remember eating the barbecued crabs, which is a shame, since I love those crabs for their sweet grease and liquid-smoke taste. I don't remember how much Mother drank in that bayou café, where you could walk to the end of the dock after dinner and toss your leftover hush puppies to hungry alligators.

My memory comes back into focus when we're drawing close to the Orange Bridge on the way home. From my spot in the backseat, I can see a sliver of Daddy's hatchet-shaped profile—his hawk-beak nose and square jaw. Some headlights glide over him and then spill onto me. I want to see Mother's face, to see which way her mood is drifting after all the wine. But I'm staring at the back of her head in its short, wild tangle of auburn curls.

All at once, the car rears back the way a horse does underneath you if it shies away from a small, skittery animal on the road, and we're climbing up the bridge. The steel webbing of the road sets the tires humming. [. . .] Lecia rolls down the window. [. . .] Her hair is spronging loose from its French twist. The wind's about to suck me out that window and over the bridge rail. The rushing sound marries with the tires humming till a big rocket fills the small car space and makes me feel little.

I muster all my courage to look out my window at the long drop down. It makes my stomach lurch. The steel girders jerk by my window in a fast staccato. In the distance, I can see two flaming refinery towers. They make a weird Oz-like glow that bleeds up the whole bottom part of the sky. It's a chemical-green light the color of bread mold, rising up the night sky like a bad water stain climbing wallpaper. Out beyond the river there are marshes and bayous. A black barge moves slow under the bridge.

Mother is shouting, shouting she wished herself dead before she'd ever married Daddy. She wished she'd been struck by lightning on this very bridge before she crossed over into that goddamn bog. Leechfield is the asshole of the universe, the great Nowhere. And Daddy is a great Nothing. I feel over for Lecia's hand, and it's a cold fist knotted shut. I set it down the way you'd put down a glass of water you don't want to spill.

Then out of all the darkness I see Mother's white hands rising from her lap like they were powered and lit from inside. Like all the light in the world has been poured out to shape those hands. She's reaching over for the steering wheel, locking onto it with her knuckles tight. The car jumps to the side and skips up onto the sidewalk. She's trying to take us over the edge. There's no doubt this time. I mash my eyes closed, and Lecia heaves herself over the top of me. Both of us topple down in the backseat well, so I can't see anything, but I can feel the car swerve while Mother and Daddy wrestle for the wheel.

Then there's a loud noise in the front seat like a branch cracking, after which the car goes steady again. I can almost feel the tires click back in between the yellow lines. The rearview mirror got knocked long-ways when they were wrestling, I guess. So when Lecia and I crane up from the backseat, our two scared faces float in it. We look like sea creatures coming up from the fathoms.

Amazingly enough, the car is off the bridge and back on the road, safe. Mother's lying slack-jawed against her window where Dad has socked her to get control of it. He's never hit her before, and the punch came from a very short distance, but she's down for the count.

When she wakes up, we'll be pulling into our driveway. She'll rake her fingernails all the way down Daddy's cheek, drawing deep blood so he looks for days like some leopard's paw has gone at him. The kids playing night tag in the Heinzes' yard will stop their game to gather at our property line and watch us spill out of the car, Mother still trying to claw Daddy, Daddy holding her wrists in his iron hands. At some point, Joe Dillard will sidle over to ask me what they're fighting about, and his brother will crack that they're fighting over a bottle. That's the last thing I remember anybody saying, Junior Dillard in his wise-assed voice saying, "Probably fighting over a bottle." Then Mother breaks loose from Daddy to stamp her foot at the group of kids, and they scatter like buckshot into their own dark yards. And that's it, that's what I remember about my birthday.

Pete Hamill

b. 1935

From *A Drinking Life: A Memoir*
(1994)

Pete Hamill's parents emigrated from Ireland in the early 1930s and settled in Brooklyn. Taverns on every street were visible evidence of the culture of drinking that permeated the neighborhood. His father, a factory worker and functioning alcoholic, was well known for the entertaining songs he sang in bars. Like most Irish American boys from observant Catholic families, Hamill attended parochial school. As a product of his neighborhood, he became aware of the gangs that operated there. Hamill stopped drinking in his thirties and has been sober ever since.

Eighth grade was a horror. Our teacher was a thick-necked Pole with a jutting jaw and a bent nose. His name was Brother Jan. In the seventh grade, we'd had a soft and saintly man named Brother Rembert as our teacher. We heard scary tales about Brother Jan, but nothing really prepared us for the reality of this snarling, vicious brute. On his desk, Brother Jan kept a thick eighteen-inch ruler called Elmer. He used it on someone every day. He used it if you were late. He used it if you didn't finish your homework. He used it if you smiled or giggled. He used it if you talked back, or copied from another kid during an exam. I would watch him when he bent one of the boys over a front desk, and there was a tremble in his face, a fierce concentration, a sick look of enjoyment as he whacked Elmer on the ass of the chosen boy until the boy dissolved in tears and pain.

He picked on some kids over and over again: a funny guy named Bobby Connors; a slow, sweet boy named Shitty Collins, who lived up the block from me; a tall sly character named Boopie Conroy. Near the end of the first term, Brother Jan started picking on me. Somehow I infuriated him. Maybe it was because I got the highest grades in the class but after school spent my time with the harder kids. I shared my homework with Shitty Collins and some of the slower kids; when Brother Jan discovered this he didn't see it as an act of Christian charity but as a case of subversion; he bent me over the front seat and whipped into me with Elmer. After the first time, he whipped me every week. He broke some other kids, reducing them to tears and humiliation; when he did that, his eyes seemed to recede under his brow and his lips curled into a knowing smile, as if he'd discovered the point at which he could destroy pride and will. I refused to cry. I would wait for the initial shock, then the cutting pain of the second blow, then wait for the next, and tighten my face, clamp my teeth together, feel it again, then again, still *again*, as many as fifteen times, thinking: Fuck you, and fuck you, and fuck you, and fuck you. And Brother Jan would swing again, grunting.

Then he'd be finished and I'd glance at him and sometimes he'd have a film of sweat on his face. And I'd think: You're sick. I'd sit down in pain, and the other kids would look at me, and I would stare up at Brother Jan, thinking: Fuck you, fuck you, fuck you.

Around this time I first sensed that I was my own version of Jekyll and Hyde. In my head, the Good Boy was constantly warring with the Bad Guy. I wanted to be a Bad Guy, tough, physical, a prince of the streets; at the same time, I was driven to be a Good Boy: hardworking, loyal, honorable, a protector of my brothers, an earner of money for the family. The Bad Guy cursed, growled, repeated dirty jokes and resisted Brother Jan; the Good Boy served Mass in the mornings and read novels in bed at night. The Bad Guy practiced walking like one of the Tigers, stole silverware from the Factory, and jerked off; the Good Boy delivered groceries to old ladies who couldn't come down the stairs, memorized poems, and drew cartoons at the kitchen table on cold or rainy evenings. It seems clear to me now that the Bad Guy was demanding respect from my father, the Good Boy acknowledging love from my mother. It wasn't at all clear when I was in my early teens.

There were times when the existence of the Good Boy forced the appearance of the Bad Guy. In the final three years of grammar school at Holy Name, I always finished at the top of the class in grades, averaging 98 or 99, was placed on the honor roll and granted awards for general excellence. But there was an assumption that if you got good grades you must be soft, a sissy, or an AK—an ass kisser. This was part of the most sickening aspect of Irish-American life in those days: the assumption that if you rose above an acceptable level of mediocrity, you were guilty of the sin of pride. You were to accept your place and stay in it for the rest of your life; the true rewards would be given you in heaven, after you were dead. There was ferocious pressure to conform, to avoid breaking out of the pack; self-denial was the supreme virtue. It was the perfect mentality for an infantryman, a civil servant, or a priest. And it added some very honorable lives to the world. But too often, it discouraged kids who aspired to something different. The boy who chose another road was accused of being Full of Himself; he was isolated, assigned a place outside the tribe. Be ordinary, was the message; maintain anonymity; tamp down desires or wild dreams. Some boys withered. And the girls were smothered worse than the boys. They could be nuns or wives, brides of Christ or mothers of us all. There were almost no other possibilities.

But the Bad Guy in me resisted the demand for conformity that was so seductive to the Good Boy. I hated being called an AK. For one thing, it wasn't true. I polished no apples, sought no favors. But worse, to say that I was an AK was to imply that what I had actually done was a fraud. I knew that I got those grades by doing the homework, reading the books, and above all, by paying attention; I didn't get them by kissing ass. So, after a while, whenever I was called an AK, I struck back: punching and hurting my accusers. The Bad Guy shoved the Good Boy out of the way and went to work. By the time I was subjected to Brother Jan's sick furies, nobody again called me an AK. And I'd acquired a vague notion in my head that I could be like Sugar Ray Robinson: a boxer *and* a puncher, smart *and* tough.

By the spring of 1949, seething with anger at Brother Jan, I started hanging out in a different part of the neighborhood, two blocks from Holy Name. In a way, it was a matter of choosing my own place, rather than having it chosen by my parents; they had moved to Seventh Avenue but I didn't have to hang around there. There was another aspect to it too; my brother Tommy was eleven and I was thirteen; eight and ten are somehow much closer than eleven and thirteen; so I was moving away from Tommy too.

The place I chose was called Bartel-Pritchard Square, and it was more a circle than a square. Three different trolley lines converged here, turning around a center island before heading off to Coney Island, Mill Basin, or Smith Street. Off the square on one side were the two tall Corinthian columns that marked the entrance to Prospect Park; we called them the Totem Poles, or the Totes. They rose from cleanly carved granite bases, and in the evenings that spring, after work at the grocery store and after finishing my homework, I would walk up from Seventh Avenue and see the others and we'd gather around the bases, sitting on them, looking at girls, cursing, smoking, making jokes, and drinking beer. First, the Good Boy attended to his chores; then the Bad Guy went out into the evening.

That was when I really started drinking. There were a lot of us hanging around the Totes that spring and summer: Boopie Conroy, Shitty Collins, Mickey Horan, Vito Pinto, Jack McAlevy. Among my friends was a thin, handsome guy named Richie Kelly. He was smart and tough but he always seemed cautious about drinking. Later in the summer, I learned why. His father, Jabbo Kelly, was one of the public rummies, a small group of men who'd been thrown out of their homes and lived on the streets. They slept in the park, or in the subways. They were filthy and panhandled for wine money. There was no way that Richie could avoid seeing Jabbo, because the rummies were always around the park, but I never saw them talk. I admired the way Richie handled a fact of his life that would have shamed others. He was cool and indifferent. For a while, we were close. I thought that with any kind of bad luck, my father could join Jabbo Kelly on his aimless wanderings.

Richie was also our liaison to the older guys, who owned the benches in the center of the traffic island, across the street from the Totes. They played football together as the Raiders and fought occasional gang battles in Coney Island or in the park. Richie's older brother, Tommy, was one of the Raiders. He was built like a safe and was a ferocious puncher but never went out of his way to fight. I never saw him talk to Jabbo either.

I don't know who bought the beer, but it was around, in cardboard containers or quart bottles. At first I didn't join in the drinking. It was as if I knew I would be crossing a line in some permanent way. But I didn't make a big deal out of this; I just shrugged and passed on the offered bottle. Then one evening, all of us laughing and joking, a guy named Johnny Rose handed me a container, casually, easily, and I took a sip.

The first swallow triggered a vague remembrance of the beer I'd sipped when I was a little boy, and was accompanied by a yeasty smell I associated with Gallagher's [bar]. I didn't like the taste; unlike the sweet wine I'd drunk in the woods at Fox Lair Camp, the beer had a sourness to it. I passed the container to Boopie Conroy, who took a long swallow. After a while, it came back to me, I took another sip, and this time I picked up a repulsive odor that reminded me of my father's breath when he was sleeping late on weekend mornings.

But as the beer kept coming around to me, I felt oddly proud of myself. The taste and smell didn't matter as much as the act. I was doing something I wasn't supposed to do—drinking under the legal age of eighteen. Just by drinking beer, I was a certified Bad Guy. If the police saw us, and caught us, we'd be in trouble. We stayed on the side of the Totes that faced the park, safe from the scrutiny of passing cars. But several times, I wandered out under the streetlight with my container in my hand. That spring night, and on later evenings in summer, when I had graduated from Holy Name, I *wanted* to be seen. I wanted to be seen by one person: Brother Jan. I wanted him to come over to me. I wanted him to try to stop me from drinking. And then I would crash into him, I'd beat and batter him, I'd stomp him and kick his balls out his ass. He was bigger than I was, heavier, with a fullback's neck; I didn't care. I wanted to hurt him back. On my turf. On the street.

For the first time I began to experience a transformation that would later become familiar: the violent images grew larger in my head and everything else got smaller. It was as if the beer were editing the world, eliminating other elements, such as weather, light, form, beauty. I could hear talk bubbling around me from the others, random words colliding in my head, then a tightening of focus, the faces closest to me having the most solid reality. A few of us talked about Brother Jan and how we'd like to give him a good beating. But all sorts of other talk flew around the beer-tingling air: the Dodgers, the gangs, girls, prizefighters, the songs we heard on the radio. [. . .]

Up on the Totes, even while I was learning to like the taste of beer, I never mentioned cartooning. I never tried to discuss the books I was reading. I never let the Good Boy get in the way of the apprentice Bad Guy.

At first, I didn't get drunk. At least I didn't think I was getting drunk. I was always conscious of where I was. I always walked home and didn't stagger (chewing gum or Sen-Sen so that my mother couldn't smell the beer on my breath). I didn't fall down inside the park to sleep, the way some of the others did. But I knew I was being changed. I talked more, postured as badly as the others, tried on different attitudes as if they were suits. I watched the Raiders—we called them the Big Guys—and the way they dressed (in T-shirts and chino pants, in contrast to the pegged pants of Seventh Avenue) and the way they wore their hair (in crisp crew cuts, instead of the pompadours and sideburns of the Tigers and the South Brooklyn Boys), and I tried to look like that too. I liked the way they held their containers of beer; casually, firmly, passing them around in an open generous style.

I also watched the way they walked up to the Sanders with a girl on a Saturday night, paying for two, the girl waiting to the side, then taking the guy's hand as they walked inside to the dark balcony. I wanted a girl too and had tried to talk to girls in my grade at Holy Name; they didn't share classrooms with us but they were our age and knew the same songs we knew. In their presence, however, I felt clumsy and awkward, and the girls seemed always to be holding back some secret knowledge, exchanging glances with other girls, prepared to dismiss me with a sigh or some form of mockery. It was as if they knew more about me than I did. They certainly knew more about me than I knew about them. I kept hearing about periods and sanitary napkins and didn't understand what any of it meant. I don't think any of the other guys knew either, as they played at being Bad Guys on the Totes on those long summer evenings.

Then one evening that summer, I was home after dinner, drawing at the kitchen table. I had sketched a cartoon in light blue pencil and was drawing with a fine-haired brush, dipping into the Higgins india ink. My father came in. He was drunk and lurching and his eyes were opaque. He bumped into the kitchen table and my hand jerked, ruining a line. And I rose in a fury. I tore up the drawing and threw the ink bottle against the sink and stormed out. I couldn't do this! I wanted to be a cartoonist and this drunk, *my father*, made it impossible! I hated him then, with a white, ear-ringing, boyish hatred, and my rage and hatred carried me to the Totes. Among my friends, I drank to get rid of something.

That gave me a delicious sense of joy. I could drink until I got drunk because it was someone else's fault. If I downed too many beers, it was my father's fault; if I staggered, it was his fault; if I fell down in the grass in the park: it was his fault. The son of a bitch. I didn't say any of this to the other guys. I kept thinking of Bogart in *Casablanca*, sitting at the bar in a pool of bitterness, drinking his whiskey. I would be like that. I would just drink, quietly and angrily, and say nothing. Sitting on the Totes, with the others laughing and grab-assing around me, I sipped the beer, telling myself that I enjoyed the taste. I didn't want to go home. I didn't want to clean up the mess I'd made with the ink. I didn't want to confront my father or explain to my mother. I wanted to sit there forever, drinking in bitter satisfaction, using someone else as a license. In the years that followed, I did a lot of that.

Brent Staples

b. 1951

From *Parallel Time: Growing Up in Black and White* (1994)

Brent Staples grew up in an African American family in the industrial city of Chester, Pennsylvania, where as a teenager he became involved in a theater group and spent hours chatting with a black sociology professor at the downtown office of the League of Women Voters. Brent's father drank away the good money he made as a truck driver. Brent's mother, the "perfect comforter," stayed with her husband to raise their nine children but finally escaped when Brent was in graduate school, taking with her his younger brothers and sisters. Staples's book begins and ends with the shooting death of his younger brother Blake by a rival drug dealer and its repercussions.

My father eavesdropped on my phone calls. He greeted callers with obnoxious expressions like "Your dime, my time!" or "Hello, Grand Central Station!" then lingered to sample the conversation. It piqued his interest to hear his once timid son using lines and pitches, trying to get girls to come across. The call that found him out was from Chickie Mayo. I was talking to Chickie from the bedroom upstairs and speaking in my sexiest voice. I was supposed to be making time, but was bad-mouthing my father instead. "He couldn't be that bad," Chickie said. I responded, "Oh, no, you don't understand. My father is a veritable monster." My father let loose a howl of laughter. It was tinny laughter, the kind that covers hurt.

I crossed the line on my sixteenth birthday. That's what led to the fistfight. The subject was beds, which chronically went to splinters in our house. They collapsed from too many occupants. They also collapsed when younger children trampolined them to death. I was supervising the replacement brigade when my father appeared in the doorway and complained we weren't working fast enough. His eyes were as red as fire from a day at the bar. He barked at me, "I thought I told you to put up these beds!" I barked back, "What's it look like we're doing? We're working as fast as we can!" The edge in my voice frightened even me. My father ate up the room in two quick strides and was on me. He snatched my glasses from my face and put them aside. "I guess you think you're a man now." I deflected the blows but was smart enough not to punch back. The blows hurt my arms but less so than if they'd landed on my body and head. I was pleased to be holding my own, so pleased that I smiled at him from behind my guard. This was a big mistake. He stopped punching and raised his hands above his head and smiled clownishly, baring his teeth. I let my guard drop, and then he sucker-punched me. The punch came in slow motion: the left hand snapping into a fist, his weight shifting to get behind the fist, the fist speeding toward my face, the ceiling falling away into blackness.

I woke up and stumbled to the bathroom to have a look at my face. The right eye was hideously swollen, the white of it red with blood. I was leaving the house that minute. I stalked back to my bedroom, gathered as many trousers, sports jackets, and shirts as I could carry, and stomped downstairs.

"Put the clothes back," my father snapped. "I paid for all of them."

"The hell you did! I paid for every stitch," I said and kept stomping.

My mother cried and persuaded me to stay. Then she got one of my older cousins to drive me around until I calmed down.

That night, as my brothers slept, I lay awake seething. I parted company with my family. Physically I remained with them, but mentally I was gone. I arranged to be out of the house at every possible minute. I prowled the city, banging against its limits.

Sandra Scofield

b. 1943

From *Occasions of Sin: A Memoir*
(2004)

Sandra Scofield was sent to a Catholic boarding school
at the age of twelve because her chronically ill mother,
a devout Catholic, was unable to care for her. The man
Sandra thought was her father was actually her stepfather; she never knew the identity of her biological
father. Her mother died at age thirty-three when Sandra
was sixteen. When her stepfather remarried, his second
wife, Phyllis, recommended that she get a job instead of
going to college. At age seventeen she was admitted to
the University of Texas in Austin.

The saint I knew and loved best was the recently canonized Maria
Goretti, who as a girl only eleven years old had died defending her
purity in an assault by a boy from a neighboring farm. Of course I
loved her! *She could be me.* She was a saint of my century. Smitten
like millions of girls all over the world, I had recently chosen her for
my confirmation namesake. I had a clear picture in my mind of her
heaped on the back of a farmer's wooden cart. I thought that her ho-
liness lay not just in her virginity (after all, I was a virgin and hardly
holy at all), and not just in her violent death (people are murdered
every day), but in her generosity *(I pray he will repent!)*, and especially in the way she saw clearly what she had to do. Her vocation
had been martyrdom and she had welcomed her bloody death. I am
appalled now to remember thinking of this eleven-year-old peasant girl as capable of such self-aggrandizing projection—in the mo-

ments of a brutal attack, no less—but not only was I immature, I was a Catholic [. . .] and was enthralled with the concept. The hagiographers were pushing hard this child who had died for virtue, and I simply couldn't conceive of a girl around my age being so good, so brave, and so full of conviction, that she would act *without having to think about it.*

I thought that what had made Maria brave was her belief that she had been blessed with her violent fate, *as my mother had been blessed with her afflictions.* I loved that word, afflictions. (That night I would write Mother these thoughts, and she would answer that I had made her weep with pride love.) Those brave, good girls who were martyred for their faith (Cecelia, Agnes, Perpetua) *had been at that window when God called.* Simple acceptance—that was how you learned to do the right thing, even if you didn't understand everything about what you embraced. Somehow acceptance became faith; your patience and humility got you God's prize—bestowed, not won (Sainthood!). It was heady, romantic stuff, a kind of Prince Charming story in which God himself came along to rescue you, not from death, but from anonymity. I was thrilled by the simple virtue of having a fresh thought of my own at age twelve. I wasn't mature enough to turn around and evaluate it, too. [. . .]

[At age seventeen] I had to decide myself about boys: Romance was a dead end but I thought sex would be fine. I thought maybe I could be good at it and I thought that sex might be the way to find someone I could talk to, the thing I really wanted. I was lonely. I was going to a university in a great college town where there were hundreds of parties every month and someone would like me. [. . .] Mostly I was sunny about my prospects. I was a good dancer. One of my roommates was a licensed beautician and she was glad to bleach my hair. It wasn't really me, but it sure wasn't Phyllis, either.

The trouble was I really didn't have any way to meet anybody. Most of those parties were fraternity-sorority mixers. I didn't belong to any clubs. I lived in the back carriage house of a big boarding-house in one of four rooms, each with four girls. Next door there was a similar arrangement for boys, and the two groups became friends. During the evenings, the house owners would unlock the gate into the alley, and the boys could come into the courtyard and hang around. Sometimes a group of us went to the movies or out to eat on Saturday night. One by one, pairs formed. There was one boy I liked a lot, Bobby, but he fell for a New Jersey girl and began dating her. Bobby and I became close friends anyway and have kept in touch ever since, but for all his good feelings toward me, it did nothing for my Saturday nights.

So I asked a couple of the girls in the house to see if their boyfriends knew anyone who might want to double. They paid more for their rooms, wore great clothes, and had dates every Friday and Saturday, so I knew they would come through eventually, and the girls were flattered. Sure, they said.

Right away boys started calling. I heard you're a good dancer. Want to go to a party, and so on. They all ran together, those boys, too dull for words, but I didn't lose my optimism. People have to click, I thought. [. . .]

One Saturday in late October I walked over to the 7-11 to get some Cokes. I was at the register when a boy tapped me on the shoulder and said, "Glad to see you on your feet."

I turned to see who it was saying something so dumb, and instantly I remembered how we knew one another. During registration, which took place in ninety-degree weather with high humidity, I had had to wait outside on the steps for two hours, and just before my group was due to go into the building for registration, I passed out and fell straight back into the arms of two guys behind me. People started fanning me, someone got a cup of water, and in no time I was on my way. Later I wished we had exchanged names.

Now there they were, both of them. They had fake IDs to buy beer. There was a football game on TV that afternoon, the University of Texas against I don't know what team. We chatted for a moment and they invited me to come home with them to watch the game. They were going to order pizza. "There's not going to be a Texan on the streets, you know!" they said.

I had not been to a game. As a student, I was able to draw tickets and then turn around and sell them—not legal, but done widely, and a very nice supplement to my small income as a tutor in the speech lab. I told them I would come if they would explain a few things about football first, and they agreed. Off we went merrily on what had to be a classic Austin fall afternoon, doing just what thousands of students were doing all over the city.

I got drunk for the very first time. They had two cases of beer and they kept throwing them back. I could only sip, but I did so steadily, mostly to combat my utter boredom. By the time the pizza arrived, it smelled disgusting to me. I made it through halftime and then I began to feel sick. I said the room was going 'round and 'round. One of the guys pointed to a door and said, "Pick either bed and go lay down until you feel better. It's cool." So I did.

There was an air-conditioner in the bedroom, and heavy shades. In the cool dark, I sat on the edge of the messy, unmade bed for what seemed like a long time, too sick to lie own. I peed and I threw up, something I later was sorry for though it made me feel better at the time. I was still too drunk to do anything but go to sleep.

This has to be the most ordinary of tales. On that same day it was probably happening to at least ten other girls in Austin, and hundreds on campuses around the country. I was drunk and dumb and I went to sleep. The game ended. The boys were drunk and decided they were horny; after all, there was a girl in their bedroom. A third guy had turned up, too.

I woke to the sensation of suffocation. I was naked except for my bobby socks. One of the boys was on me, then in me. I moaned, No! but I had no strength. I didn't really feel much with the first boy, but the second one hurt me. I was dry and tight and scared. He was big, and maybe he was more drunk, or less drunk than the first boy, and he kept at it a long time. He held himself up with his hands flattened on my breasts, leaning so hard against them I thought they might tear away. I cried and begged him to stop but my protests were feeble. I tried to gag but I couldn't even do that. I stopped pushing and striking him and threw my arms straight out at my sides, off the bed. One hand slid across the crotch of another boy and he giggled and hopped back. I tasted the sour beer again, I remembered where I sat on the couch when I first entered the apartment, I imagined myself leaving before anyone scored—and then the big boy was done with me.

I heard the third say, "There's something I always wanted to do." More talk, and some guffaws. Someone spitting. I remember them shoving me and turning me over, pulling me up from behind and spreading my legs apart; and suddenly there was a pain unlike anything I had ever felt in my life, a searing, tearing pain that went up the center of my body and came out in my hoarse cries and pleas. One of the other boys wanted to try it, too. It was the big boy. He hooted and laughed at the surprise of the ride. I thought I was screaming, but no sound came out. Then there was silence, and dark.

I lay there for hours, in and out of consciousness. When I finally got up, the apartment was dark. I turned on the light, a dim bulb overhead. My skirt and panties were on the floor. I had bled on the sheets. I dabbed at myself with a towel in their filthy bathroom and dressed, then I stumbled out onto the street. I felt as if I had been turned inside out. I walked home slowly in the dark, crying. I passed hordes of drunk college boys and I stepped off the walks to make way for them, sometimes backing into darkness behind trees.

In my room, I showered and scrubbed my body hard except for those parts that were horribly abraded. I sat on the floor of the shower and let tepid water run on me. I dried by touching myself gently with a tee shirt over and over, then I put Vaseline on the outside of my vagina. I couldn't bear to touch myself on the other places. I took five or six aspirin and went to bed.

There were no words in my head. I was as empty of language as a feral child. My roommates came in at curfew and asked me if I was sick, if I needed anything, and I said I just wanted to sleep. I lay half-awake all night, kept awake by the burning pain, knowing that everything had changed for me. Who had I thought I was?

And it came to me that I was my mother. Something like this had happened to her all those years ago, something she could never tell anyone, not even her own mother, because it was too shameful to be so vulnerable and so stupid. She had married Daddy because he was a gentle person. Ever after, she had wanted something more, something better, because the core of her was gone. Somebody had hurt her when she was younger than I was, and from that, came me.

You can't make your life into something you have dreamed about. It comes to you. Whether you wait for it by the window or you go out looking, life comes to you as it will and it gives you your chance at sainthood or happiness or it shorts you and you have to make the best of what you've got. I knew that what had happened was my fault, but what I felt was not guilt and not quite shame. It was the simple absence of pride. Those boys gave my name away, and we had so many ugly calls we had to change the phone number to an unlisted one. I told my roommates that I didn't know who was doing it, or why, but they didn't believe me.

It never occurred to me to tell someone in authority what had happened, and I didn't go to a doctor then. It took a long time for the abrasions and tears to heal, and some damage had to be repaired much later, but I went back to classes after a few days. I didn't date again until after the Christmas holidays, and I did so out of stubbornness. In Odessa, Daddy told me that Phyllis's son was coming from Canada to live with them, and [my stepsister] Karen; there wasn't room for me. They'd like to see me, of course, he said; I could drive over from Aunt Mae's.

I came back to school and discovered that my roommates had asked the housemother to move me out of my room. I wasn't the kind of person they wanted to live with. All my stuff was piled harum-scarum in the laundry shed, off the courtyard. The housemother talked to me kindly. She said she didn't make much of what they said, but sometimes it was easiest to start over. *They had no right!* I screamed. They had never said anything to me. *What had I done to them, what had I done to deserve this?*

The housemother moved me into a much nicer room for the same price. I shared it with one other girl, Darlene, whose friendship invited confidences. Within a week I had told her what had happened. She said she was sorry, but really it was nothing and I would get over it. She had been a cheerleader in high school, and a virgin when one night half the team had raped her, then rolled her out onto her lawn. She had to be hospitalized. Everyone knew about it but nothing happened to the boys. Her parents didn't want to create a scandal. She had a little boy her parents were raising as her brother. You never would have guessed. I stared at her and I thought, *Everybody has stories and most of them don't count for much.* That's why we loved Maria Goretti. All the factors fell into place for her martyrdom; her death made her story perfect, the one we would tell over and over, knowing none of us could ever be like her.

commentary for chapter seven: **ABUSE**

Stories in this section present the complex and malignant relationship between substance abuse—alcohol, in these cases—and physical abuse, domestic violence or, in Sandra Scofield's passage, sexual assault. For Pete Hamill, drinking starts in his teens as a way of self-medicating the profound psychic wounds left by a sadistic teacher's abuse. In Mary Karr's account, alcohol abuse spoils a family occasion—the author's seventh birthday—and turbocharges what could have been a tame disagreement over family finances into near-catastrophe. Brent Staples links his father's alcoholism to the brutal domestic violence that Brent endured until he disengaged emotionally from his family.

In all four readings, alcohol abuse and its consequences play out against a backdrop of economic or class anxiety, sometimes severe. Karr's father has been on strike for a month and the family is almost out of money. Staples's father works as a trucker, but the family lives on the edge of poverty, their beds collapsing from too many people sleeping in them, in a declining factory town. Scofield has come from a working-poor family and admires the wealthier girls' fine clothes in her freshman year at the University of Texas, where male students quickly exploit her eagerness to fit in and, in a shockingly graphic account, rape her. Hamill comes from a financially strapped immigrant family. Yet economic anxiety is only one stressor associated with alcohol abuse and its toxic aftermaths. With a complex admixture of depression, resentment, and longing fueling it, alcohol abuse brings about its own unique form of destruction.

Although physical or sexual abuse scars the young psyche, these writers also show that it can also have a strangely maturing effect. Abuse can wrench children into adulthood. Karr, only seven when she was subjected to her parents' alcohol-fueled fights, adopted the "parentified child" behavior characteristic of children forced to act grown up when their parents no longer function as adults. After they quarrel over her mother's extravagant purchase of a party dress for Mary, the girl tries to make peace by sensibly suggesting that they take the dress back for a refund. But sensible measures are ineffective against alcohol abuse. As an eighth-grader, Hamill endures the blows that teacher Brother Jan inflicts on his buttocks with a ruler. Hamill takes this abuse as a kind of personal challenge, a temptation to cry to which he would not yield as other children did, as if trying to show his adulthood at least to himself.

After being gang-raped, Scofield reflected on her past and tried to put the catastrophe into a context that allowed her to proceed constructively. She took responsibility for getting drunk with unfamiliar young men but, importantly, did not feel guilty or blame herself for the crime. She gained a deeper understanding of her beleaguered mother who had conceived Scofield under similar circumstances, and she resolved not to be defined in her own mind by the assault she had suffered and to continue her education.

Alcohol is central to Hamill's story of himself as a Good Boy turned bad, spending evenings hanging out in a park with beer-drinking friends. From his mature perspective as an author in his fifties with years of sobriety behind him, Hamill reflects on the antecedents to his alcoholic behavior. Already in his teens, he saw himself becoming an angry, bitter old drunk who blames his failings on his heavy-drinking father. Violent images began to appear in his head—the "beer editing my world"—and that included stalking Brother Jan and crushing him to a pulp. Hamill's and other stories in this section suggest that at the core of alcohol abuse lies a self-destructive impulse.

QUESTIONS FOR DISCUSSION

1. Mary Karr wishes that her family was more like the one on the TV sitcom *Leave It to Beaver*. Do you see any evidence that her parents also aspired to a normal family life like the one depicted on *Leave It to Beaver*? If so, what? How do you explain that her family deviated so far from the norms of middle-class American family life?

2. Pete Hamill's account of student life at Holy Name includes a teacher's violent abuse. What, according to Hamill, is the relationship between those assaults and his superior intelligence? And how does he connect that violence with his later alcoholism?

3. Brent Staples "parted company with his family," as though there was no other solution to his family problems. Was he right? If so, why?

4. Sandra Scofield describes the story of her sexual assault as "the most ordinary of tales." What does she mean by that? How could a rape be "ordinary"?

5. Scofield cites two rapes: her own and the rape of her roommate Darlene. Both were treated as secrets, in a manner that was typical at the time they occurred. While rapes like these still occur today on campuses, their concealment is less likely. What role do you think today's greater openness about sexual violence plays in reducing the likelihood of sexual abuse?

chapter eight
INTIMACY

Kim Barnes

b. 1958

From *Hungry for the World: A Memoir*

(2000)

Kim Barnes's family was active in a Pentecostal church
in Idaho that demonized sexual contact before marriage. Her father was a rigid authoritarian who intimidated both his daughter and his wife. When Kim
became deeply infatuated with Tom, another teenage
parishioner at the same church, she was reaching out
for two forbidden fruits: sex and freedom. She tasted
both, but only temporarily, and with unexpected consequences.

The fall of freshman year in high school, I came to believe that
what held my greatest allegiance was not my family or my church
but Tom, a thin, fair-haired boy who had begun his courtship while
holding my hand during prayer, so that, even now, when I remember my voice rising in praise that early September, I feel the tingle of
something new about to happen, something sparking, traveling my
knuckles, settling light and electric beneath my breastbone.

He was the son of a deacon, a good boy a year older than I was
who didn't smoke or drink or cuss, who, like me, wore glasses and
spent too much time reading. We began sitting together during
Sunday school, walking hand in hand from the foyer. Hand-holding
in and of itself was not a sin, but, we'd been warned, it could lead to
disastrous things. (I still have several of the "hand-holding sticks"
various young suitors carved for me at church camp, abiding by the
rules set by our elders: the boy could hold one end, the girl the other,

and in this way their flesh would not be tempted toward further engagement.)

Our parents were friends, and so there were afternoons when we were able to gaze at each other with great longing across the dinner table, and I began to believe that I might not survive more than a few hours away from Tom. My father, I knew, was watching me carefully: my overt preoccupation with a boy was new territory for both of us.

Could I go with Tom for a Coke after choir practice? Yes, my father said, as long as I returned home by the designated hour. Sundays after church, Tom took me to the gravel pit just south of Lewiston, where we fired round after round from his .22 revolver. The further I stood from the target, the more shots I placed in the tightest space, the more he praised me. He taught me to load and unload, sight in, compensate for distance and trajectory. He bought a .357, and l learned to allow for greater recoil, the concussion through my wrists and shoulders.

Those long afternoons alone with Tom, hidden from the road by a cirque of basalt, gave me my first taste of true freedom. The reflected warmth of the rock, the heavy gun in my hands, Tom's soft words of direction and praise, the red-tailed hawks winging lazy loops overhead—I felt both independent and protected, stronger, and strangely new.

Tom lived in a large house with his parents and numerous siblings. As long as there were adults on the premises, my father said, I could go there, and I soon became a fixture at Tom's dinner table, happy to be part of his raucous family, in rooms that seemed vibrant with television and music—less silent, less rigid than my own somber home. Tom and I spent hours listening to the rock-and-roll albums I was not allowed to possess, mesmerized by the flashing colored lights he had wired to his speakers. We talked of things that, aboveground, were taboo—the rumors and stories that fascinated us: the symbolism of Paul's barefooted march across the Beatles' *Abbey Road* album cover; the eerie accurateness of my cousin's Ouija board; the article I had read about epileptic seizures bringing on visions. Though neither of us suffered from the disorder, we wondered if Tom's chronic migraines might not serve to bring on an otherworldly aura, transport him to another plane.

It might have been there, in his bedroom, or perhaps in the cold interior of his car, or even in the alley behind the church, that we began to feel our virginal resolve weaken. It was a sin to move beyond the feverish kissing that kept us occupied for long minutes in the parking lot's dark corner while our parents chatted after evening service. Tom's hand would find my breast, I would murmur that he mustn't, and then he would profess to great misery and guilt, and we would both pray for strength and forgiveness. I don't remember at what point the prayers quit working. I know that we were very young and very determined to save ourselves for marriage and that there came a moment when none of this was enough to smother the fire we had kindled in each other's body. We agonized at first, and then we didn't but simply began to allow ourselves the pleasure of consummation.

We rationalized and reasoned: we were in love; we would be married the moment I turned eighteen, if not before. We imagined illicit escapes and elopements. Tom gave me a thin gold ring in which a single diamond chip was embedded, a promise that we would soon be engaged. When I showed it to my mother, she shook her head, said it was too much, too soon.

"But you were married when you were sixteen," I argued. "Why should it be any different for me?"

"It just is, Kim. I didn't know any better."

This meant nothing to me. All I saw was hypocrisy, unjust criticism, and restriction. My father said only one thing: I must give the ring back. I could not imagine such infidelity, and so I hid the ring in my pockets and purse, slipped it on my finger the moment I left my parents' field of vision. I believed that nothing they could do would be punishment enough to separate me from Tom. He was the one with whom I could share every part of myself, the intimate who knew me better than any mother, father, or friend. We spent hours whispering our secrets, feeding ourselves to each other in bits and pieces, until we seemed less two people than a single, unified self. I was besotted by the intensity of Tom's attention, the way he kissed me, took my breath into his lungs, touched each hidden part of me. How could we not call this love?

It must have been apparent to everyone that what we were about was no longer simple infatuation but something bordering on obsession. My father's growing disapproval of the time we spent together only strengthened my resolve to remain loyal to my lover.

Soon there was little I would not do to gain a few more minutes with Tom. We wove elaborate plans to meet, skipping school, dodging teachers, urging our friends to cover for us should our parents discover that we'd sneaked from the back pew during the minister's long-winded sermon. At one point Tom and another young man from the church consolidated their savings—enough to pay for one month's rent of an airless apartment beneath the eaves of a crumbling Victorian mansion—a place of privacy, where we could lie together and love without interruption.

The other boy and his girlfriend reserved the even days, Tom and I the odd. Tom presented the key to me as a gift, pleased with himself for daring such adult maneuvers. I was amazed and frightened by such risk. What if my father were to find out? How could I ever explain?

Tom interpreted my hesitation as an insult. He'd worked hard for the money, taken chances so that we could be together. I talked myself into believing that we deserved this hideaway, that the oppression of parents and church had driven us to take such a step, forced us to take our love into hiding.

But if the idea of such a retreat was romantic, the reality was not. I remember the lack of light and the cold darkness. The rooms smelled of spoiled food and mildewed linens. There was a small wooden table and two chairs, a rough-edged counter, a rust-ridden sink. The bed was a thin mattress with blue-striped ticking, discolored with sweat and urine. When I told Tom that I could not lie on it, he scowled, then spread his shirt and coat to cover the most offensive stains. He was, I could tell, not happy with me. As I lay beneath him, I felt nothing of the liberation such space had promised. What I felt instead was disgust. How many others had lain in this same room, for an hour, a night? What kind of woman would come here? I felt cheap and dirty, as though the soiled bedding had bled into my skin.

"You're ruining this," Tom said. He sat up, his shoulder blades sharp in the shadows of afternoon light.

"I'm sorry." I did not know what else to say. His anger made me feel as though I could not breathe. Men were dangerous if made angry. It was my job to soothe, to make things right. I placed the palm of my hand against his spine, let two fingers trace the vertebrae's path.

"I'm just a little nervous, that's all." I pulled gently at his arms. "I'm cold."

"Maybe I should just take you home."·

"No," I said, "I want to stay here." I moved my hand across his back. "Next time I'll bring a blanket. We'll have a picnic lunch. We'll say we're going to the river." I imagined a checkered tablecloth, a Mason jar of dried flowers. Maybe I could sneak a sheet or two. Maybe I could find a curtain for the kitchen window, a rug for in front of the sink, bring softness and color to this place my lover had chosen. I thought of all the houses my mother had remade with little more than a swatch of gingham and a bucket of Pine-Sol.

"Maybe," I said, "I just need to learn how to *be* here, how to act."

"We can be whoever we want here. We can act however we want." He pulled me against him roughly. "There are no rules."

There was a new insistence in him. Before, our times together had held a certain balance—both of us eager, both of us taking, both of us giving. But this was different. Now our roles were more defined: he was the taker, I the giver. I felt disconnected, separated from my body, unable to feel the rush and rise of blood, unable to focus on anything other than the fly-specked ceiling, the room's webbed corners, the bare bulb hung from its wire.

When he was done, we lay together, listening to the sounds of traffic, the distant whistle of the mill train, and I had a sudden sense of impending loss. What if Tom were to become impatient, tire of me? What if I no longer pleased him? I was fifteen, maybe sixteen years old, and already I was wondering how I could keep this man— how I might reshape my own desire to more convincingly reflect his, become the lake he might fall into, enchanted by his own image in the mirroring surface.

Even though he may not have known the intricacies of my relationship with Tom, there is no mystery to my father's reasons for doing what he could to keep me home. It was not simply the obvious intimacy between Tom and me that alarmed my father but something perhaps even more dangerous. My father saw what I could not: Tom's intensifying possessiveness, his demands that made my father's rules seem nearly enlightened.

Tom insisted that, as the man, it was he who should determine my boundaries, and one of those boundaries was that I could go nowhere without his attendance. If I could not be with him, Tom said, then he didn't want me with anybody, and I could only see this as a manifestation of his affection: wasn't this the way I had come to know all great love, through what it asked of me, through my adherence to the giver's conditions? My father's love, just like that of the Heavenly Father, necessitated that he guide and confine my behavior; I returned that love by concession and obedience. It was, I understood, for my own good.

Yet who would I obey? If I went against my father, I was grounded, left without recourse; if I attended a high school football game or a church prayer rally without Tom, he became enraged, ranted that I was a whore, threatened to abandon me.

Increasingly, my fear of Tom's disapproval outweighed the threat of my father's censure. I could, I believed, live without paternal love, but I could never survive losing Tom. What could I say or do that would prove to him my faithfulness, my allegiance? I pledged and promised, soothed him with words, touched him with my lips and fingers. I no longer thought of sin or damnation or even pleasure but instead wondered if this would be enough to win his tolerance and favor for a while longer, make him see that I was wholly his. Sex became something other, something more than a shared journey toward physical delight; it became a coin that I could use to buy back his approval.

I believed I had given every part of myself to Tom, yet his jealousy increased, as did his policing of my attire and activities. He hectored and harassed, his anger turning more and more menacing until one night he wrapped his fingers around my throat and I thought he would kill me.

Even then, it was he who ended the relationship, left me crying and hysterical, believing that I had not given enough, or taken enough, that somehow it was my fault that he'd turned mean. If I hadn't worn that dress, talked to those other boys, if I'd stayed home like he'd asked—weren't these the things I'd been taught would save a woman?

My parents were relieved, but I felt an enormous loss, not only of Tom but of some part of myself. I had thought I would marry this boy, but now I was alone and no longer a virgin—a state that forecasted despair for any woman who hoped to win an honest man. I was "ruined"—I had heard my mother and grandmother pronounce it of other women—and I envisioned a life of sorrowful decay and abandonment.

After Tom, there were other boys I believed I might love, and so I kept myself from them, thinking that to do so would shield my secret transgression and ensure their fidelity, win from them the respect and admiration such chastity attracted. Instead of approval, what my abstinence brought me was, at first, steady imploring, then anger and scorn. Why had I agreed to go out to a movie, for dinner, if I wasn't ready to give something in return? I was a prude, a prick tease, not worth their money and time. Some part of me—that part that Tom had tended so well—believed them. It seemed that no matter which path I chose, I was doomed to rejection.

Rosemary L. Bray

b. 1955

From *Unafraid of the Dark: A Memoir*

(1998)

Rosemary Bray is the granddaughter of southern share-croppers. Her parents came north to Chicago during the Great Black Migration. Although they themselves never achieved financial security—in fact, the family was on public assistance—they knew that education was how their children would achieve it. Bray's mother taught her how to read when she was three, and her father stressed to her the importance of a diploma: "White people respect pieces of paper." She graduated from an elite private school to which she was admitted on full scholarship. The day that she left for her freshman year at Yale was a big family occasion. Everybody in the family got dressed up to go to the airport to send her off. That day was the first time that she had been in an airplane.

One of the things I learned early on was that the personal style I had cultivated in high school—iconoclastic and plainspoken, unadorned and feminist—was anathema [at Yale]. I particularly remember an argument one night at dinner, when several of the men at the black table were discussing their plan to go "road tripping" to Smith or Vassar. The Yale sisters, they agreed, weren't being very cooperative sexually, and they were feeling a bit deprived. I found their expressions of horniness pretty insulting, and said so. Several of the men and I got into a fierce argument, and the confrontation ensured my reputation as a hostile bitch. Some part of me was hurt and grieved by this, and another part of me was pleased. I'd had a taste of popularity toward the end of my high school career, and I wondered whether I could expand it. But the part of me that didn't care if people liked me was actually entertained by the idea that I was scary to some of these guys. I couldn't imagine why they thought the black women they studied with had spent years writing papers and taking exams so that they could come to Yale and provide sexual relief for men. I wanted a man to sleep with myself, but some conversation afterward would be nice, along with some basic respect. These requirements, it seemed to me, eliminated all of the undergraduates. I would have to seek out a grown man. [. . .]

Most of us had come to Yale to study law or medicine or engineering; it was important to be prepared for the revolution we were sure was imminent. Gil Scott-Heron's political music played on WYBC, the college radio station, and on the phonographs in rooms that had them, advising us all that the revolution would not be televised—it would be live. By the start of my sophomore year, however, [. . .] I doubted that I was fit for the law. A year of freedom from my parents had opened my mind to an unconsidered possibility: I might choose a career because I loved it, because it was fun. For the first time in my life, I gave a lot of thought to what I loved, and discovered that my pleasures came from arenas I had always considered frivolous before.

I joined the staff of the college radio station as a producer on the afternoon segment *Black Spectrum*. I wanted to learn about radio, and I had just discovered jazz. I helped produce the news shows, and because I was a night owl, I eventually did the midnight-to-three-a.m. jazz show. I didn't have a license, so an engineer had to be on hand, but I did play the music I had learned to love—lots of Freddie Hubbard and Herbie Hancock in those days—and took requests. At least once, I called the campus police to walk me home after my show, after an enthusiastic fan said he wanted to meet me and promised he'd be waiting for me. He wasn't there, but I wasn't prepared to risk someone's actually trying to meet me. It turned out that someone on campus was a fan of my show, but I wouldn't learn about him for some time. [. . .]

The other thing I loved was writing. Even amid all the pressures of school, it was still my great joy to sit with a notebook and sketch out short stories on lazy afternoons while I did laundry or didn't feel up to more studying. I was already taking English courses, but they were reading courses in the classics of English literature; they were not about the nuts and bolts of storytelling. In the second semester of my sophomore year, I took a class jointly sponsored by the English and Afro-American studies departments, taught by the writer and poet Larry Neal. He was an active and invigorating teacher who assigned us such exercises as retelling a Greek myth in contemporary terms. As I worked on assignments for his class, I could feel a sense of contentment in me that I never felt when doing anything else. By the time the class was over, I had decided to change my major to English. I would follow my first love; I would see whether there might be a way to make a living as a writer.

Even among my peers at school, this was not a well-received choice. By this time, Yale was entering what was popularly known as the era of grim professionalism, the wholehearted pursuit of a lucrative career in a traditional field. Black students were even more captured by this attitude. It was too hard to get into Yale, too hard to stay there, too expensive for our families, not to commit to a career that would pay back some of the enormous investment we had all made. So when I announced one night that I was thinking about abandoning my choice of the law for the more creative arena of writing, I was met with a goodly amount of scorn. One of my classmates went so far as to say that black America needed serious leaders with serious skills. He said I was as bad as the handful of our black classmates who wanted to sing or dance or make movies or act. "The last thing we need," he said, "is more singing and dancing black people."

Some part of me agreed with him: I recalled a moment in high school when one of the black students was performing at Morning Exercise, his bass voice filling the room. It was beautiful to hear him, but it was difficult, too, to watch the delight on the faces of white people. I was always so suspicious of their happiness as they enjoyed an expected spectacle—someone black doing what he was supposed to be doing. I sometimes felt that way when I saw black members of the football team. But I also knew that people couldn't help what their talents were, no matter how white people might seek to make that talent a prison. I knew that I had been writing most of my life.

And I wasn't convinced that the white world was so comfortable with creative black voices, especially literary ones.

In fact, there were several black students like me who weren't rushing off to graduate and professional schools. I knew them very well, and as I thought more about what I wanted to do with my life, I found myself spending more and more time with them. In many ways, we were all pretty eccentric. We liked all the music our friends listened to, but we also liked classical music and Broadway show tunes and jazz. We frequented the Yale Repertory Theater as well as the local movie houses, and we even auditioned for plays put on at the Yale Dramat.

Some of these students were writers in training, like myself. Others were budding filmmakers and still others were actors. My friend Austin was the glue that held us all together. Attractive and urbane, Austin possessed a wicked sense of humor and a horror of the ordinary. Austin and I had met the first week of school, standing in line at the president's reception, and had been running buddies ever since. He had directed plays in dining hall productions at Timothy Dwight and Calhoun, including a version of Lorraine Hansberry's *To Be Young, Gifted and Black*. I was a member of that cast, and the play did so well that we performed it off campus for a short run at the end of sophomore year. The experience had helped to give me the bug—not necessarily to perform, but to create in some way.

Because Austin's great love was the stage, we were always trying to write something that would get us out of school and make us rich and famous. At the same time, there was a part of me that agreed deeply with the need for black professional people with a serious commitment to the future of black America. Once again, I felt at odds, and went home that summer with the idea of persuading my parents to let me take a year off to think it over. It didn't help that Yale was getting more expensive by the year, and the amount of my scholarship was decreasing exponentially. I figured that a semester or two off would let me think things through while I made some money.

Later that week, the Afro-American Cultural Center (known to all of us as the House) was giving its last party of the year. I went to say good-bye to people, find out about their summer plans, and get my mind off studying for finals. As I walked into the Enormous Room, a Stevie Wonder album was playing, and amid the dim red lights I could make out the figures of many of the folks. Some people were dancing, some were drinking, others were chatting in the halls, or were in the next room shooting pool. I started wandering toward the punch bowl when a man's voice asked, "Would you like to dance?"

The voice belonged to a guy named Bob McNatt. I'd seen him before; he was part of the artistic group I hung around with. But he rarely came to parties, so I was surprised to see him here. He was tall and dark and quiet; he held a lit cigarette between his fingers and kept it with him as we started to dance. We danced and talked about exams. I told him I was looking for a summer job and thinking about taking a semester off. Bob was hoping to put together a junior year abroad; he wanted to study at the London School of Economics.

"I thought you liked the theater," I said over the music.

"I do. But I'm an economics major. Besides, it would give me a chance to go to Europe."

We danced together the rest of that night, talking about acting and writing. When I told him I was thinking about being a writer, he said that was a good thing. And when I mentioned that a lot of people thought it was a waste of talent for the black community, Bob scoffed.

"That's nuts. Black people need art and music and good books, too. Besides, if you don't try writing, how will you ever know if you're any good at it?"

We ended up walking home together, since his college and mine were right across the street from each other. At one point, he asked me if I was the woman he sometimes heard on the radio late at night. I said I was, flattered that he recognized my voice. "Well, you have a great voice," he said simply. We wished each other a good summer, and I especially wished him well in London. His encouraging words about writing stayed with me on the trip home to Chicago. What a shame, I thought. I meet a nice guy, and he ends up going to London for a year. [. . .]

At the start of our junior year, it was Austin's idea to form a theater group with several of the other creative outcasts among us. We wanted to perform plays written by black authors as well as put on productions of other popular works with a multiracial cast—something that rarely happened on campus. We agreed to meet and talk it over at a dinner meeting in Silliman College, the dorm across the street from mine.

By the time our group had hashed out its fantasies, we had become a black repertory company called Shadowbox. We divided into two sections. One was to put on a stage version of *Casablanca*, written and directed by Austin. The other group would do a production of James Baldwin's *The Amen Corner*, directed by a sophomore from Chicago named Charles Jones. Charles was a member of the wrestling team, a serious opera fan, and a student of Russian. I had not decided which group I would work with, but for the time being, I agreed to be the company photographer, recording for posterity all the cast members of our productions.

Among the people who joined the group was Bob, the young man who'd been on his way to London the last time I saw him. It turned out that the London School of Economics was not as thrilled to meet him as he'd hoped, so he'd returned to Yale. But the quiet, gentle person I remembered from that night seemed to have disappeared. In his place was an arrogant and opinionated man who grated on my nerves in the worst way. I think it was because Bob was impossibly blunt in his opinions. If he didn't like an idea, it stank. If he thought someone didn't understand something, he or she was dumb. I thought he often acted like an intolerant snob, and I often told him so. He didn't know what to make of my not-so-gentle critiques of his style, and there were times when we would snipe at each other all through the meetings.

One evening I arrived at Silliman for an early-dinner meeting of the Shadowbox group and took a seat at our usual table, where Bob already was. To make conversation, I noted that I hadn't seen him around that weekend. He told me he'd gone home to see his parents, since it was his birthday.

"You should have said something to us," I chided him. "We could have taken you out for a drink, or gotten you a cake."

"Oh, I didn't think it mattered," he said carelessly.

I felt a funny little pull at the nonchalance in his voice. Of course it mattered, I thought to myself; he's one of us. For the first time, it occurred to me that Bob might be lonely. Whenever I saw him, I saw him alone. He'd gone home, I guessed, because he didn't want to be by himself on his birthday. I'd always thought he preferred his self-induced solitude. But now I found myself wondering about that, and resolved to be a little kinder to him.

Later that week, I was working on cast photographs for *Casablanca* in the common room at Calhoun. The drapes were open and I could see students passing as I worked. Bob was walking by—alone as always—and I waved to get his attention. He caught the wild motion of my hands as I beckoned to him to drop in. He ambled in, his knapsack on his shoulder, and asked me how things were going.

"I'm probably going to have to stop for the night; I'm nearly out of film," I told him, positioning one of the cast members against the wall.

"If you want, I could get some for you," he said, giving me a smile that made his face look quite handsome.

I thought that was pretty nice of him, and took him up on the offer. When he returned with three rolls of Tri-X and my change, something mischievous in me made me reach up for his face with one hand and pull him down for a gentle kiss on the cheek. The two of us were mildly surprised, and I went back to work, wondering what was up with me. I didn't ever do things like kiss guys on the cheek. Besides, I was sure Bob had a girlfriend. I'd noticed his frequent trips home, and the picture of a woman he kept in his wallet—"someone I know from high school," he'd once said. The fact that he didn't give more details made me suspect he was involved with her.

Bob stayed on my mind a lot, enough for me to transfer my dinner meals to Silliman several nights a week and sit at the round table with several of our friends, wondering if I might see him. He had a habit of placing his green canvas knapsack on a table near the serving line; it was how I knew whether he had already come to dinner before I arrived. If the knapsack was there, I scanned the room for his profile and to see whether there was an empty seat near him. If there was, I'd wander over with my own books and say hello. He would always smile and say hi, as I surveyed his tray to see how close he was to finishing dinner. He was almost always with people I knew, so it didn't feel especially strange to ask the general question, "Are you all going to be here awhile?" And almost always, the answer was, "Sure, go get your food."

So I would get dinner and pick at it while I listened to Bob excoriate Nixon as a liar and a traitor to his country (his resignation had occurred only a few months earlier) or talk about a recent play he'd seen on Broadway during one of his visits home, or a concert he'd been to. He seemed to know something about nearly every topic; he always had an opinion he was willing to defend. When I interjected a thought of my own, he listened to me seriously, even if he disagreed. What I had earlier considered arrogance in him, I now viewed as a passionate, often impatient, self-assurance.

By now it was clear to everyone what was happening—clear to everyone but me, that is. I persisted in the belief that Bob was just so much more interesting than the other guys my age. It was a pleasure to talk with him, that's all. If I never ate dinner in TD anymore; if I asked about Bob's whereabouts at the check-in desk so often that Mary, the middle-aged Irish woman who worked there, had taken to giving me status reports as I entered; if I tried out for a part in *The Amen Corner* (Bob had agreed to be assistant director) rather than work with my friend Austin on *Casablanca* as I had planned— well, it was just because he was so funny and pleasant.

I became the production manager of *The Amen Corner*, after losing the lead to a senior named Allyn, an incredibly beautiful woman with a singing voice like an angel's and an equally wonderful body. Her physical attributes didn't go unnoticed by Charles, the play's director. He offered me a secondary part, which I turned down, but promised that I would work on the nuts and bolts of the production itself. And so each night after dinner, I would grab my notes and walk across campus to the Cultural Center, which had provided us rehearsal space in a large open area on the second floor.

I was sitting on the floor in the House library one night after dinner, taking notes on a scene Bob was rehearsing with the main characters. I found myself watching him a lot more than I was watching the scene—the quiet, passionate way he spoke about the material, the way he moved his hands as he spoke. I liked watching his hands; they were large and graceful, with long fingers that, at that moment, were holding a cigarette, which he waved to emphasize a point. It suddenly came to me that I was feeling something very different about Bob than I thought—and the revelation plunged me into despair.

I had no way of knowing that I was even on Bob's radar. I wanted to pursue him, pursue the feelings I had, but I was too afraid to say or do much of anything. My feminist sensibilities were appalled; I knew I should just say something to him about my feelings and take the consequences. But the rest of me was too insecure to be direct. Suppose he didn't like me? Suppose he laughed at me? Suppose he gave me that most terrible of all speeches: "I think you're a very nice person, but . . ." The best thing to do, I decided, was to live with the feelings and say nothing while I considered what to do.

But once I had realized that I was attracted to Bob, it became harder and harder to act nonchalant. We all had a habit, after each rehearsal, of walking back together and stopping at Durfee Sweet Shop for a snack. Now I searched for ways to delay my departures with the rest of the cast, maneuvering so that Bob and I would end up walking a little behind the others, taking stock of the evening's work and trying to figure out what might be left to do. It didn't take more than a few evenings for this to become a kind of ritual for us. Even after I'd run out of excuses to lag behind, Bob and I walked each night along High Street alone, toward Old Campus, talking sometimes about the play, sometimes about school or our families. I realized during our nightly talks that we were becoming friends.

One evening at the House, rehearsals were especially tense. A rivalry for the affections of the lead actress in *The Amen Corner* had been brewing for a while between the director and the male lead. Finally, as Charles rehearsed the scene, a fight broke out between him and Pierre, and Bob had to break it up. I had never seen Bob angry before—neither had anyone else—but it was an episode to remember. He delivered a blistering speech on the collective responsibility of actors in a small production, excoriated everyone involved for their immaturity, and dismissed rehearsals for the night. We were all so shocked to hear Bob raise his voice that everyone scurried to disappear. But when he looked at me, he said only, "You almost ready to go?"

As we walked back along the darkness of High Street, the only sounds I could hear were our footsteps and the distant clacking of typewriters from open dormitory windows as students worked late into the evening. Finally, Bob spoke—he wanted to know if I thought he'd gone too far. I demurred, on the grounds that I was just the production manager and it didn't matter what I thought.

But Bob disagreed. "It matters to me what you think," he said. "If it didn't, I wouldn't have asked you."

The blood came to my face in a rush of pleasure. It just so happened that I thought he'd been quite right to read everyone the riot act, and I told him so. "Actually, you probably should have done it a while ago," I said.

"I know," Bob told me. "But I was hoping things would work themselves out. Now, we probably won't even have a play."

"Oh, that's not true," I said, in a rush to reassure him. "They know they were wrong. And it's not like you to jump up and start throwing fits every night. Everything will be fine by tomorrow."

"You think?" he asked, and I could tell he was worried about it.

"I really do. It'll be all right."

It was, too. The next night, Charles and Pierre apologized to the cast and crew, and rehearsals went on a lot more smoothly. Later that week, while Charles and I were meeting before dinner about production details, I decided to tell him about my new crush. He didn't seem all that surprised.

"Do you want me to find out what he thinks about you?" Charles said.

I was panicked that Charles would do something horrible and embarrass me for life. So I cautioned him to be as subtle as possible in his inquiry. I wanted to know for sure who that girl in the picture was. And I thought it would be nice to know whether Bob had ever considered thinking about me "that way."

Meanwhile, I was gathering up my courage to ask him out on a date. I had noticed in *The Yale Daily News* that an off-campus movie theater was showing one of Bob's favorite movies, *Love and Anarchy*, directed by Lina Wertmuller, along with Bertolucci's *The Conformist*. I had made up my mind to suggest our going together as soon as I heard from Charles that Bob was a free man. I got my answer in a few days.

"He likes you," Charles announced to me one night before dinner in the Silliman common room.

"What do you mean, he likes me?" I asked, with growing horror.

"I mean he likes you. He told me so himself," he said with great pride.

"How did he come to tell you that?"

"I asked him," said Charles. "It seemed like the best way."

I let out a scream that caused heads to turn, then lowered my voice to hiss at Charles. "You told him? How could you tell him? How I can ever look him in the face again!" I was absolutely mortified. But Charles was unsympathetic. He herded me toward the check-in desk, where I absentmindedly said hello to Mary. She smiled back and said in a confidential whisper, "He's here already!"

I moaned in despair while Charles laughed. "Rosemary, stop worrying. It's not like it's a big secret or anything."

"Why, did you tell everybody else, too?"

"No, we all knew anyway. You're always coming here for dinner; you hang on to everything he says. It was impossible not to know. I'm telling you it's all right."

I could have died. But I couldn't leave now; I didn't have a good enough excuse. So I decided to get a grip on myself long enough to make it through dinner. There was, for once, no rehearsal that night, so I could go back to my room and cry for a couple of hours.

There was a seat right next to Bob, saved for me by my thoughtful friends and meant to complete my humiliation, no doubt. Bob was in the middle of talking to someone else when I sat down, but he turned to me and gave me his usual quiet smile. Perhaps it wouldn't be so awful to be near him if he wasn't going to treat me like a lovestruck fool. In a few minutes, he turned to me again and asked me about my day. I made some mindless comment about it being uneventful, and tried to keep my eyes on my plate. At the other end of the table, someone had started discussing what movies were in town the next few days, and I found myself blurting out, "*Love and Anarchy* is playing at the Lincoln."

Bob said, "Well, I guess we'd better go see it, then."

I'm sure I looked completely stupid as I asked him, "What did you say?"

The smile Bob gave me that time was not quiet at all, but very sweet and knowing. He said, "I said, I guess we'd better go and see it, don't you think?"

I smiled back at him. "Yes, I think we should."

I've always intended to rent those two movies so that I could actually see them; all I remember about that night was sitting next to Bob in the darkened theater, conscious of his arm draped casually across the back of my chair. Later, as we walked home in the fall

New Haven drizzle, he put his arm around my shoulder to steady my steps over a puddle—and left it there. When we got to my back gate, he kissed the top of my head and said good night, then ambled toward his own room.

I didn't know what to think. I'd prepared myself for the usual wrestling match at the door. Part of the fallout from the movement toward sexual liberation was that women often had to justify why they weren't having sex with a man who'd asked. But Bob didn't even ask, and that threw me. I didn't know if he'd had a terrible time. I didn't know if he'd want to go out again.

We saw each other a lot, in fact. There was still the play to work on, and the same group of us still met for meals and went to parties at the House. But more and more, he and I spent time together alone. One night, he climbed with me to the roof of Silliman College, through a skylight in the ceiling of one of its towers. It was a brilliant night, and Bob was showing off his knowledge of astronomy by pointing out all the constellations he could see amid the hazy lights of campus and downtown. No matter what we did or where we went, our time together ended the same way. We'd talk, we'd laugh, we'd have a wonderful time—then he'd say good night and leave. It was beginning to make me worry: was there something wrong with me? After a few weeks of this, I made a decision to come right out and ask him. I knew him well enough by now to know that he would tell me the truth. And no matter what he said to me, he wouldn't be mean or hurt my feelings.

He'd come over one afternoon to pick up a book I'd promised to let him read, and for once he was planning to have dinner at TD with me. Standing in my living room, I asked him pointblank. "You've never once tried to sleep with me. Is it because I'm not attractive?"

Bob looked a little surprised that I'd just blurted out my question, but mostly he looked thoughtful. After a pause he said, "It's not that at all. I guess I'm still not over my old girlfriend. And I guess I didn't want to start sleeping with you until all of me was with you, not just my body. You understand what I mean?"

I had never heard a man say anything like that in my life. I said I understood completely and left it at that. What I understood most was that I was irrevocably in love. Another young woman might have found this revelation exhilarating, even a cause for celebration.

But I had always imagined myself alone; no, I had promised myself that I would stay alone. Men were for convenient sex; involvement was something to shun like the plague. I was so frightened by this overwhelming rush of feeling that I was thrown into a major depression in the days that followed. I did a minimal amount of schoolwork to keep myself from falling behind in my classes, and I put on a reasonable façade in front of others, even Bob. But I cried myself to sleep each night. In my heart, I was terrified.

Thanksgiving was coming up, and I couldn't afford to go home before Christmas. So I would be having Thanksgiving dinner in the Commons with the other students too poor or too alienated to see their families. Bob explained to me that he had to go home, but that he would be back to see me as soon as he could. I chafed a bit at his not asking me to come home with him, but how could he do that without making it look as though I were his girlfriend? Part of my annoyance stemmed from the fact that I didn't know what I was to Bob. I guessed he would just drift along with me until he recovered from his last heartbreak, but he gave me no clue as to how long that would be.

The upshot of my lonely weekend was that I had worked myself into a fine state of hurt and rage by the time Bob returned to campus Saturday afternoon. We went to the movies, but I met his conversational overtures with terse answers or stony silence. Finally, he'd had enough. On the walk back home, he asked me what was wrong, which only infuriated me more. What was he, blind? He asked again, and I exploded with all the hurt feelings and loneliness of the past week and a half. Bob looked more baffled than upset, and when I had finished, he walked me upstairs to my room.

"I didn't think you would be upset; you told me you would be here for Thanksgiving, and I told you I'd be back as soon as I could. And I'm here," he said gently.

"Well, I didn't think it was going to bother me as much as it did," I confessed. "It was lonely without you here."

"But I'm here now," he reminded me, and finally got around to kissing me for real.

We were lovers by the time school was back in session. I felt completely transformed, sure that everyone could tell I was in love by gazing at my radiant countenance. I was happy, confident, filled with all kinds of energy. On the nights when I did not see Bob, I sat with my friends in TD, listening to their agonies and triumphs with a kinder ear, joining in without defensiveness as I talked about my writing classes. On the nights when I did see him, we were together the way we had always been—not pawing each other in public, since it was not our way—but being silly together, with lots of teasing and very bad jokes. [. . .] For the first time in my life, I considered the notion of happily-ever-after as something other than a misogynist plot.

Daisy Hernández

b. 1975

From *A Cup of Water under My Bed: A Memoir*

(2014)

Daughter of a Cuban father and a Colombian mother, Daisy Hernández grew up in suburban Union City, New Jersey. Her father was a factory worker and her mother sewed at home for pay. Her aunts (*tías*) were an important part of her family's life. For Daisy, college was a turning point in her understanding of herself and her sexuality.

The women in my family do not talk to me about sex, and women's magazines do not mention poverty or race. My mother and tías tell me that men either work for you or they do not. Romance happens between seven and nine in the evening on Spanish soap operas. Sex comes later.

But at the library, I read the truth about multiple orgasms in *Cosmo*. I rely on a library copy of Judy Blume's novel *Forever* to tell me I can have sex with a boy and not marry him. Something can happen between a broken hymen and baby showers. College and a career, of course, but mostly it will be a lot of sex. My best friend and I spend our teenage summers reading Judith Krantz novels and watching porn videos from her father's collection. We see that women can have sex in swimming pools and hotel rooms and even on a spaceship. They can do it with different men and with each other. I observe this, analyze it, and come to my final conclusion: sex is good.

By the time I watch women have sex with each other on my

friend's nineteen-inch TV set, I have already heard about women like them.

I am ten years old and sitting at the kitchen table when a friend of my mother's tells her and the tías the latest *chisme* [gossip]: a woman they all know from the neighborhood has left her husband and children to be with another woman. Gasps make their way around the kitchen table where *café con leche* is being served.

"Can you believe it?"

"She's that way?"

"I never would have thought it!"

Everyone is shocked that a woman was so moved by love that it flung her into the arms of another woman. I, for one, find it terribly romantic. It's like a Harlequin romance novel but without the stoic, rich guy, or like *Romeo and Juliet* but without the suicides. Two women in love confirms for me that there is a love that can push you beyond what everyone else says is possible.

I am also not sure why the women in my family are so startled about a woman going off with another *mujer*. Besides discussing how Colombian men don't work, all we ever do at home is talk about women.

There are two types of women in this world. The telenovela one is a fair-skin lovely who works as a maid, suffers public humiliations, and marries her well-to-do man in the last episode. Then, there is Iris Chacón.

On Saturdays, my family gathers to watch a variety show on Spanish-language television, where Iris Chacón is all sequined thong and big brown ass, and salsa is a side note. She is a curve of glitter on the screen, an exaggeration turned into art of what it means to be a woman, and we are very much in love with her. Or at least, my father and I are.

My mother and tías talk endlessly about Iris Chacón.

"Look at her *tetas!*"

"*Qué grandes, no?*"

"And her backside!"

"*Cómo lo mueve!*"

They discuss other dancers and performers, debating who has silicone implants and fake behinds. I stare at the screen, wondering how real Iris Chacón is.

"She might as well wear nothing!" my mother declares, as if to chastise us for looking. My father and I nod but keep our eyes on the screen, grateful that the reception is good on the old television set.

After a year of dating, I am very much in love with Julio, his old white Camaro with its black doors, and the tender way he kisses me. He takes me down the shore at night when the world is flooded with stars and the sound of crashing waves, and life feels so much bigger than what I ever imagined. I am seventeen and in love.

I am also beginning to resent my mother and tías for finding any fault in a man who takes me to the movies, the mall, and up-scale versions of McDonald's, like Houlihans. The more they raise their dark eyebrows and ask if Julio ever plans to attend college and amount to anything more than a fast-food job, the more I call him and tell him I will love him forever.

Sex is a different matter.

Growing up in a small town where love easily means nine months of *gordura* [fatness] and no high school graduation, I am determined not to become a teenage mother. I tell Julio that sex between us shall happen after my high school graduation, when I am on my way to college with a four-year scholarship.

I then go about sex like the overachiever from a workingclass home I truly am. First, I start taking the pill. Then, I drag Julio to the local clinic to be tested for HIV. There, I carefully read the pamphlets on STDs and abortions. I pepper the counselor with questions. I check the expiration dates on the condoms and examine the rubbers for visible signs of tears. Finally, I am ready.

Sex with a man is like what I have read in books and *Glamour*. There is suspense and need, an aching and much throbbing. There is *el* spot, and when Julio touches it, I understand immediately that this is the reason women cheat on their men, risk their corporate jobs, and abandon their children. And that Judy Blume was right, too. Something else could happen.

By the time I start wearing a fake gold chain that proclaims "Julio [heart] Daisy 2-14-91," my mother and aunties refuse to speak to him. It only makes me want him more. At nineteen, I move in with him, setting up our home in a basement apartment while commuting to college and working two part-time jobs. I love Julio against all odds, but mostly against the wishes of my mother and tías.

When we break up a year later, Julio says my mother was right. He feared what she desired: that I would leave him for the guy with more money and a better car. Guilt-ridden, I tell him he's wrong. The other guy understands me better. He's also in college and a writer.

But Julio is right. The other guy does have a better car. He didn't emigrate from Colombia and he has the money to attend college. He's not Italian, but his grandmother is.

How did I end up heeding my mother's warnings? Were the romance novels wrong? Does love follow the lines of race and class?

To the degree that I am disturbed, my mother and tías are delighted. Finally, I am listening to them. I am in college, living back home, working part-time at a newspaper and dating a gringo.

The sign in the student center at William Paterson College reads "Workshop on Sexuality for Women * Hosted by the Feminist Collective."

I would like to say now that the afternoon, which changed my life, was cinematic. But it wasn't. One night, I was in the arms of my new boyfriend; the next afternoon, I was sitting in a carpeted room with other college girls, giggling, fully clothed, drawing portraits of our vulvas.

The facilitator, a woman from Planned Parenthood, is genuinely cheerful and unfazed by our work. "That's it everyone! You're doing great!" she calls out. "Fanny, that's beautiful! I love the colors. Keep going! We've got crayons for everyone! Don't be shy."

I glance up and down the table. All the women are drawing vulvas in startling shapes and colors and spending time on the size and details of their clitorises. So engrossed in staring, I almost don't hear the Latina sitting next to me when she starts talking.

Fanny is the president of the Feminist Collective and she's encouraging me to attend the group's weekly lunch meetings. I nod politely, but I'm too preoccupied with the portrait of another woman's vulva, which looks like strawberries that have been plucked, washed, and pried opened.

Fanny introduces me to the white woman sitting next to her, saying, "This is my girlfriend."

Maybe it's the rich colors of all those vulvas in one room or the slow and purposeful way she says "girlfriend," but I understand her immediately. And as I nod at Girlfriend, I think, "I have never met one." A lesbian.

Lesbians happen on television like Iris Chacón. They belong to another country. The idea of actually kissing a girl has never occurred to me. As Fanny and Girlfriend peck each other ever so lightly on the lips, I feel so embarrassed and enthralled that I frantically look around for a place to put my eyes. Finding nothing, I stare down at the crayon drawings of their vulvas.

What is wrong with me? *Qué me pasa?* Why had it never occurred to me? A girl. I love kissing boys, but a girl. I could kiss a girl. The facilitator passes by, murmuring, "Daisy, why don't you add some colors, open it up."

I look down and it's there for the whole world to see: my vulva. I have drawn a small brown mound, a little hill speckled with black ants for curls.

Not sure of where to meet a girl I can kiss, I head for the weekly meetings of the Feminist Collective. I dress in what I think are my best plaid shirts, but instead of meeting a girl, I find myself immersed in women's rights. We talk about sexual abuse, organize our school's Take Back the Night, and analyze the importance of lube. The women's studies professor gives us impromptu talks about the fluidity of gender identity and desire, and it is all I can do to sit still next to the girl who looks like a boy.

It is the mid-nineties and multicultural everything is in. I have the books, the teachers, and the new friends to teach me that being queer is about as normal as me being a Latina at a predominantly white college. Sure, Latinas and queers are outnumbered, but now the laws are on our side, and we have a small but visible community.

The more I listen to Fanny talk about her life with a woman, the more comfortable I also feel. She knows about Audre Lorde and *arroz con frijoles*, and she throws a Spanish word into the conversation every now and then. She is close enough to remind me of home, the equivalent of my mother and aunties in one woman, with the lesbian and feminist added.

The worst part about trying to date women is that I don't have my mother's warnings. There is no indicator if I am doing it right or wrong. And so, my queer friends and the spoken-word artists in New York are my teachers, and they know the formula.

Sleep with your friend, sleep with her friend.

Break up and get back together again.

Write her a poem, show her the piers, pretend you want less than you do.

One-night stands, one-night nothing.

You'll see her at Henrietta's again and again.

My friend is Dominican, and she reminds me of Iris Chacón. When we make love, I can't tell what's more exciting: her large, naked breasts against my own B-cup-sized ones or the inversion afterwards of gender roles. I am now the one buying dinner, picking up the flowers, driving us upstate. Every time she mixes Spanish and English in the same sentence, a part of myself collapses into what I am sure is eternal love.

Within months, however, the relationship sours. So, I try dating another friend. She e-mails that she isn't interested.

I go out with a Puerto Rican butch, who drinks about as many Coronas as my father. My mother and aunties would be horrified. I am too, after two months.

I meet another Dominican femme, but this one drives an SUV, has her hair straightened once a week, and keeps a butch lover in the Bronx. After three times in bed, I get tired of being on top.

Dating a transgender man, I get tired of being on the bottom.

I go back to what I know and try dating a Colombian woman. But she lives across the Hudson River and doesn't have a phone with long distance.

I persevere though—drinking flat Diet Coke at lesbian bars and giving women my phone number—because I do not believe my mother. I have read the romance novels, seen the movies, and heard the songs. Love will work no matter what job I have, what nationality I claim, or what street I want to live on. It will work even if I kiss a woman.

And it does.

For a few months, I fall in love with a dark-haired woman who has a way of tilting her bony hip that gives her ownership of the room. Men hit on Lisette and she snaps, "I don't think my girlfriend would appreciate that." She is the most feminine woman I have dated (hours are spent dabbing eyeshadow in multiple directions), but also the most masculine. She carries my bags, buys me overpriced jeans, leans in to kiss me. She talks to me about the films she will make one day and the books I will write. She follows me into the dressing room at Express and whispers that she wants to go down on me right there. "I like it when you scream," she tells me in bed. "I need you to do it like this morning. Scratch my back when I'm fucking you."

I had heard those lines before from men and from women, but it's different this time. I am sure I will never date anyone else ever again.

When she breaks up with me (yes, by e-mail), I don't know if I am crying over her or because I can't talk about it with Mami and Tía Chuchi and Tía Dora and Tía Rosa, the first women I loved. Instead, I tell them it is the rigors of graduate school that now make me sob in my mother's arms in the middle of a Tuesday afternoon.

After another night of crying about lost love, I call my mother into my bedroom. Unsure of where to begin, I choose the logical. "Mami," I begin in Spanish, "it's been a long time since I've had a boyfriend."

She nods and gives me a small smile.

I look at the pink wall of the bedroom I have in my parent's home, the writing awards, the Ani DiFranco CDs, the books. *"Estoy saliendo con mujeres."* I'm dating women.

Her mouth opens, but no sound comes out. She covers her heart with her right hand in a pose similar to the one of the Virgin Mary that hangs over the bed she shares with my father.

"Mami, are you ok?"

"Ay, Dios mío."

When she doesn't say anything else, I fill the silence between us with a concise history of the LGBT, feminist, and civil right movements, which combined have opened the door to higher education, better laws, and supportive communities of what would be otherwise marginalized people. "It's because of how hard you worked to put me through school that I am fortunate enough to be so happy and make such good decisions for myself."

By this time, my mother is hyperventilating and fanning herself with her other hand. She stammers, "I've never heard of this. This doesn't happen in Colombia."

"You haven't been in Colombia in twenty-seven years."

"But I never saw anything like this there."

In the days that follow, Tía Chuchi accuses me of trying to kill my mother.

We're on the phone. She's at Tía Dora's apartment. As if it's not enough that I am murdering my mother, Tía Chuchi adds with grim self-satisfaction: "It's not going to work, *sabes?* You need a man for the equipment."

For this, I am ready. I am not being sassy. I really do believe she doesn't know and that I can inform her. "Tía, you can buy the equipment."

She breaks out into a Hail Mary and hangs up the phone.

My mother develops a minor depression and a vague but persistent headache. She is not well, the tías snap at me.

"Don't say anything to her!" barks Tía Dora over the phone. "The way this woman has suffered I will never know."

But she wants me to know.

Tía Dora stops talking to me. She throws away a gift from me because she can see that the present (a book on indigenous religions in Mexico) is my way of trying to convert her to loving women. Tía Chuchi begins walking into the other room when I arrive home. Tía Rosa alludes to the vicious rumors the other two aunties have started about me. "It's terrible," she says, and then: *"Siéntate, siéntate. I made you buñuelos just the way you like. Are you hungry?"*

Tía Rosa still complains about the back pains from the accident of years before, but she is living in her own apartment again. In her sixties now, she is a short, robust woman with thick eyeglasses and hair the color of black ash. Her husband is long gone, and since the bed is half empty, Tía Rosa has covered the mattress with prayer cards. Every night, she lies down on that blanket made of white faces, gold crosses, and pink-rose lips.

That my romantic choices could upset my mother and tías had been a given since high school. A lot can be said about a woman who dates the wrong man. But dating the same sex or dating both sexes has no explanation.

My mother now is hurt. More than anything, she is bruised, and she wonders what she did wrong. "This isn't what we expected," she says quietly one day as we walk toward Bergenline Avenue to catch the bus.

I keep thinking that if only I could tell my mother how it works with women, she would understand. The problem is I don't know.

The closest I have to an explanation is a Frida Kahlo painting titled *The Two Fridas*, where the artist is sitting next to her twin who holds her heart, an artery, and a pair of scissors. That is how I feel about loving women. They can dig into you and hold the insides of you, all bloodied and smelly, in their hands. They know you like that. But this is nothing I can say to my mother.

I miss the conversations now. More than anything, I long for the days when I came home to report that Julio had given me flowers or promised to take me to Wildwood. We have, my family and me, including my father (who demanded to know if Julio was gay the whole time), settled into a region called "Don't Ask, Don't Tell." And it is hard, I imagine, for people who have not experienced this to understand the weight of that silence and how the absence of language can feel like a death.

Often when my mother tells me about those early days in her relationship with my father, she mentions the *postres*.

"He would bring pastries from the bakery," she recalls, smiling and then adding with a warning, "That's how they get you."

Kristina does it with *dulce de leche*.

Our first date is a month after September 11. The city is struggling to be normal. The subways are running and the *New York Times* is publishing its "Portraits of Grief." Kristina and I eat burritos on Christopher Street and walk to the piers. In the summers, brown butches and black divas light up the area, their bodies pretzeled around their loves and friends and strangers, but tonight the piers are empty, muted, *solitos*. With the bone skeleton of lower Manhattan near us and Jersey's lights across the river, Kristina and I kiss for the first time.

She's mixed: white, Chicana, Californian, New Mexican. She reminds me of the women in my family, the shape of their bodies, *ni gorda ni flaca*. It's how quick she lights up when I say, "I've got *chisme*," and the way she talks to her mother on the phone and then laughs and says to me: "I'm on hold. [Astrologer] Walter Mercado's on."

This is our routine: I take a bus from Jersey, then switch to the 1 train. She meets me at the stop near her apartment in the Bronx. We make love. Afterwards, Kristina rolls over on her side and asks, "You want some ice cream?"

She dresses and crosses the street to the deli for small cups of *dulce de leche*. I eat the cold caramel on her sofa, my head on her shoulder, crying into the *helado*, because Halle Berry has won the Oscar.

My mother would like Kristina. She would probably like her more than she likes me. Kristina believes in diplomacy. Like my mother, she doesn't see why I need to write about sexuality. She values privacy. My mother would appreciate that.

When Kristina and I break up, almost five years after we first ate *dulce de leche* together, I call Tía Chuchi to deliver the news. "We've ended," I say in Spanish. "For good this time."

I don't know what to expect from my auntie, but I'm figuring she will say something along the lines of good riddance. Instead, she exclaims, "That's why you're taking the martial arts class!"

"What?"

"That's why you're taking martial arts. I knew this woman who rented a room once from a lady and it turned out the lady was, *tú sabes*, gay." The lesbian had terrible fights with her partner. "It was horrible," my auntie recalls, as if she had been in the room when the arguments exploded. "They threw pots and pans at each other and fought with their fists." Tía sighs. "It's good you're taking the martial arts classes to defend yourself."

I start laughing and crying, because my ex-girlfriend couldn't face a kitchen mouse let alone strike another woman, because I loved her so much and walked away, because I glimpse in my tía's words some deeper emotion, some love that struggles to be steady even when it hurts.

commentary for chapter eight: INTIMACY

Sex and intimacy are famously difficult subjects for writers to tackle, even when writing about their own lives. Describe it too closely and a writer can sound lurid and voyeuristic; too distantly, and he sounds chilly or mechanical.

In these brave and unflinching passages, three women from working-class families tell how their early experiences with sex and, sometimes, romance brought not just passion but a sublime sense of freedom over their own bodies and fates. In the cases of Kim Barnes and Daisy Hernández, sex also meant liberation from their stifling or uncomprehending families. But love in these accounts also carries dangers—of heartbreak, or of exposing some of our deepest insecurities.

Daughter of a lumberjack-turned-truck driver, Barnes is fifteen or sixteen when she falls hard for a boy she meets at church. Both are determined to stay virgins until marriage, but they soon yield to an intense mutual attraction. Taking care not to let their romance be known to Barnes's disapproving father, they meet in cars, an alley, and Tom's bedroom. Their relationship sours after Tom rents a small apartment for trysts. Barnes is disgusted by the squalid room and its dirty mattress, and sex, once "a shared journey toward physical delight," becomes instead an instrument by which she must prove her commitment to the increasingly possessive Tom. He finally breaks off the relationship, leaving a terrible legacy. For years afterward, Barnes writes, she has trouble with intimacy. Men expected sex and she did not want to give it, drawing the same scorn she had faced from Tom.

Hernández also writes about sex as a window into the soul and our deepest desires, in her poignant and funny account of discovering her bisexuality as a college student. Her immigrant family, so proud of her as their first to go to college, reacts with shock and then, by the end of the account, a grudging acceptance of her lesbian relationships. Hernández's account reminds us that early sexual foibles can seem comical in retrospect but, for the teenagers living them, can feel deathly serious and consequential. Breakups leave her sobbing. She describes the mantle of silence that came over her family after she declared her sexuality, how "the weight of that silence and how the absence of language can feel like a death."

When Barnes and Rosemary Bray were young, the sexual revolution of the 1960s was still quite recent (or, in the case of Barnes's rural community, still hadn't completely arrived). The birth control pill, modern feminism, and women working outside the home were new realities that the older generation had not fully accepted. Bray alludes to these new, shifting mores when she writes that part of "the fallout from the movement toward sexual liberation was that women often had to justify why they weren't having sex with a man who'd asked." New ideas about sex have brought expectations of their own, she suggests. In her case, however, her boyfriend Bob turns the tables on her by not asking for sex until they were surer of their commitment to each other. Traditional gender roles grow even murkier later when Bray writes that, until she met Bob, she viewed men as objects "for convenient sex; involvement was something akin to the plague."

Her moving account of falling in love suggests that gender roles are not as fixed as either the older generation's values or feminist ideals might claim; rather, they are created daily in our interactions with our romantic partners. Like religious faith in Barnes's account and sexual orientation in Hernández's, gender roles and sexual attraction are fluid and constantly evolving. They defy rigid categorization.

QUESTIONS FOR DISCUSSION

1. By the end of Kim Barnes's relationship with Tom, what has she learned about herself? Did she derive anything beneficial from that relationship and if so, what?

2. Both Daisy Hernández and Kim Barnes are keenly aware of the attitudes of their parents and other relatives toward their ro-

chapter nine
CLASS CONSCIOUSNESS

Roxanne Dunbar-Ortiz
b. 1939

From *Red Dirt: Growing Up Okie*
(1997)

The daughter of a truck driver and an alcoholic mother, Roxanne Dunbar graduated first in her class from high school. She worked at a bank before starting college at the University of Oklahoma. There she met her future husband, Jimmy, an engineering student, whose father was an executive in a construction company. At college she and Jimmy had in common a love for the Beats and for the jazz they heard together at a smoky coffeehouse. They also shared physical handicaps: hers were asthma and migraine headaches, his was a gimpy leg from rheumatoid arthritis. Roxanne dropped out of college to marry Jimmy.

Despite fantasies of becoming a movie or sports star and get-rich-quick schemes, the two most successful means of class-climbing for poor whites, like other poor groups, is marrying up and out and/or education. Marrying up and out is probably more possible for women than men, and is certainly something my mother preached to my sister and me. Indeed, marriage was my way out of my class and into the middle class. It was during those six years of marriage and that transformation that I slowly comprehended the class question.

I was eighteen and Jimmy was nineteen when we married. Jimmy had grown up on the family estate outside Oklahoma City. The house, which his father had built himself, was to me a fantasy world, the kind of place I could only imagine from reading Jane Austen novels—a rambling five-bedroom, two-bath, native-stone mansion with a stone fireplace, thick carpets, fine antiques, chandeliers, and cut-glass crystal and bone china displayed in mahogany "breakfronts," as they called the glass-front display cabinets. The place was surrounded by a stream and woods and gardens. At the end of a long stone path was a huge stone patio and barbecue pit. Unlike in a Victorian novel, there were even two working oil wells on the property.

As Jimmy showed me around the first time he took me to meet his family, he was suddenly a stranger to me. I could not even comprehend growing up like he had; and, of course, he could not even imagine how I'd grown up. The land had been homesteaded by his mother's Scots-Irish family who farmed it. When his mother married his father, who was descended from Dutch Protestants, they lived there, then inherited the land. They were simple farming people, potentially poor whites, but during the Depression and World War II the construction company Jimmy's father worked for grew huge and rich off government contracts, and he climbed from journeyman carpenter to chief superintendent. After the war he sold some of the land to the state to build the Tulsa Turnpike, invested in real estate, then built the new house. Jimmy grew up rich. The only blight on his and the family's perfect world was that his mother—he called her "an angel"—had died. I suppressed a tiny warning signal that I now interpret as the fear that I was repeating what my mother had done marrying up and never being able to be as "good" as the mother/matriarch; because she was dead, Jimmy's mother shone all the brighter, her angelic and righteous presence never absent. She was the model I was supposed to imitate.

Jimmy's father fit my image of a patriarch or an English country gentleman out of one of my favorite novels at the time, Galsworthy's *The Forsyte Saga*—a man of property. He wore a fine cashmere overcoat and a fur cap. I had never seen anyone with a fur cap. He greeted me by shaking my hand, a gesture I had never before experienced—shaking hands was not something we did in Piedmont [Oklahoma].

A strange thought passed through my mind as I walked down the aisle holding my father's arm. It occurred to me that my father may have had my new father-in-law for a boss when he worked for the

WPA during the thirties. The thought made me feel like a traitor and haunted me during the marriage.

At my wedding, if Daddy had asked me, "Do you really want to go through with this?" maybe I would have said, "No, Daddy, oh no, please save me from this fate." I knew I was not getting married for anything but protection and class-climbing. But Daddy did not ask and instead of taking me away, he gave me away. Years later he would tell me that indeed he came close to objecting.

One reason I married Jimmy was so I could continue at the university. His father offered to pay our tuition and provide a free place for us to live and a car. Yet within a week after the wedding Jimmy announced that he wanted us to be self-supporting and persuaded me to work.

"You support me until I graduate, then I'll support you to go back to school. It's only three years," he argued, adding the clincher: "My sisters think you might be a gold-digger just looking for a free ride off the family, but if you work they would know that's not true."

What Jimmy's older sisters thought of me mattered a great deal, to him and to me. I agreed to work. So began the pattern that would doom our marriage. With a huge sense of humiliation, after having left to make something better of myself, I returned to the bank to beg for a job. [...]

Within the bank, as in all corporations, a class system existed among the workers. Below management, the tellers were at the top of the pyramid in status, although their pay was very little more than those at the bottom. Now back at the bank I realized that Central Files had been second in status after the tellers; next came Bookkeeping, and at the very bottom was the Proof department. I had fallen into a hole from which there was no escape.

Many evenings I worked until seven or eight and even up to midnight a few times. We stayed until we balanced the deposits and withdrawals of over a hundred small banks around the state that used our bank as a clearinghouse. There were no buses to the family place where we lived, so Jimmy drove the ten miles to downtown Oklahoma City to pick me up after work. By the time I cooked dinner and we ate, it was bedtime. The morning started at five so I could be at work by seven, an hour early. Jimmy dropped me off and drove to Norman for his eight o'clock class. On Fridays when the bank was open until six we rarely balanced before midnight. Instead of paying us overtime when we worked late, the supervisor gave us the afternoon off.

Already thin, I lost weight and fell below a hundred pounds. Migraines plagued me. I suffered agonizing menstrual cramps. Asthma struck rarely, but colds and flu wracked my body. Boils erupted all over my body and bladder infections flared, yet I never missed a day of work. One day an operator about my age next to me screamed, jumped up and began pounding her machine. She threw checks in the air laughing hysterically. Two male supervisors took her away, kicking and screaming. The next day at lunch the other operators said that she had been committed, that she'd had a nervous breakdown and would receive shock treatments.

Reading Marx some years later, I had a pretty visceral reaction to his term "alienated labor."

Very early I had signed up with an employment agency to find another job, but there were no jobs in the midst of the economic "recession," as Eisenhower called it. After nearly a year of that work routine I was fired one Friday in June after lunch.

As usual, a half-dozen of us women operators sat together in the cafeteria, eating and griping about having to work late without overtime, griping about speed-ups and our low pay, some of them complaining about the bosses making passes.

"We need a union," I said.

My co-workers abruptly left the table. I walked back into the huge noisy workroom and my supervisor beckoned me to his desk. He pantomimed cutting his head off and pointed to me. I felt dizzy.

"What?" I yelled.

He wrote on a notepad and held it up: "Do not pass Go. Collect your final paycheck in Personnel."

During the following two scorching summer months I pounded the sidewalks looking for a job. The recession was lifting and more jobs were advertised, but I didn't get any of them. On several occasions, I was practically hired and given a starting date only to receive a call telling me someone more qualified had been hired or that they'd decided they didn't need anyone.

One day I received that kind of call from the Oklahoma Natural Gas Company where I had applied. Then the secretary said, "By the way, are you related to Hank Dunbar?"

"My brother."

"Yes, well, in that case Mr. Sands, the personnel director, would like to see you," she said.

The downtown office of the gas company's personnel manager was chock-full of gold and silver baseball trophies on mahogany pedestals—the gas company had one of the best semi-pro baseball teams in the region.

"Hi, I'm Sam Sands. Besides being in charge of personnel I'm the coach of our ball club."

"I've watched your team play. My brother used to pitch for the Stockyards team last summer," I said.

"Yeah, missy, I know all about Hank Dunbar. What an athlete. I said to myself, no sister of Hank Dunbar could be a bad egg, least of all a communist."

"A communist?" I giggled nervously.

Mr. Sands slid a sheet of paper across his desk toward me, watching my face closely. I picked it up and saw my name at the top.

Troublemaker; union organizer; agitator; Urban League member; subscribes to *The New Republic*; father-in-law long-term union and integration advocate.

"What is this, where did this come from?" I thought he was joking for some unfathomable reason.

"Sister, that there's a blacklist and you be on it," he said.

"But how, why?" I thought I must be in the middle of a nightmare.

"Don't worry. I plan on hiring you-all. Like I said, no sister of Hank Dunbar could be like that there. But listen up, if you even breathe union, or make any trouble, you walk that day. Got the message?"

"Yes sir," I said. As I started to fold the paper to take with me, he grabbed it, winking.

Mr. Sands placed me in the Oklahoma Natural Gas Company's service center, which was in an industrial park on the northeast edge of Oklahoma City, only three miles from where we lived. No overtime, nice working conditions—even free coffee and lunch—but still at minimum wage and no medical benefits. [. . .]

There were only eight of us white-collar employees in the huge plant and only one other woman in my department, an older woman who was the personal secretary of the plant manager. But some three hundred men worked in the meter repair shop, and the meter readers and gas line repairmen, the troubleshooters and installers, all men, worked out of there. The plant had its own radio tower and a dispatcher to choreograph service.

My job was to assist the meter records clerk. I noted on familiar three-by-five index cards the placement and removal of gas meters and the model and capacity of the meters. (To this day, I notice every gas meter wherever I am, registering whether it is an ironclad or aluminum and what capacity; despite high-tech transformation during the past four decades, gas meters have remained the same, a fact that always gives me some comfort.)

The job was so easy that it crossed my mind that Mr. Sands had made up the job to bail me out of being blacklisted because he admired my brother.

The best part about working at the gas plant was that two of our Arab acquaintances from Oklahoma University were interning there as petroleum engineers. Every day I had lunch with Rafic, a Jordanian, and Nouri from Syria, and they told me the latest news from the Middle East. It was the time of the Suez crisis and they admired Nasser. Before I came to work, they said, their only friends at the plant had been Howard, Lorenzo and Red, the three black employees, an elderly man and his two nephews who cleaned and made coffee and lunch. So they became my friends as well. At Christmas when the company gave each employee a ten-pound cured ham for a bonus, Rafic and Nouri, who couldn't eat pork because they were Muslims, gave theirs to our black friends, so I did, too. And Saïd, our Palestinian friend, visited every weekend.

The meter records clerk, my supervisor, was a fanatic Nazarene who'd grown up in Bethany, west of Oklahoma City, an evangelical-founded town with a Bible college. Next to my Church of Christ grandmother, Neal was the most self-righteous person I'd met in my life. He "suggested" that I not wear tights under my skirt because "the men will wonder how far up they go."

I ignored his "suggestion." He preached to me all day and cautioned me not to fraternize with the black and Arab employees: "Some people might get the wrong idea."

Each day Neal greeted me with a new racist joke. I told him I liked Senator John Kennedy and hoped he would run for president. Neal was outraged and railed about the "Papists" and communists taking over America.

I always brought a novel with me to read on my breaks. Neal said that reading fiction was sinful and was horrified when I brought *Lolita* and *Lady Chatterley's Lover* on purpose to rile him.

But I never mentioned the word "union." [. . .]

Life was much easier with my new job and growing confidence that I successfully had escaped my class fate and was fully accepted into my new family.

Jimmy and I lived in the three-room garage apartment—near the "big house"—which had once been the servants' quarters; now they hired day laborers and housekeepers to maintain the house and the grounds. I idolized Jimmy's family and adopted them as my own, especially his sister Helen, who lived with her husband in a cottage they had built nearby. She called me "a diamond in the rough." I accepted the role and submitted to being polished. Helen said I was from good peasant stock like Tolstoy's characters and embodied the nobility of the peasantry, enriched by being part Indian. I shivered with pleasure when she told me these things.

The whole family opposed racism and segregation. Despite his wealth and being a boss, Jimmy's father was a trade union advocate, and thought, as ridiculous as it sounds to me now, that the ignorance of poor white people, my kind of people, was responsible for racism. Even before the Supreme Court decision on school segregation, he'd fought for integration, not very successfully in the Carpenters' Union, and as a superintendent on projects that hired black laborers and hod carriers. He invited his construction workers and their families, including the blacks, to his famous barbecues. I imagined that my new father-in-law was like my Wobbly grandfather, although when I asked him once what he thought of the Wobblies he said they had been anarchists and crazy and un-American.

Everyone in the family read *Time* and *The New Republic*, and knew all about what was happening in the world. I soaked up everything they said, and I read and read. [. . .]

I read everything I could find about being alienated—Ralph Ellison's *Invisible Man*, Camus' *The Stranger* and *The Plague*, Kafka's *The Metamorphosis*, *The Castle* and *The Trial*, Kerouac's *The Subterraneans*. I identified with J.D. Salinger's alienated characters in "A Perfect Day for Bananafish," *The Catcher in the Rye* and especially *Franny and Zooey*. I read Dostoyevsky's *Crime and Punishment* and *The Idiot* for the first time. I realized that I had been the *idiot* in my family, that the Family itself, not just *my* family, was at the root of the problem.

I began to observe Jimmy's family more critically.

Some symptoms I suffered ever since my family fell apart grew far worse after I got married. For no apparent reason I would be overcome by a blinding white rage. I could see and hear and control my movements, and it seemed that I chose to scream or to run and hide or to kick a chair or slam a door. Yet I couldn't prevent or stop it. The fits would last from a few minutes to hours. Inside the fit I felt terror and sometimes a strange euphoria, a feeling of safety. The first time it happened with Jimmy, before we married, I thought he would leave me but he wrote me a page-long note saying I was too good for the evil world around me, that I had a pure mind and soul, that I was perfect except for that tiny flaw in my personality that came from my inferior background, and that it was his destiny and mission in life to protect and care for me.

On other occasions, Jimmy would shake me awake, saying I was grinding my teeth. Once he recorded it for me to hear. The sound was loud and eerie. Insomnia plagued me. I was afraid to go to sleep, not knowing what I would do. During those times I had blinding, disabling migraine headaches and nausea.

The more I read the more my fits and migraines diminished in number and intensity. It was then that I realized that self-knowledge and education are curatives, and it was then I believe that I determined to become a teacher one day. I tried to talk to Jimmy about what I was learning, but he was lost in differential equations and strength of materials. Our mental worlds diverged. He was relieved that I was better but he thought all my problems were caused by a bad family life and could be cured with a good family, his family. Helen gave me books to read that made me understand the madness of the world around me. A book called *The Nature of the Non-Western World* explained colonialism. *The Great Fear in Latin America* by John Gerassi, a former *Time* reporter who had been fired for writing it, was a tract against U.S. imperialism. Helen's favorite books, which became mine, too, were Rachael Carson's *The Sea Around Us*, and Vance Packard's *The Hidden Persuaders*, which showed how unbridled capitalist development was poisoning our food and water, and how advertising manipulated people. [. . .]

I followed the news of the United Nations closely, as reported on television by Pauline Fredericks, who became my new role model. That fall, day after day, heads of newly independent states of Africa arrived at UN headquarters to take their seats as equals among nations. The sight was more thrilling than seeing Elvis Presley four years before. I had new heroes and dreams. [. . .]

I began to wonder about the price I had to pay for my new status when one really hot summer Saturday afternoon Jimmy and I with his sister and her husband went to drink beer in a joint we hadn't been to before, attracted by the air-conditioning sign. The barmaid turned out to be Darla. I hadn't seen or talked to her for nearly two years.

"Darla, what are you doing here? How are you and the kids?" I asked. I was surprised by my own joy in seeing her.

Darla wore a tight-fitting red sundress. Her bosom, which I knew to be false, protruded seductively. She looked different, not so much older but somehow hard, her skin rough. Yet she remained strikingly beautiful with her mane of thick black hair and her smoky skin. Darla hesitated and I thought she didn't remember me. I followed her eyes—she was studying my companions.

"Fancy seeing you here. How are you, stranger?" she said, a teasing tone in her voice. Then I realized she was shocked because she had known me as a devout teetotaling Baptist. She looked amused and approving.

"I got married. Darla, this is Jimmy, and his sister and brother-in-law," I said.

Jimmy looked up at her sideways and said, "Howdy do." Suddenly I was aware that Jimmy did not approve of Darla. He glared at me as if I were a stranger, or a traitor.

When Darla returned to serve us, she handed me a slip of paper with her phone number on it. "Give me a call. I'm off now." She left with a man who had been sitting at the bar.

"You got some outstanding old friends, Roxie," Jimmy said, not with a smile.

"She's from my hometown. I used to babysit for her, you remember me telling you about her." There was apology in my voice, and shame.

Later, when we were alone, Jimmy said, "You're not going to call that woman, are you?"

"I thought I might. Why not?"

"She's a prostitute."

"She's my friend."

"Not any more. You associate with lowlife like that and you will become like them," he said.

I said nothing and never called Darla and never saw her again.

Other warning signals alerted me to the class chasm between Jimmy and his family and me—for instance, on that trip to Colorado to meet [his] Uncle Bob. All along the highways were broken-down cars and pickups with women and children and old people sitting in the shade while a man worked under the hood. They beckoned for us to stop and help. Jimmy passed them by.

"Why don't we stop?" I asked. No one in my family would ever have passed up a stranded motorist, but then we never strayed far from home.

"They're hustlers, rob you blind, highway bandits," Jimmy said.

"How do you know?"

"I just know. They use the kids and old people for bait to get you to stop, then rob you. They're transients, fruit pickers, white trash."

I stared at the sad faces as we passed by and tried to see the con artists and criminals behind the masks. But they merely looked familiar, like my own relatives. Yet we got plenty of help on the highway. Practically everything that could go wrong with a car plagued ours—the radiator burst, the voltage regulator busted, the carburetor spewed gas, even the ignition wire broke, and we had flat tires on several occasions. Each time we broke down, always in the middle of nowhere, someone stopped to help us or gave Jimmy a ride to the next station.

"How come they don't think we're highway robbers?" I asked. The people who stopped to help us were invariably driving old cars or pickups and looked a lot like the people who tried to get us to stop. New cars whizzed on by.

"They can tell," Jimmy said. As Ken Kesey, himself an Okie, notes: "It isn't a new car that pulls over to help you when you are broke down with the senile carburetor; it is somebody who knows what it is to be broke down with a hurt machine."

Then one autumn day in the third year of my marriage I was home sick with the flu and found myself the only person on the grounds. I had never been alone there before. The place was so serene and lovely, the oak leaves bright yellow, a maple tree flaming red, the blackjacks burnished copper. The huge lawn that sloped down to the creek was still a carpet of green thanks to the sprinkler system. I sat down on the stone bench in the patio that was halfway between the creek and the big house. Even though I was only thirty-five miles from where I grew up it was so different, rolling hills with trees rather than flat and barren, no cannibalized old cars and junk around.

"How lucky I am," I said aloud and felt like yelling it since no one would hear. I could never have dreamed of being a part of that kind of life three years before. Jimmy's family had taken me in as one of their own. Forever and ever I would be safe and secure and loved. I loved my sisters-in-law and father-in-law as if they were my own flesh. I would never be poor or want for anything again. I tingled with happiness, tears of joy streaming down my face.

The sound of a car startled me out of my reverie. The mail carrier: he always brought everyone's mail to the big house and put it on the back porch where we could each fish out our own. I strolled up the hill to check. I pulled out a manila envelope, exactly like many others I had received, from the White Citizens' Council. Inside was a pamphlet dated 1958, which began:

> We are proud of our white blood and our white heritage of 6 centuries. If we are bigoted, prejudiced, un-American, etc., so were George Washington, Thomas Jefferson, Abraham Lincoln, and other illustrious forebears who believed in segregation. We chose the old path of our founding fathers and refuse to appease anyone even the internationalists.

I tore the pamphlet in half and rifled through the rest of the mail. There was a letter to Helen from the sister who had moved to California. The envelope was barely sealed, just at the tip. I stuck my little finger under the flap and it popped open. I slipped the letter out of the envelope and unfolded the two pages. My eyes fell on the middle of the first page and the words hit me like a blast of icy wind:

> I think you are right that it remains to be seen if Roxie will drag Jimmy down to her level or if he can pull her to his. Coming from her background she may be beyond rescue. I wish Jimmy would leave her.

I had to sit down to keep from falling. I could not believe what I was reading, and that there had been other letters and conversations, letters about me ruining Jimmy. The letter was almost entirely about me, mostly a discussion of the condition of "white trash," whether it was genetic or social, and the "complication" that I was part Indian. I read the letter a second time, telling myself they were concerned about me because they loved me and wanted to help me. But it wasn't there, only concern for Jimmy and the wish that I would disappear or had never appeared. The letter ended by saying that Jimmy had met me at a vulnerable time in his life just after their mother's death, and I, being a gold-digger and devious, had entrapped him for a quick marriage.

I felt like running, packing a suitcase and leaving without a word. I would not be able to tell Jimmy because he would know I'd opened the letter. I vowed to remain quiet. [. . . But finally] I acknowledged that my destiny would not be with Jimmy. I would have to find my way alone somehow, someday, without family or protection.

Howard Zinn

1922–2010

From *You Can't Be Neutral on a Moving Train: A Personal History of Our Times*
(1994)

Howard Zinn's parents met as immigrant factory workers, his father from Austria, his mother from Russia. Howard was the oldest of four boys in a Brooklyn household where cockroaches were ubiquitous, employment was precarious, and it was "always a battle to pay the bills." But the marriage between his parents was passionate, and his mother was "ingenious at making sure there was enough food."

My father, looking to escape the factory, became a waiter, mostly at weddings, sometimes in restaurants, and a member of Local 2 of the Waiters Union. While the union tightly controlled its membership, on New Year's Eve, when there was a need for extra waiters, the sons of the members, called juniors, would work alongside their fathers, and I did too.

I hated every moment of it: the ill-fitting waiter's tuxedo, borrowed from my father, on my lanky body, the sleeves absurdly short (my father was five-foot-five and at sixteen I was a six-footer); the way the bosses treated the waiters, who were fed chicken wings just before they marched out to serve roast beef and filet mignon to the guests; everybody in their fancy dress, wearing silly hats, singing "Auld Lang Syne" as the New Year began and me standing there in my waiter's costume, watching my father, his face strained, clear his tables, feeling no joy at the coming of the New Year. [. . .]

His name was Eddie. He was always physically affectionate to his four boys, and loved to laugh. He had a strong face, a muscular body, and flat feet (due, it was said, to long years as a waiter, but who could be sure?), and his waiter friends called him "Charlie Chaplin" because he walked with his feet splayed out—he claimed he could balance the trays better that way.

In the Depression years the weddings fell off, there was little work, and he got tired of hanging around the union hall, playing cards, waiting for a job. So he became at different times a window cleaner, a pushcart peddler, a street salesman of neckties, a W.P.A. worker in Central Park. As a window cleaner, his supporting belt broke one day and he fell off the ladder onto the concrete steps of a subway entrance. I was perhaps twelve and I remember him being brought, bleeding, into our little flat. He had hurt himself badly. My mother would not let him clean windows again.

All his life he worked hard for very little. I've always resented the smug statements of politicians, media commentators, corporate executives who talked of how, in America, if you worked hard you would become rich. The meaning of that was if you were poor it was because you hadn't worked hard enough. I knew this was a lie, about my father and millions of others, men and women who worked harder than anyone, harder than financiers and politicians, harder than *anybody* if you accept that when you work at an unpleasant job that makes it very hard work indeed. [...]

From the age of fourteen I had after-school and summer jobs, delivering clothes for a dry cleaner, working as a caddy on a golf course in Queens. I also helped out in a succession of candy stores my parents bought in a desperate attempt to make enough money so my father could quit being a waiter. The stores all failed, but my three younger brothers and I had lots of milkshakes and ice cream and candy while they existed.

I remember the last of those candy store situations, and it was typical. The six of us lived above the store in a four-room flat in a dirty old five-story tenement on Bushwick Avenue in Brooklyn. The street was always full of life, especially in spring and summer when everyone seemed to be outside—old folks sitting on chairs, mothers holding their babies, teenagers playing ball, the older guys "throwing the bull," fooling with girls. [...]

The Civil War in Spain, just ended with victory for the Fascist general Franco, seemed the event closest to all of us because several thousand American radicals—Communists, socialists, anarchists—had crossed the Atlantic to fight with the democratic government of Spain. A young fellow who played street football with us—short and thin, the fastest runner in the neighborhood—disappeared. Months later the word came to us: Jerry has gone to Spain to fight against Franco.

There on Bushwick Avenue, among the basketball players and street talkers, were some young Communists, a few years older than me. They had jobs, but after work and on weekends they distributed Marxist literature in the neighborhood and talked politics into the night with whoever was interested.

I was interested. I was reading about what was happening in the world. I argued with the Communist guys. Especially about the Russian invasion of Finland. They insisted it was necessary for the Soviet Union to protect itself against future attack, but to me it was a brutal act of aggression against a tiny country, and none of their carefully worked out justifications persuaded me.

Still, I agreed with them on lots of things. They were ferociously antifascist, indignant as I was about the contrasts of wealth and poverty in America. I admired them—they seemed to know so much about politics, economics, what was happening everywhere in the world. And they were courageous—I had seen them defy the local policeman, who tried to stop them from distributing literature on the street and to break up their knots of discussion. And besides; they were regular guys, good athletes.

One summer day they asked me if I wanted to go with them to "a demonstration" in Times Square that evening. I had never been to such a thing. I made some excuse to my parents, and a little bunch of us took the subway to Times Square.

When we arrived it was just a typical evening in Times Square—the streets crowded, the lights glittering. "Where's the demonstration?" I asked my friend Leon. He was tall, blond, the ideal "Aryan" type, but the son of German Communists who were also nature worshippers and part of a little colony of health-conscious German socialists out in the New Jersey countryside.

"Wait," he said. "Ten o'clock." We continued to stroll.

As the clock on the Times tower struck ten, the scene changed. In the midst of the crowd, banners were unfurled, and people, perhaps a thousand or more, formed into lines carrying banners and signs and chanting slogans about peace and justice and a dozen other causes of the day. It was exciting. And nonthreatening. All these people were keeping to the sidewalks, not blocking traffic, walking in orderly, nonviolent lines through Times Square. My friend and I were walking behind two women carrying a banner, and he said, "Let's relieve them." So we each took an end of the banner. I felt a bit like Charlie Chaplin in *Modern Times*, when he casually picks up a red signal flag and suddenly finds a thousand people marching behind him with raised fists.

We heard the sound of sirens and I thought there must be a fire somewhere, an accident of some kind. But then I heard screams and saw hundreds of policemen, mounted on horses and on foot, charging into the lines of marchers, smashing people with their clubs.

I was astonished, bewildered. This was America, a country where, whatever its faults, people could speak, write, assemble, demonstrate without fear. It was in the Constitution, the Bill of Rights. We were a *democracy*.

As I absorbed this, as my thoughts raced, all in a few seconds, I was spun around by a very large man, who seized my shoulder and hit me very hard. I only saw him as a blur. I didn't know if it was a club or a fist or a blackjack, but I was knocked unconscious.

I awoke in a doorway perhaps a half-hour later. I had no sense of how much time had elapsed, but it was an eerie scene I woke up to. There was no demonstration going on, no policemen in sight. My friend Leon was gone, and Times Square was filled with its usual Saturday night crowd—all as if nothing had happened, as if it were all a dream. But I knew it wasn't a dream; there was a painful lump on the side of my head.

More important, there was a very painful thought in my head: those young Communists on the block were right! The state and its police were not neutral referees in a society of contending interests. They were on the side of the rich and powerful. Free speech? Try it and the police will be there with their horses, their clubs, their guns to stop you.

From that moment on, I was no longer a liberal, a believer in the self-correcting character of American democracy. I was a radical, believing that something fundamental was wrong in this country—not just the existence of poverty amidst great wealth, not just the horrible treatment of black people, but something rotten at the root. The situation required not just a new president or new laws, but an uprooting of the old order, the introduction of a new kind of society—cooperative, peaceful, egalitarian.

Perhaps I am exaggerating the importance of that one experience. But I think not. I have come to believe that our lives can be turned in a different direction, our minds adopt a different way of thinking, because of some significant though small event. That belief can be frightening or exhilarating, depending on whether you just contemplate the event or *do* something with it. [. . .]

When I was eighteen, unemployed and my family desperate for help, I took a much-publicized Civil Service examination for a job in the Brooklyn Navy Yard. Thirty thousand young men (women applicants were unthinkable) took the exam, competing for a few hundred jobs. It was 1940, and New Deal programs had relieved but not ended the Depression. When the results were announced, four hundred of the applicants had gotten a score of 100 percent on the exam and would get jobs. I was one of them.

For me and my family it was a triumph. My salary would be $14.40 for a forty-hour week. I could give the family $10 a week and have the rest for lunch and spending money.

It was also an introduction into the world of heavy industry. I was to be an apprentice shipfitter for the next three years. I would work out on "the ways," a vast inclined surface at the edge of the harbor on which a battleship, the USS *Iowa*, was to be built. (Many years later, in the 1980s, I was called to be a witness at the Staten Island trial of pacifists who had demonstrated against the placement of nuclear weapons on a battleship docked there—the USS *Iowa*.)

I had no idea of the dimensions of a battleship. Stood on end, it would have been almost as tall as the Empire State Building. The keel had just been laid, and our job—thousands of us—was to put together the steel body and inner framework of the ship. It was hard, dirty, malodorous work. The smell caused by cutting galvanized steel with an acetylene torch is indescribable—only years later did we learn that the zinc released in such burning also causes cancer.

In the winter, icy blasts blew from the sea, and we wore thick gloves and helmets, and got occasional relief around the little fires used by the riveters. They heated their rivets in these fires until the rivets were glowing globules which they then pulled from the fire and pounded into the steel plates of the hull with huge hammers driven by compressed air. The sound was deafening.

In the summer, we sweated under our overalls and in our steel-tipped boots, and swallowed salt pills to prevent heat exhaustion. We did a lot of crawling around inside the tiny steel compartments of the "inner bottom," where smells and sounds were magnified a hundred times. We measured and hammered, and cut and welded, using the service of "burners" and "chippers."

No women workers. The skilled jobs were held by white men, who were organized in A. F. of L. craft unions known to be inhospitable to blacks. The few blacks in the shipyard had the toughest, most physically demanding jobs, like riveting.

What made the job bearable was the steady pay and the accompanying dignity of being a workingman, bringing home money like my father. There was also the pride that we were doing something for the war effort. But most important for me was that I found a small group of friends, fellow apprentices—some of them shipfitters like myself, others shipwrights, machinists, pipefitters, sheet-metal workers—who were young radicals, determined to do something to change the world. No less.

We were excluded from the craft unions of the skilled workers, so we decided to organize the apprentices into a union, an association. We would act together to improve our working conditions, raise our pay, and create a camaraderie during and after working hours to add some fun to our workaday lives.

This we did, successfully, with three hundred young workers, and for me it was an introduction to actual participation in a labor movement. We were organizing a union and doing what working people had done through the centuries, creating little spaces of culture and friendship to make up for the dreariness of the work itself. [...]

When I became a second lieutenant in the Army Air Corps I got a taste of what life was like for the privileged classes—for now I had better clothes, better food, more money, higher status than I had in civilian life.

After the war, with a few hundred dollars in mustering-out money, and my uniform and medals packed away, I rejoined Roz.

We were a young, happy married couple. But we could find no other place to live but a rat-infested basement apartment in Bedford-Stuyvesant ("rat-infested" is not a figure of speech—there was that day I walked into the bathroom and saw a large rat scurry up the water pipe back into the ceiling).

I was back in the working class, but needing a job. I tried going back to the Brooklyn Navy Yard, but it was hateful work with none of the compensating features of that earlier time. I worked as a waiter, as a ditch-digger, as a brewery worker, and collected unemployment insurance in between jobs. (I can understand very well the feeling of veterans of the Vietnam War, who were *important* when soldiers, coming back home with no jobs, no prospects, and without the glow that surrounded the veterans of World War II—a diminishing of their selves.) In the meantime, our daughter, Myla, was born.

At the age of twenty-seven, with a second child on the way, I began college as a freshman at New York University, under the G.I. Bill of Rights. That gave me four years of free college education and $120 a month, so that with Roz working part-time, with Myla and Jeff in nursery, with me working a night shift after school, we could survive.

Whenever I hear that the government *must not* get involved in helping people, that this must be left to "private enterprise," I think of the G.I. Bill and its marvelous nonbureaucratic efficiency. There are certain necessities—housing, medical care, education—about which private enterprise gives not a hoot (supplying these to the poor is not profitable, and private enterprise won't act without *profit*).

Starting college coincided with a change in our lives: moving out of our miserable basement rooms into a low-income housing project in downtown Manhattan, on the East River. Four rooms, utilities included in the rent, no rats, no cockroaches, a few trees and a playground downstairs, a park along the river. We were happy.

While going to N.Y.U. and Columbia I worked the four-to-twelve shift in the basement of a Manhattan warehouse, loading heavy cartons of clothing onto trailer trucks which would carry them to cities all over the country.

We were an odd crew, we warehouse loaders—a black man, a Honduran immigrant, two men somewhat retarded mentally, another veteran of the war (married, with children, he sold his blood to supplement his small pay check). With us for a while was a young man named Jeff Lawson whose father was John Howard Lawson, a Hollywood writer, one of the Hollywood Ten. There was another young fellow, a Columbia College student who was named after his grandfather, the socialist labor leader Daniel DeLeon. (I encountered him many years later; he was in a bad way mentally, and then I got word that he had laid down under his car in the garage and breathed in enough carbon monoxide to kill himself.)

We were all members of the union (District 65), which had a reputation of being "left-wing." But we, the truck-loaders, were more left than the union, which seemed hesitant to interfere with the loading operation of this warehouse.

We were angry about our working conditions, having to load outside on the sidewalk in bad weather with no rain or snow gear available to us. We kept asking the company for gear, with no results. One night, late, the rain began pelting down. We stopped work, said we would not continue unless we had a binding promise of rain gear.

The supervisor was beside himself. That truck had to get out that night to meet the schedule, he told us. He had no authority to promise anything. We said, "Tough shit. We're not getting drenched for the damned schedule." He got on the phone, nervously called a company executive at his home, interrupting a dinner party. He came back from the phone. "Okay, you'll get your gear." The next workday we arrived at the warehouse and found a line of shiny new raincoats and rainhats.

That was my world for the first thirty-three years of my life—the world of unemployment and bad employment, of me and my wife leaving our two- and three-year-olds in the care of others while we went to school or to work, living most of that time in cramped and unpleasant places, hesitating to call the doctor when the children were sick because we couldn't afford to pay him, finally taking the children to hospital clinics where interns could take care of them. This is the way a large part of the population lives, even in this, the richest country in the world. And when, armed with the proper degrees, I began to move out of that world, becoming a college professor, I never forgot that. I never stopped being class-conscious.

commentary for chapter nine: CLASS CONSCIOUSNESS

Every reading in this book is about socioeconomic class to some degree. In this section, two writers make class the main subject of their story as they explore how the difference between rich and poor, or poor and poorer, can become a chasm that is impossible to bridge. Class becomes an unspoken code in these stories, the source of an intangible but ever-present tension that corrodes much of human interaction.

Roxanne Dunbar-Ortiz tells the story of her first marriage, at the age of eighteen, to nineteen-year-old Jimmy, who is from a wealthy family. She anticipated that his family's money and connections could lift her out of the working class or at least pay for her college, but instead she found in them a virulent class snobbery. In its story of rural-class envy and family drama, complete with landed gentry, Dunbar-Ortiz's account recalls the Jane Austen novels she read at the time but with a tougher, meaner edge. Howard Zinn's consciousness of class and exploitation began when he was a boy, when his Jewish immigrant father put him to work with him at a fancy restaurant. Patrons dined sumptuously on filet mignon while the waiters were fed chicken wings and the country was mired in the Great Depression. His father was hard working and adaptable, toiling through the Depression years as a pushcart peddler and window cleaner but never climbed much on the economic ladder.

Despite the differences in their backgrounds—Dunbar-Ortiz lived in small-town Oklahoma, Zinn in gritty neighborhoods of New York —the two writers' views and experiences have many commonalities. They voice disillusionment with traditional liberal politics. Dunbar-Ortiz describes how her father-in-law's progressive opinions on race and labor translated into chilly condescension toward the author at family gatherings and failed to transfer at all to Jimmy, whose views toward the poor ranged from mistrust to outright contempt. In Zinn's case, the experience of seeing police charging a peaceful demonstration in Times Square and being beaten into unconsciousness set him on a lifelong path of political activism and class awareness. Much later, Zinn would develop his radical critique of American society as a best-selling writer and historian.

Both accounts suggest that class exploitation can lead to debilitating physical ailments. Dunbar-Ortiz describes a coworker's nervous breakdown and her own fits of "blinding white rage," as well as incapacitating migraines, nausea, and insomnia. Zinn describes the exhaustion and "hateful work" he was obliged to take after returning from fighting against the Nazis in the U.S. Air Force—ditch-digger, brewery worker, and, again, waiter. Their accounts can have multiple interpretations, and the maladies they describe could be caused by many factors, but they take place against a backdrop of feeling belittled or exploited for being poor.

Both writers see labor unions as one of the few avenues for workers to improve their lives. Dunbar-Ortiz is fired and blacklisted after she casually suggests to coworkers at a bank that they form a union. Taking a job at a shipyard in 1940, Zinn discovers that many of his coworkers share his readiness to organize but are excluded from the skilled-workers' guild. They form their own apprentices' union.

These accounts also point to how the realities of class can reach deeply into the family. Love takes a backseat to social ambition in Dunbar-Ortiz's union with Jimmy ("I was not getting married for anything but protection and class-climbing"), suggesting that, in her case, marriage grounded in love and affection would have to wait until later in life. In Zinn's account, one of the few reliefs from dreary jobs and unemployment is his happy marriage to Roz and the birth of their two children. Still, they are forced to turn over the toddlers to the care of others while Zinn and his wife studied or worked, showing again how, in his view, the working poor are forced to make compromises in even the most intimate areas of their lives.

QUESTIONS FOR DISCUSSION

1. We have heard the phrase "internalized sexism" to describe a tendency among women and girls to absorb and hold sexist

ideas even when they believe they are not prejudiced. "Internalized racism" and "internalized homophobia" are also well-known terms. Do you think there might be such a thing as internalized classism and, if so, do you see evidence of that in Roxanne Dunbar-Ortiz's attitudes or behavior?

2. Both narratives in this section refer to communism: Zinn in the 1930s, Dunbar-Ortiz in the 1950s. How did negative attitudes toward communism affect the two writers personally? How is Zinn's attitude toward communism nuanced?

3. Both authors refer to the discrimination faced by African Americans in the workplace and society at large. What evidence do they give for that discrimination, and how does racism interact with class divisions in these stories?

4. Both authors caused trouble at work and upset their bosses by supporting the right of workers to organize. Do their stories make you, as the reader, sympathize more with labor unions, or less, or neither?

career biographies

Maya Angelou (1928–2014), after an itinerant childhood in California, St. Louis, and rural Arkansas, was working as a dancer and theater actor when, in the 1950s, she met and became a close friend of James Baldwin and turned to writing. Encouraged by him and the Harlem Writers Guild, she wrote and published her memoir *I Know Why the Caged Bird Sings* when she was forty-one. It became a phenomenal success. She wrote six more autobiographical works as well as poetry and essays—more than thirty books in total, including the acclaimed poetry collection *And Still I Rise*. At her death, Angelou was one of the most powerful black voices in America. She helped Malcolm X set up the Organization of African American Unity and taught American studies at Wake Forest University. She won the country's highest civilian honor, the Presidential Medal of Freedom, in 2010 and read her poem "On the Pulse of Morning" at Bill Clinton's first inauguration in 1993.

Russell Baker (1925–2019) won two Pulitzer Prizes, one for his memoir *Growing Up* and one for his *New York Times* column The Observer, which was syndicated to more than one thousand newspapers across North America. After graduating from Johns Hopkins, he worked for the *Baltimore Sun*, becoming its London bureau chief, and then for the *New York Times* as a member of its Washington bureau. He was the author of six collections of essays, three memoirs, a novella, and a children's book, and editor of *Russell Baker's Book of American Humor* and *The Norton Book of Light Verse*. From 1993 to 2004 he was the host of the PBS TV series *Masterpiece Theatre*.

Kim Barnes (1958–) has written two memoirs, *In the Wilderness: Coming of Age in Unknown Country*, which was nominated for a Pulitzer Prize, and *Hungry for the World*, as well as three novels. A professor in the MFA program at the University of Idaho, she graduated from Lewis-Clark State College in Idaho and has master's degrees from Washington State University and the University of Montana. Like many memoirists, she began her writing life as a poet, but as a high-school student, she had to hide her poems from her parents. "Not because they contained anything that was dangerous, except emotion observed," she said in a 2012 radio interview. "In my family and many families, especially rural families and families that are marginalized, that is often the case. Do not speak what you feel most deeply." Her poems, essays, and reviews are widely published.

Rick Bragg (1959–) teaches in the journalism department at the University of Alabama and is author of three memoirs. He worked as a reporter for various Alabama newspapers and for the *St. Petersburg Times* in Florida before joining the staff of the *New York Times* in 1994. His feature writing there earned him a Pulitzer Prize and the Distinguished Writing Award twice from the American Society of Newspaper Editors. A former Nieman fellow in journalism at Harvard, he wrote *Somebody Told Me: The Newspaper Stories of Rick Bragg* (2000) and *I Am a Soldier Too: The Jessica Lynch Story* (2003). In 2012 he won the Last Lecture Award at the University of Alabama, the only lecture on campus whose speaker is determined solely by students.

Rosemary L. Bray [McNatt] (1955–) made a significant career change from editor and writer to minister and is now president of the Starr King School for the Ministry, a Unitarian Universalist (UU) and multireligious seminary in Berkeley, California. After graduating from Yale, she held various writing-related positions, including as an editor at *Essence* magazine and at the *New York Times Book Review*. She felt a calling as an active lay leader in her UU church and decided to attend Drew Seminary. From there she became senior minister for thirteen years at the Fourth Universalist Society in New York. In her current position as seminary head she still finds time to write book reviews and other pieces. She and Bob McNatt, whose courtship she recounts in her memoir *Unafraid of the Dark*, have been married for more than thirty years.

Mary Childers (1952–), who has a doctorate in English from the State University of New York, Buffalo, currently consults to colleges and universities, government agencies, and companies on employment practices. She provides workshops, policy reviews, grievance investigations, and mediation. She has held administrative and teaching positions at Dartmouth, Brandeis, Vanderbilt, Oberlin, and the University of Cincinnati. Using her memoir *Welfare Brat* as a departure point, she lectures widely on "climbing out of poverty and the ethics and aesthetics of life writing" and has spoken on National Public Radio, the *Diane Rehm Show*, and *PBS Newshour*.

Paul Clemens (1973–) followed up his acclaimed memoir *Made in Detroit* with a deeply researched account of the dismantling of the massive Budd Detroit Automotive Plant in his 2010 book *Punching Out: One Year in a Closing Auto Plant*. In a 2011 radio interview, he referred to the latter book as "not really a Detroit story. Detroit is the setting, but the subject is blue-collar decline." He won a Guggenheim fellowship in 2008 and, in 2011, a Whiting Writers' Award for exceptionally talented emerging writers.

Roxanne Dunbar-Ortiz (1938–), a historian, activist, and author, has a doctorate from UCLA and is professor emerita of ethnic studies at California State University. Her books include *An Indigenous People's History of the United States, Loaded: A Disarming History of the Second Amendment*, a study of American gun culture, and *Blood on the Border: A Memoir of the Contra War*, which was based on her travels in Honduras and Nicaragua. Active in the American Indian Movement, she wrote *Indians of the Americas: Human Rights and Self-Determination*. Her book *Outlaw Woman: A Memoir of the War Years, 1960–1975* drew on her experiences with left-leaning and radical organizations, including Students for a Democratic Society and the Weather Underground.

Vivian Gornick (1935–) has published eleven books, including, most recently, a collection of autobiographical essays, *The Odd Woman and the City*. She earned a BA from City College and an MA from New York University. One of her first books, *In Search of Ali Mahmoud: An American Woman in Egypt*, was nominated for a National Book Award in 1974, when she was still a reporter for the *Village Voice*. She has written books on feminism, women in science, and the art of personal narrative, as well as biographical studies of Elizabeth Cady Stanton and Emma Goldman. *The End of the Novel of Love* and *The Men in My Life* were finalists for the National Book Critics Circle Award for Criticism. She has taught nonfiction writing at institutions around the country, including the University of Iowa, the University of Arizona, and the New School in New York.

Pete Hamill (1935–), a journalist and novelist, was named one of the "400 Most Influential New Yorkers in the Past 400 Years" by the Museum of the City of New York. A winner of journalism awards for lifetime achievement, he has been editor-in-chief of both of the city's major tabloids, the *New York Post* and the *Daily News*. In his early career he was a graphic designer, having studied at Pratt Institute, and wrote a book on Diego Rivera. Closely associated with New York City, he was the subject of a *New York Times* profile called "Sunday Routine." Commenting on not seeing kids during his Sunday walks in downtown Manhattan, he said children are having "virtual childhoods, instead of childhoods." He added, "They don't play ball or hang out with the wrong people or get in fistfights, all the things that once made childhood."

E. Lynn Harris (1956–2009) wrote twelve novels, ten of which were *New York Times* best sellers; more than four million copies of his books are reported to be in print. His first book, written while he was an IBM salesman, was initially self-published, but Harris recruited an agent who sold it to Anchor Books, which published it in 1994. His books are often about successful and self-confident black men with inner conflicts about their sexuality (like Harris himself, as described in his memoir, *What Becomes of the Brokenhearted*). He graduated as a journalism major from the University of Arkansas, where he was also a cheerleader. Before his death at age fifty-four, he was a professor and writer-in-residence at the university, and also a coach of the cheerleading team.

Daisy Hernández (1975–), who has master's degrees in journalism and in creative writing, teaches in the creative writing program at Miami University in Oxford, Ohio, and has been a visiting writer at the University of North Carolina in Chapel Hill. She was a columnist for *Ms.* magazine, a reporter on the *New York Times* metro desk, and an editor of *ColorLines*, a magazine on race, culture, and politics. She is the coeditor of *Colonize This! Young Women of Color on Today's Feminism*, a collection of essays from around the globe that is used in women's studies classes. She has spoken at colleges and conferences about feminism, race, immigration, and media representations and on NPR's *All Things Considered*.

Oscar Hijuelos (1951–2013), a son of Cuban immigrants, wrote eight novels but was best known for *The Mambo Kings Play Songs of Love*, a melancholy story of musicians and loss that won the Pulitzer

Prize for fiction in 1990, the first time a novelist with roots in Latin America won it. He earned a bachelor's and a master's degree in creative writing from City University in New York. From 1977 to 1984, he worked in advertising while writing fiction at night. The *Washington Post* quoted him as saying that he wrote *Mambo Kings* "as a long poem to musicians everywhere." It was translated into thirty languages. He received grants from the National Endowment for the Arts and the Guggenheim Foundation. For the last six years of his life, he was on the faculty at Duke University.

Richard Hoffman (1949–) is senior writer-in-residence at Emerson College and the author of two memoirs, three poetry collections, and a book of short stories. His first memoir, *Half the House*, originally published in 1995, was reissued in 2005 and 2015. The second, *Love & Fury*, was a finalist for the New England Book Award from the New England Booksellers Association. His book of poetry *Gold Star Road* won the 2008 Sheila Motton Award from the New England Poetry Club. His verse and prose have appeared in *Agni, Hudson Review, Poetry, Harvard Review* and other magazines.

bell hooks (1952–) is the founder and director of the bell hooks Institute at Berea College in Berea, Kentucky. She was formerly Distinguished Professor of English at City College in New York and has taught at UCLA, Yale, and Oberlin. She has a BA from Stanford and a PhD from the University of California at Santa Cruz. Her first book *Ain't I a Woman: Black Women and Feminism*, published in 1981, was followed by *Yearning: Race, Gender, and Cultural Politics, Teaching to Transgress: Education as the Practice of Freedom*, and *Outlaw Culture: Resisting Representation*, the last two published in 1994. She has also written children's books including *Happy to Be Nappy*. Her ideas focus on interconnections among race, class, and gender and have reached a wide audience through her prolific writing, public lectures, and appearances in several documentary films.

Mary Karr (1954–) is the Peck Professor of Literature at Syracuse University and has taught at Tufts, Emerson, Harvard, and Sarah Lawrence. Her first memoir *The Liars' Club* (1995) was on numerous best-seller lists. She has since written two other memoirs—*Cherry*, about her teenage years, and *Lit*, about her alcoholic drinking and eventual recovery—and four books of poetry. Her writing has been supported by fellowships from Harvard's Radcliffe Institute, the National Endowment for the

Arts, and the Guggenheim Foundation and a Whiting Award. She was the winner of a PEN/Martha Albrand Award and was a National Book Critics Circle Award finalist.

Michael C. Keith (1948–) is associate professor of communication at Boston College, having received his PhD from the University of Rhode Island in 1988. He is the author of more than twenty books on broadcast and electronic media, including *The Radio Station*, a widely adopted text on American radio. Before becoming a full-time academic in the late 1970s, he worked as a broadcast professional for more than a decade. He was cited in the book *Blast from the Past: Radio's First 75 Years* as the teacher "who has trained more [broadcast] professionals than any other single person." Besides writing media books and academic articles, Keith has published a coming-of-age novel called *Life Is Falling Sideways* and short stories. His fiction has been nominated for a Pushcart Prize and the O. Henry Award.

Michael Patrick MacDonald (1966–) is the honors writer-in-residence at Northeastern University and its professor of the practice of writing. After winning acclaim with *All Souls: A Family Story from Southie*, he wrote *Easter Rising: A Memoir of Roots and Rebellion* (2006) which recounted his experience in Boston's punk rock movement and traveling with his mother to their Irish homeland. As an activist, he worked to establish a gun buyback program in Boston and support groups to counter violence. He lectures widely on these topics, among others: "Finding Your Voice: Helping Young People Transform Trauma into Leadership"; "Our Common Ground: Race and the Unspoken Issue of Class in America"; and "Cross-Cultural Community Building."

Bich Minh Nguyen (1974–) directs and teaches in the MFA in Writing Program at the University of San Francisco and has taught at Purdue, the University of North Carolina at Greensboro, and the University of Michigan, from which she has an MFA. She is the author of two novels, *Short Girls* and *Pioneer Girl*, coeditor of three anthologies, and contributor to periodicals, including the *New York Times*, the *Chicago Tribune*, and *Gourmet*. Her memoir *Stealing Buddha's Dinner* received the PEN/Jerard Fund Award, and *Short Girls* won an American Book Award. *People* magazine describes her work as "a poignant look at immigrants and their children finding their identity as Americans."

Joe Queenan (1950–) is the author of eleven books, mainly essay critiques of American culture. After graduating from St. John's University in 1972, he became a film reviewer and political commentator for *Spy* and *Rolling Stone*, a writer for the business journal *Barron's*, and a senior editor at *Forbes*. Since becoming a freelancer in 1990, he has contributed to *GQ*, *Time*, and the *Wall Street Journal*, among other publications, and has appeared on several TV shows such as *The Late Show with David Letterman* and *Today*. Known for his satirical critiques of American culture and personalities, he once described himself as "an acerbic, mean-spirited observer of the human condition."

Luis J. Rodriguez (1954–) was born in Texas and raised by Mexican immigrant parents in Los Angeles, the city for which he was named poet laureate. A writer across many genres, he has written two memoirs, a novel, a book of short stories, articles and essays, and a children's book, in addition to four books of poetry. After attending college and universities within the California public system, he worked as a journalist for Los Angeles newspapers. Throughout his career he has been involved in community activism and peacemaking with gangs, and his 2003 book *Hearts and Hands: Creating Community in Violent Times* draws on that experience. He founded Tía Chucha's Centro Cultural and Bookstore, a successful cultural center that promotes art and education for the Latino community. He is a winner of the PEN/West/Josephine Miles Award for Literary Excellence.

Richard Rodriguez (1944–) was born and raised in northern California and has written four autobiographical books, of which *Hunger of Memory* was the first. Others are *Days of Obligation: An Argument with My Mexican Father* (1992) and *Brown: The Last Discovery of America* (2002). The fourth, *Darling: A Spiritual Autobiography* (2013), is a collection of essays. A *Boston Globe* reviewer praised the author's "deeply humanistic voice that is politically hard to place" and called him "as ardently Catholic as he is proudly gay." Rodriguez came out after the publication of *Hunger of Memory*. He has degrees from Stanford and Columbia and a PhD from Berkeley. He was a frequent commentator on *PBS NewsHour* and won a George Foster Peabody Award for his work on that program.

Esmeralda Santiago (1948–) is a magna cum laude graduate of Harvard and has an MFA from Sarah Lawrence. She is the author of two novels: the historical *Conquistadora* (2011) and *America's*

Dream (1996). Her autobiographical trilogy begins with *When I Was Puerto Rican*, followed by *Almost a Woman* (made into a show for PBS's *Masterpiece Theatre*) and *The Turkish Lover*. The writer of two screenplays, she won the Gold Award from the Houston Interstate Film Festival in 1984. *Las Mamis: Favorite Latino Authors Remember Their Mothers* and *Latina Authors Share Their Holiday Memories* are titles of anthologies that she has coedited.

Sandra Scofield (1943–) published her first novel the year she turned forty-six and then wrote six more, one of which—*Beyond Deserving*—was a finalist for the National Book Award. In addition to *Occasions of Sin: A Memoir*, she has written on the craft of writing in *The Last Draft: The Novelist's Guide to Revision* and *The Scene Book: A Primer for the Fiction Writer*. She has also written short stories, book reviews, and scholarly articles. Her *Mysteries of Love and Grief: Reflections on a Plainswoman's Life* is a memoir and biographical portrayal of her maternal grandmother, a widow and mother of three children who worked as a farmer, a railroad cook, a millworker, and a nurse in four western states.

Kate Simon (1912–1990) graduated from Hunter College, then worked for the Book of the Month Club, *Publishers Weekly*, and publisher Alfred A. Knopf, later reviewing books for the *New Republic* and *The Nation*. Esteemed for her travel writing ("exceptionally literate and highly trustworthy," in a reviewer's words), she wrote about New York, Italy, Mexico, Paris, Rome, and London. Asked to advise travelers on how best to enjoy a trip, she suggested regular eavesdropping on conversations in cafes, and also, "Walk slowly, look, listen, smell." *Bronx Primitive* was followed by two more memoirs, *A Wider World* and *Etchings in an Hour Glass*, which was published the year of her death.

Brent Staples (1951–) has been an editor and editorial writer at the *New York Times* since 1985, as well as the author of op-eds, reviews, blog essays, and other articles at that newspaper. He graduated from Widener University in 1973 and the University of Chicago with a PhD in 1982, having received doctoral fellowships from the Danforth and Ford Foundations. He worked as a science writer at the *Chicago Sun-Times* and taught psychology at colleges in Pennsylvania and Chicago. A prolific and influential opinion maker, he has written on a wide range of subjects including politics, racism in professional sports, film, and

his own ancestry as the descendant of Virginia slave owners in
the nineteenth century, "my nearest white forbears."

Michelle Tea (1971–) has written five memoirs, including *How to Grow Up*,
which a reviewer in the *Boston Globe* described as a "no-holds-
barred cautionary tale written by someone who has lived and
learned, and hit rock bottom only to develop a rewarding career on her own terms." Some of her writing chronicles her
battles with drug addiction and alcoholism, which she kicked
in her early thirties. She is also the author of three novels and
the editor of the essay anthology *Without a Net: The Female
Experience of Growing Up Working Class* (2003) and *Baby Remember My Name: An Anthology of New Queer Girl Writing*
(2007). In 2018 she published a collection of her articles titled
Against Memoir: Complaints, Confessions & Criticism.

Tobias Wolff (1945–) teaches English and creative writing at Stanford. A
winner of the PEN/Faulkner Award for Fiction, he has written
several short-story collections, including *In the Garden of the
North American Martyrs* (1981) and *Back in the World* (1985),
a novel, and the award-winning novella *The Barracks Thief*.
His articles have appeared in the *Atlantic, Granta, Esquire*,
and the *New Yorker*. He has a BA from Oxford and an MA from
Stanford and was a Guggenheim fellow. One of two memoirs
he has written, *This Boy's Life*, was made into a 1993 movie
in which Robert De Niro played the part of his stepfather,
Dwight. Wolff served a one-year tour of duty in Vietnam.

Monica Wood (1953–) is the author of four novels, including *The One-in-a-
Million Boy* (2016), a volume of short stories, and the memoir
When We Were the Kennedys. She is the editor of a short-story
anthology and the author of two books on the craft of writing:
The Pocket Muse: Endless Inspiration: New Ideas for Writing
(2006) and *Description: Elements of Fiction Writing* (2000).
A graduate of Georgetown, she was a fellow at the MacDow-
ell Colony and Virginia Center for Creative Arts. The winner
of a Pushcart Prize, she has taught workshops on writing for
over a decade. Her 2015 play, *Papermaker*, was performed on
the Portland Stage, where audiences included many residents
from Maine mill towns like her own.

Howard Zinn (1922–2010) wrote about two dozen books, but none came
close to the success of his *A People's History of the United
States*, which retold American history from the point of view
of workers, racial minorities, women, and others marginalized

from the usual narratives. Published in 1980, *A People's History* was a finalist for the National Book Award and became a publishing phenomenon, selling over a million copies in more than twenty editions and earning praise from Matt Damon's character in the Oscar-winning movie *Good Will Hunting*. A tireless political activist, Zinn spoke into his eighties at rallies and teach-ins, was jailed for civil disobedience ten times, and, as a professor of political science at Boston University, twice led faculty votes against the university's controversial president John Silber. His memoir was made into a History Channel documentary.

selected bibliography

OTHER IMPORTANT MEMOIRS

We list here other significant memoirs about family and class in America. In drawing up this nonexhaustive list, we have excluded some fine works by authors now based in the United States but writing about their childhoods elsewhere (Jill Ker Conway and Trevor Noah, among others). All illuminate American society through the lens of personal memory.

Arana, Marie. *American Chica: Two Worlds, One Childhood.* New York: Dial Press, 2001; New York: Delta, 2002.

Braestrup, Kate. *Here If You Need Me: A True Story.* Boston: Little, Brown, 2007; New York: Back Bay Books, 2008.

Carter, Jimmy. *An Hour Before Daylight: Memories of a Rural Boyhood.* New York: Simon & Schuster, 2001.

Chast, Roz. *Can't We Talk About Something More Pleasant?* [graphic memoir]. New York: Bloomsbury, 2014.

Conley, Dalton. *Honky.* New York: Vintage/Random House, 2000.

Dickerson, Debra J. *An American Story.* New York: Pantheon/Random House, 2000.

Graham, Katharine. *Personal History.* New York: Alfred A. Knopf, 1997.

Greenberg, Michael. *Hurry Down Sunshine: A Father's Story of Love and Madness.* New York: Vintage/Random House, 2008.

Hart, Moss. *Act One: An Autobiography. New York: Random House,* 1959; New York: Vintage/Random House, 1976.

Hochschild, Adam. *Half the Way Home: A Memoir of Father and Son.* New York: Viking, 1986.

Jamison, Kay Redfield. *An Unquiet Mind: A Memoir of Moods and Madness.* New York: Vintage, 1996.

Knapp, Caroline. *Drinking: A Love Story.* New York: Dell, 1996.

Kovic Ron. *Born on the Fourth of July.* New York: McGraw-Hill, 1976.

Lynn, Loretta, with George Vecsey. *Coal Miner's Daughter.* Chicago: Contemporary Books, 1976.

Mar, M. Elaine. *Paper Daughter: A Memoir*. New York: Perennial/ Harper-Collins, 1999.

McBride, James. *The Color of Water: A Black Man's Tribute to His White Mother*. New York: Riverhead Books, 1996.

Merullo, Roland. *Revere Beach Elegy: A Memoir of Home and Beyond*. Boston: Beacon Press, 2002.

Monette, Paul. *Borrowed Time: An AIDS Memoir*. New York: Avon Books, 1988.

Moody, Anne. *Coming of Age in Mississippi*. New York: Dell Publishing, 1968.

Murphy, Finn. *The Long Haul: A Trucker's Tales of Life on the Road*. New York: W. W. Norton, 2017.

Nies, Judith. *The Girl I Left Behind: A Narrative History of the Sixties*. New York: HarperCollins, 2008.

Nuland, Sherwin B. *Lost in America: A Journey with My Father*. New York: Alfred A. Knopf, 2003.

Obama, Barack. *Dreams from My Father: A Story of Race and Inheritance*. New York: Three Rivers Press, 1995.

Somers, Suzanne. *Keeping Secrets*. New York: Warner Books, 1988.

Villaseñor, Victor. *Burro Genius: A Memoir*. New York: Rayo/HarperCollins, 2004.

Wamba, Philippe. *Kinship: A Family's Journey in Africa and America*. New York: Dutton, 1999.

Wright, Richard. *Black Boy*. New York: Perennial/HarperCollins, 1945.

SOCIAL CLASS IN THE UNITED STATES: PERSPECTIVES FROM JOURNALISM AND ACADEMIA

Ault, James M., Jr. *Spirit and Flesh: Life in a Fundamentalist Baptist Church*. New York: Vintage Books/Random House, 2004.

Bageant, Joe. *Deer Hunting with Jesus: Dispatches from America's Class War*. New York: Three Rivers Press, 2007.

Broughton, Chad. *Boom, Bust, Exodus: The Rust Belt, the Maquilas, and a Tale of Two Cities*. Oxford: Oxford University Press, 2015.

DeLuca, Stefanie, Susan Clampet-Lundquist, and Kathryn Edin. *Coming of Age in the Other America*. New York: Russell Sage Foundation, 2016.

Dews, C. L. Barney, and Carolyn Leste Law, eds. *This Fine Place So Far from Home: Voices of Academics from the Working Class*. Philadelphia: Temple University Press, 1995.

Dodson, Lisa. *Don't Call Us Out of Name: The Untold Lives of Women and Girls in Poor America*. Boston: Beacon Press, 1999.

Ehrenreich, Barbara. *Nickel and Dimed: On (Not) Getting By in America*. New York: Metropolitan Books, 2001.

Grimes, Michael D., and Morris, Joan M. *Caught in the Middle: Contradictions in the Lives of Sociologists from Working-Class Backgrounds.* Westport, Conn.: Praeger, 1997.

Harrington, Charles C., and Susan K. Boardman. *Paths to Success: Beating the Odds in American Society.* Cambridge, Mass.: Harvard University Press, 1997.

Lareau, Annette. *Unequal Childhoods: Class, Race, and Family Life.* 2nd ed. Berkeley: University of California Press, 2011.

LeBlanc, Adrian Nicole. *Random Family: Love, Drugs, Trouble, and Coming of Age in the Bronx.* New York: Scribner, 2003.

Liu, William Ming Lie. *Social Class and Classism in the Helping Professions: Research, Theory, and Practice.* Thousand Oaks, Calif.: Sage, 2011.

Lubrano, Alfred. *Limbo: Blue-Collar Roots, White-Collar Dreams.* Hoboken, N.J.: John Wiley & Sons, 2004.

Lucas, J. Anthony. *Common Ground: A Turbulent Decade in the Lives of Three American Families.* New York: Vintage Books, 1986.

Putnam, Robert D. *Our Kids: The American Dream in Crisis.* New York: Simon & Schuster, 2015.

Rose, Mike. *The Mind at Work: Valuing the Intelligence of the American Worker.* New York: Viking, 2004.

Rubin, Lillian B. *Worlds of Pain: Life in the Working-Class Family.* New York: Basic Books, 1992.

Sennett, Richard, and Jonathan Cobb. *The Hidden Injuries of Class.* New York: Random House, 1972.

Shipler, David K. *The Working Poor: Invisible in America.* New York: Alfred A. Knopf, 2004

Smarsh, Sarah. *Heartland: A Memoir of Working Hard and Being Broke in the Richest Country on Earth.* New York: Scribner Books, 2018.

Williams, Joan C. *White Working-Class: Overcoming Class Cluelessness in America.* Boston: Harvard Business Review Press, 2017.

Woodard, Colin. *American Character: A History of the Epic Struggle Between Individual Liberty and the Common Good.* New York: Viking, 2016.

credits

index

Authors whose work is featured in this volume appear in small caps.